"NO ONE WILL LISSEN"

"NO ONE WILL LISSEN"

How Our Legal System Brutalizes the Youthful Poor

Lois G. Forer

The Universal Library

GROSSET & DUNLAP

A NATIONAL GENERAL COMPANY

New York

To my young clients
whose brief doomed lives,
bruised bodies and brave spirits
form the substance of this book

UNIVERSAL LIBRARY EDITION 1971
BY ARRANGEMENT WITH THE ORIGINAL PUBLISHER,
THE JOHN DAY COMPANY, INC.

ISBN: 0-448-00260-4

PUBLISHED SIMULTANEOUSLY IN CANADA

PRINTED IN UNITED STATES OF AMERICA

CONTENTS

ACKNOWLEDGMENTS

A lifetime of the study, teaching, and practice of law provides the background of this book. I owe so much to so many, especially the lawyers with whom I have been associated. I can mention only a few: Judge John Biggs, Jr., senior circuit judge of the Court of Appeals for the Third Circuit for whom I had the privilege of serving as law clerk, who showed me the dynamic role that the law can play in ameliorating injustice and promoting a better social order; three able, dedicated attorneys general of Pennsylvania under whom I worked as deputy who demonstrated that government officials can with imagination and courage be advocates of the public interest—Herbert B. Cohen, now Justice of the Supreme Court of Pennsylvania, the late, beloved Thomas D. McBride, and the late Judge David Stahl; my husband, Morris L. Forer, who exemplifies the scholarly, ethical, public-spirited private practitioner. I am most grateful to my colleagues in the Office for Juveniles who gave unstintingly of their time, their talents, and their devotion—Almanina Barbour, Ellen Suria, Ronald McCaskill, Robert L. Finkel, Richard Ash, Arthur Cortese, Phyllis Brown, and Brenda Lumm. Florence Owens not only typed the manuscript but also gave me many helpful suggestions. My children, without whose cooperation I would never have been able to practice law, each made important contributions to this book— Stuart taught me the value of sociological method in the record keeping of the Office for Juveniles; John gave generously of his time as a volunteer in the office. Without the constant encouragement of my daughter, Hope Abigail, and her critical reading of the manuscript in progress, this book would never have been written. I am most thankful to the small group of Philadelphia lawyers who served as volunteers in the Office for Juveniles. I wish to thank Roger Donald for his valuable criticisms and encouragement, David Baker for his insights, and William Decker, Charles Mangel, and Alan Tucker for their belief that this story should be told.

LOIS G. FORER

PREFACE

What does it take to be a good parent? Love, sympathy, and understanding — certainly. Wisdom, at least for occasional moments; and common sense for the rest. Some money — enough to give the child decent food, good medical care, a safe home, and a place to play. And above all, time. Children cannot raise themselves, nor can they be raised by even the most carefully constructed machine. Every child must take a different course from childhood to maturity, and selecting the proper pathway at each day's crossroads is an arduous and time-consuming task that no child can be expected to perform without substantial help. Wrong choices are not irrevocable; but neither is any child assured of success. Our jails and our mental hospitals — and our streets as well — are filled with chronological adults who have never grown up.

Since the end of the nineteenth century, we have attempted to create a formal mechanism for helping the child whose parents are unable — or unwilling — to provide for his physical and emotional needs. The primary clearinghouse for all such attempts has been the juvenile court. In theory, children whose behavior indicates that their problems are not being solved within the family structure are brought before the court. There, a wise and experienced judge whose primary concern is the welfare of the child will aid the parents — even supplant them, if necessary — in determining and providing for the child's needs.

Of course no thinking person today should need to be told that our juvenile court systems are woefully inadequate to their tasks. If this book merely documented that fact, it would be nothing more than an interesting and well-meaning addition to a growing body of literature to the same effect. But Lois Forer has gone far beyond this elementary point of departure. In our eternal search for simple solutions that will allow us to ignore complex problems, too many of us have persuaded ourselves that the only thing wrong with our juvenile courts is that they are understaffed and undersupported. More resources, we think, will cure *all* our problems. This book shows why they will not. Of course our juvenile courts need more space, more judges, and above all more community facilities that can be called upon to aid a child in need. But the richest juvenile court in the world could do little good without understanding — and understanding is a two-way street. As this book

7

points out, communication in the juvenile system is all too often in one direction only: from the system to the child. When the child, or often his parents, tries to speak, no one will listen.

Lois Forer has listened, and she has often understood. She does not pretend to omniscience. Children are described in this book whose problems she frankly admits to be beyond her grasp. These children, however, are not the majority of those described; and one of the most important aspects of this book is its implicit testimony, from one who has dealt with so-called incorrigibles for years, that many of these children are far from being beyond salvation. On the evidence in this book, the most serious problem that many of these children face is the juvenile court system itself.

How can we tolerate a system that treats our children so badly? The answer is simple: by and large, the juvenile courts do not treat our children at all. The middle-class or wealthy boy who shoplifts has parents who can make restitution — and who could make trouble for the prosecutor who was foolish enough to try to bring the case to court. The suburban girl who sleeps around at fifteen gets contraceptives from her doctor; if she finds herself pregnant, an abortion can be quietly obtained for under a thousand dollars. If the middle-class child does, by some chance, get haled before the juvenile court, *his* case is not disposed of in a perfunctory ten-minute hearing. The system exerts its best efforts on his behalf, and a disposition is generally found that will be satisfactory to everyone.

The problems of the juvenile court system are no less complex than the problems of the children with whom it must deal. We certainly do not yet know all the answers; we may not even be asking the right questions. But our city streets are daily teaching us that we cannot long continue to ignore the problems of our cities' poor children. This book provides no easy answers, but it faces the hard problems, and presents them from a perspective unique in the literature on juvenile courts. No one who has not himself had Lois Forer's experience in trying to make someone in authority listen to a child's problems should be without this book.

— David L. Bazelon, Chief Judge
U.S. Court of Appeals, District of Columbia

INTRODUCTION

That is why I started to write. To save my soul.
ELDRIDGE CLEAVER, *Soul on Ice*

Robin, a fifteen-year-old black girl, stood at the bar of the federal court, accused of contempt because she had refused to stand up at the command of the court crier. She explained that although she was born in the United States, she felt that it was not her country and this was not her court. Judge John Lord learned that she was neither a witness nor a party to the case that was being tried. He questioned her further.

> Q. *Why are you here?*
> A. *Because I heard about it and came, you know, like these are my brothers and sisters. Like I was there the day they got beat up. I haven't slept since that day, and I wanted to come. I want to see what American justice is really like.*

Robin was taken away and put in a jail cell. (After a hearing before U.S. Judge Thomas Clary, she was later released.)

I was in the crowded courtroom with my clients, black school children of Philadelphia who had been beaten by the police. Their friends and families were present, and scores of policemen, newspaper reporters, and black and white citizens who were concerned and frightened. All of us, like Robin, were seeing what American justice is really like.

After representing hundreds of bright, alienated teenagers who were in trouble with the law, I have come to realize that it is not just poverty, race, and ignorance that have disenfranchised them and their families. Our legal system—supposedly created to provide equal protection to all citizens—exacerbates the evils of racial and economic discrimination and increases the poor person's hostility and despair. This I did not learn until I became a part of that sub-profession, a lawyer for the poor. Although I had been practicing law in every level of court, from police courts to the United States Supreme Court, for twenty-seven years and had tried all kinds of cases, from abortion to zoning, I had never realized that in the United States we do not have equal justice under law. There are two separate and unequal justice systems in the United States—due process of law for the middle class and wealthy, and a second-class justice system for the poor.

When the President's Commission on Civil Disorders published its report, many Americans were shocked by the finding that "Our country is divided into two societies, one largely Negro and poor, located in the central cities; the other, predominantly white and affluent, located in the suburbs and outlying areas." A year later the Commission found that the division into separate and unequal societies had widened.

Anyone who is not color-blind can see this obvious segregation by riding through any Northern city. What is less easy to discern is the division of the machinery of justice in America into two separate systems. There are no dramatic geographic barriers between these systems. They operate in the same courthouses, under the same judges administering the same laws under the Constitution of the United States. Because most black Americans are poor and most middle-class and rich Americans are white, the two legal systems appear to be divided on racial lines. But in fact, poor white Americans are treated almost as badly as poor black Americans. Many of the injustices that I have seen were visited upon poor blacks by middle-class blacks—judges, policemen, probation officers, and social workers.

My first glimpse of the legal system for the poor came in the spring of 1965, when Spencer Coxe, executive director of the American Civil Liberties Union, asked me to appeal the case of a fifteen-year-old poor black boy who was imprisoned after a brief hearing at which he had no notice of the charges, no counsel, and no opportunity to confront witnesses or to present a defense. The case presented interesting problems, and I hoped that the appellate courts would agree to consider the long-neglected question of the right of a child to a due-process trial. I expected to write a brief and make an oral argument; this was one case among many in a long, happy, and rather exciting career at the bar. I had not the slightest intimation that it would lead me to a critical examination of fundamental, cherished beliefs and ultimately to the abandonment of the practice of law.

After this case I began to frequent the juvenile courts. There I discovered that punishment without crime was not exceptional and that the day in court for a poor black child was a five-minute assembly-line hearing in which the state was represented by counsel but the child was not. When the Office for Economic Opportunity announced the formation of a legal services program for the poor, I urged the Philadelphia Bar Association to apply for federal funds and establish a law office to furnish counsel to poor children. In 1966 this project was funded, creating the Office for Juveniles, and I was requested to serve as attorney-in-charge.

The Office for Juveniles opened on September 6, 1966. In February, 1968, it was closed. During those eighteen months my colleagues and I represented more than three thousand indigent children. At least 90 percent of these boys and girls were black. All of them were desperately poor. A few of the boys had done horrible things—killed, raped, robbed. But most of the boys and girls were completely innocent of the crimes with which they were charged. Some were imprisoned for such heinous deeds as staying out all night, playing hookey, stealing candy, making noise on a playground, being pregnant, being emotionally disturbed. Some of these children were very bright; others dull. Many had physical ailments. Some were mentally ill. None of them had the sense of physical security which most of us take for granted; they were not safe from arrest by the police, from attack by other children, expulsion from school, beatings by adults. None of them expected that innocence would result in acquittal in a court of law, or that the law would provide redress for the wrongs they had suffered. Many times I spoke to innocent children who were in jail. "Why," I asked them, "didn't you tell the policeman and the judge what happened?" Over and over again, I heard them reply, "No one will listen."

The Office for Juveniles did not function like the traditional legal aid and public defender offices. We treated our clients precisely the way I had always treated fee-paying clients. They were people with names, not numbers in a file. We lawyers knew our clients. We investigated each case. No defense needed to protect these children was neglected or abandoned. And when a child was released we helped him return to school, to a job, and to the business of living. We still hear from these children and their parents.

Of our first one thousand clients, fewer than 3 percent were arrested again within a year. (The national recidivism rate is over 60 percent.) We obtained the release of scores of innocent children who were in jail, many for years. We slowed the assembly line of the Juvenile Court from eighty cases per judge per day to about thirty or thirty-five cases. We stopped the practice of having a probation officer decide that a child could be held in custody for days and days prior to trial. We drastically reduced the population of the juvenile correctional institutions during the time the Office for Juveniles was in operation. At one point the juvenile correctional authorities complained that they did not have enough inmates to operate the institutions—it takes a lot of children to wash the dishes, scrub the floors, serve the meals, and care for the grounds of any institution. Today all of the institutions are again overcrowded. The number of cases continues to increase.

My colleagues and I had no intention of writing a book. We had no theories of crime and punishment, race and criminology, poverty and social disorder. Our only preconception was that the law, from arrest to the final pronouncement of the Supreme Court, must afford fundamental fairness and equality of treatment to every person. This is what we had hoped to bring about in our sphere of activity. I decided to write this book to preserve the record of our experiment, and to communicate some of the things we had learned about modern society and law and their impact on the poor. I intended to narrate our collective experiences at the Office for Juveniles and to make an impersonal statement. But I soon realized that I had to speak out as an individual: the facts had impelled me to reach some very unhappy conclusions.

I saw that the present structure of the legal system—with its labyrinth of statutes, rules and regulations, filing fees, witness fees, pauper's oaths, administrative hearings, pre-trials, trials, appeals and further appeals, transfers from state to federal courts and retransfers back, and interminable delays—cannot serve the needs of poor people. The day is past when the court system can function primarily to adjust financial interests of the propertied classes and to prosecute serious crimes. Today every man, woman, and child in the United States has legal rights, entitlements, obligations—and many have legal problems. Innumerable relatively harmless acts have been made crimes. Significantly, half of the adults accused of crime and perhaps 95 percent of the children accused of delinquency are indigent. Most poor people are not capable of protecting themselves from the state and from other individuals, or of claiming their rights and benefits. They cannot afford to retain defense counsel, nor can they afford the costs of asserting their civil claims. Nothing that we five lawyers in the Office for Juveniles could do—nothing that five hundred lawyers could accomplish in an office for the poor—could possibly adapt the present structure of the litigational system to serve poor people in one city with decency and fairness. To surround a few notoriously publicized trials, such as that of Sirhan Sirhan, with the meticulous trappings of due process of law and respect for constitutional rights is a bitterly ironic jest at the expense of thousands upon thousands of innocent children and adults who are rushed to judgment and punishment simply because they are poor and unknown.

Since the closing of the Office for Juveniles, I have observed in many cities the operations of turnstile justice for poor adults and poor children. I have watched the assembly-line operations of the law offices for the poor where each lawyer functions as a cog in a machine doing one operation and no one lawyer represents a client. I have studied the reports of these law offices and the courts and read the pronouncements of the judges and the studies by armies of researchers who move in battalions across the country. They find "systemic delay" and urge more expeditious processing of cases. The American Assembly reports that "respect for law can be undermined and social order impaired if the court processes *seem* callous, mechanical or unjust to persons caught up in them" (their emphasis).* The court processes for the poor not only seem unjust, they *are* callous, mechanical, and unjust. I know that this book is not just a Philadelphia story. Similar conditions exist throughout the country—five-minute conferences between counsel and indigent client, hasty trials in "inferior" courts, indifferent processing at the preliminary hearings, inhuman conditions in detention centers and jails.

In writing this book, my purpose is not to blame individuals for the shocking miscarriages of justice that I describe. It is to reveal the basic structural defects in the legal machinery which make it almost impossible for even the wisest and best of humans to give equal justice to the poor. This is really the story of Everychild—and also Everyman—who is poor. The names and faces change. The roles remain the same, and so does the child's journey through the slough of despond of the legal system. The judge, the prosecutor, the defense counsel, each plays his appointed role. The individuals

---

* *The Courts, the Public and the Law Explosion,* Report of the American Assembly, Englewood Cliffs, N.J.: Prentice-Hall, 1965.

assuming the parts cannot change the script.

This book is not another study of crime and delinquency made by a team of researchers. We did not prepare questionnaires, tape-record interviews, compile statistics from official data, or make periodic observations "in depth" of a few days or weeks. Rather this is the intimate first-hand account of a daily struggle by lawyers to make the legal system operate to give poor children the same fair treatment and due process that it gives to the middle-class adult. This is a schizoid tale of law as it is in the books and appellate court decisions, and law as it is experienced by countless slum boys and girls. There are no shocking words describing perversions and crimes, because not one of these children ever used a vulgar expression in my presence. The reader will, however, find accounts of violence, hostility, and despair, because many of the acts that brought these children to our office and to court were violent and hostile, and the lives of these children are largely without hope. But this account includes love and humor and decency, because these are also part of the lives of our clients.

This is no trip for casual tourists—three courts in two days, and two jails on the third day, with a judge or court employee as guide. Nor am I offering a travelogue for the complacent or the squeamish. This book describes one white middle-aged lawyer's sojourn in the netherworld of the legal system for the poor.

Most lawyers who write books describe their victories. They tell of cases won, of new legal principles established, of successful careers. Five years ago I, too, might have written such a book. It would have described the opening of the Barnes art collection to the public; a successful injunction against white rioters in Levittown, Pennsylvania, and the desegregation of this lily-white enclave; the acquittal of innocent men accused of murder; the establishment of state surveillance over the misuse of charitable funds; the preservation of parks from conversion to parking lots; and, of course, the recovery of money for de-

serving and undeserving clients. Such cases are discrete incidents, episodes of significance to only a very few people. They
have little effect on the quality of life in the community or on
the basic problems of the rights of the individual and society.
And they have no relation to the problems raised in this book
—for this is not a happy success story in which virtue prevails
and cleverness is rewarded.

To repudiate one's profession and life work is a sad and
difficult choice. I am reminded of an American who went to
Russia years ago, filled with enthusiasm for the future in a
society which, he thought, worked. As he lived through the
terror of Stalinism and saw his neighbors, who he knew were
good and decent citizens, being eliminated one by one, he did
nothing.

"Why didn't you speak out if you knew these people were
innocent?" I asked.

"I had read John Reed; I believed in the ideals of Com-
munism," he explained. "I dared not allow myself to think that
the system was so wrong. If this were true, what was the meaning of my life?"

I have been forced to ask myself the same question. What
is the meaning of my life, dedicated as it has been to the law?

The public is overwhelmed with statistics, studies, and
reports—and this applies to our judicial system as well as to
other aspects of society. The significance of what is happening
to individual human beings is lost in the welter of figures and
theories. It is estimated that six million people are arrested in
the United States each year and that 80 percent of them plead
guilty. A New York City Rand Institute study of the criminal
courts reveals that only 7 percent of the 200,000 persons found
guilty of offenses in 1967 were actually tried. The others
pleaded guilty. More than 350,000 people are put in jail each
year. Almost 40 percent are nonwhite. One in every six boys in
America has contact with the law before he is eighteen years

old. In many urban areas 70 percent of the boys will be found delinquent at least once. These are alarming statistics. Are all these people guilty of crimes? Are there too many or too few in jail? How can one know?

In fact, we know very little about the operation of the other legal system, the one to which some thirty million poor Americans are relegated. Few lawyers are even aware that there are two legal systems, because they see only the system in which they participate. The other law, like the other America, is largely ignored by those fortunate enough not to be a part of it. This secondary legal system for the poor has its own special lawyers, its own ethics, and its own practice. Lawyers for the poor grow inured to the daily injustice of ill-prepared trials, quick guilty pleas, and the unending stream of clients who are not people but cases or numbers.

The mainstream of the law gives its practitioners little opportunity to see the poor people's legal system. Law is one of the traditional learned professions and tends to maintain itself as an elite. A lawyer is licensed by the state, investigated and certified as to his good moral character. Today he is usually required to be a graduate of a three-year law school; first he must have a college degree or at least three years of college education. Very few ghetto dwellers can acquire the money or devote the time necessary to become a lawyer. The nonwhite lawyers, approximately 2 percent of the bar, are also predominantly middle-class.

A lawyer is not permitted to solicit clients. Except upon request by an organization such as the ACLU, he can represent only those people who seek out his services. Obviously, white attorneys of middle-class or wealthy backgrounds are likely to have clients from the same stratum of society. Lawyers, like other workmen (whether professionals, white, or blue-collar), expect to be paid for their labors. Most members of the bar seldom encounter an indigent client. A person without money, even though he has a most meritorious claim or defense, rarely

consults a lawyer. We lawyers do not see what is happening in
police stations, jails, schools, legal aid offices, and courts which
we have never entered. We do not see the innumerable poor
people who have been injured, cheated, defrauded, and rail-
roaded to prison.

The economics of our society serves to widen the split
between the two legal systems. Percy Foreman, the distinguished defense lawyer, nobly declared: "Justice doesn't have
a price tag on it." But on another occasion he was quoted as
saying that it costs fifty thousand dollars to defend a man accused of murder. Most trial lawyers would agree that the cost
of an adequate defense to a serious charge is in five figures. The
American people have accepted as an immutable law of nature
that "you get what you pay for." Those who cannot pay top
prices receive inferior goods and services. Those who pay nothing naturally receive the most inferior.

There is no undue strain on the fabric of society when
rich men buy Cadillacs, the less affluent Fords, and the poor do
without automobiles. These are choices of goods in the private
sector. But there are many public facilities and necessities paid
for by public monies which should be equally available to all of
the people. It is indisputable and deplorable that the public
schools, the garbage collection, and police protection available
to the poor are inferior to those provided at public expense for
the middle-class and wealthy. Most dismaying is the fact that the
law in every respect gives less protection to the poor than to the
middle-class. It is undesirable but it is possible to have second-
class medical care, second-class education, and second-class
housing in a democratic society. But there cannot be second-
class justice. For if justice is not equal to rich and poor, to black
and white, to young and mature, it is injustice.

Although the legal profession and society at large appear
to be unaware of this fact, the poor know the truth. Representatives of the Poor People's March on Washington told Attorney
General Ramsey Clark: "There is no justice for the poor in

America." No one listened. That bitter accusation has been buried in the mud of Resurrection City. But it should not be forgotten; it is true. The injustice to the poor is endemic in American law because the structure of the legal system is not designed for the indigent.

Halfway measures will not help to change this systematized abuse. No decisions of the U.S. Supreme Court, no antipoverty programs, or random legal innovations superimposed on the time-honored processes of the common law will give the poor the kind of protection enjoyed by the middle-class and wealthy.

Legal rights are but a piece of paper until they are enforced by a court order. But only those who can afford to go to court and litigate can protect and defend these rights, whether they be guaranteed by the Constitution of the United States or by a bailment lease.

Anglo-American law is predicated on an adversary theory of justice. As a refinement of the ancient trial by battle, it contemplates that two opponents shall contend for their rights before an impartial referee, the judge and jury. Throughout the centuries elaborate rules of evidence and procedure have been developed in order to weight the scales so that the adversaries shall be equally matched in the arena of the court. The lawyer, like the Hessian troops who fight for their employer, is expected to do battle vigorously, within the limits of the rules, on behalf of his client. If all parties have equal access to the courts and to competent counsel, equal opportunity to institute lawsuits, and equal ability to carry them through to the ultimate appeal, the system works in a tolerable fashion. It is of course essential to its functioning that all parties shall have competent counsel, single-mindedly prosecuting and protecting the interests of their respective clients. But many people cannot afford to retain lawyers to prosecute their claims or to defend them in civil or criminal courts. Some of these people forgo their rights. Others, if sufficiently impoverished, turn to the special law offices established to provide counsel for the poor.

These lawyers hired as an act of charity by a niggardly society are overworked and underpaid. With few exceptions they simply are not able to give the masses of clients, whom they are expected to represent, the careful, scholarly, and vigorous advocacy that the middle-class client receives from his attorney. Many of the agencies that provide lawyers for the poor impose policy limitations on these lawyers. Certain cases they may not take. Certain arguments must not be made. The salaried lawyer transgresses at his peril the rules laid down by his employer. Furthermore, the lawyers hired by society to represent the poor do not receive the same treatment from the judges as private counsel does.

Two young volunteer lawyers lent to our office for three weeks by one of the large law firms told me this story.

At 3:30 one afternoon they finally finished trying their cases and went to the corner sandwich shop for lunch. A juvenile court judge sat down beside them to have his belated lunch. To make conversation, one of the lawyers remarked, "Judge, it's been an amazing few weeks. I'll never forget this experience."

The judge looked at him in astonishment. "Do you mean you're a volunteer? Why didn't you tell me? I would have been nicer to you."

Not only the lawyer for the poor gets inferior treatment. His clients do. They get the last place on the list and the least amount of time. The five- or ten-minute hearings that channel poor children and poor adults through the turnstile justice system offer a stark contrast to the days and weeks that a lawyer may take just to pick a jury to try one wealthy man.

Obviously, a system of law which depends so largely on the skill of the advocate is heavily weighted in favor of the rich and the powerful. Those who can afford to pay one hundred dollars an hour are likely to receive better representation than those who can pay only ten dollars an hour or nothing at all.

The substantive law is also weighted in favor of the non-poor. It reflects a concern with the interests of the middle-class and the wealthy and of the society in which they flourish. The vast majority of reported legal disputes involve property rights. The great early English cases involve the rights of landowners —problems of streams flooding the land, or wild beasts breaking into a pasture and inflicting damage. Young lawyers in the atomic era begin their studies by reading the opinions of long-dead judges distinguishing between *ferae naturae* and *domitae naturae* (wild beasts and tame animals). The industrial revolution was over before the common law recognized that a man's body had a compensable value. A snobbish distinction still prevails between corporation lawyers who concern themselves with important questions like stock options, and the parvenu negligence lawyers who sue to recover for the arms, legs, and eyes lost in industrial accidents and highway carnage. Criminal law is considered the least respectable branch of practice. Only in the past few years have the law schools, the practicing lawyers, and the courts recognized that there is a need for lawyers in the juvenile courts.

This concern of the law with property rights and the emphasis by scholars and practitioners on appellate opinions have diverted attention away from the operations of the legal system on those who have little or no property, those who cannot afford to appeal, and those who cannot even invoke the litigative process. Most research involves other problems. At great expense, judges and court officials are interviewed and asked how they handle cases; jury rooms have been "bugged" in an effort to learn how juries actually decide cases. Law school research centers have counted the number of minutes that courtrooms are in use and that judges are on the bench, to determine the efficiency of the judicial system. The tabulation and analysis of Supreme Court decisions as "liberal" and "conservative" and the categorizing of the individual judges and justices consume vast amounts of scholarly energy. Supreme

Court landmark cases, it appears, may often be little more than intellectual exercises for judges, lawyers, and law professors. What real relevance do all these studies have to the problems of our society, the rights of individuals, the protection of persons and property, or the maintenance of the rule of law?

Like most lawyers, I unthinkingly subscribed to a "trickle-down" system of law. This means that I placed the emphasis on the Supreme Court, which would pass justice down from above. I devoted months and years to the writing of learned articles and briefs and the preparation of what I hoped were eloquent arguments. When finally, after involved and tortuous appeals, the court pronounced from on high that the law of the land prohibits government from operating racially discriminatory institutions, that charitable foundations must have a public, not a private, function, that a testator may not tie up his money for four hundred years, that censorship cannot depend on the personal taste of the censor, that the public schools may not have religious exercises, I felt I had fulfilled the high calling of a lawyer. The law had been nudged into the proper niche through the orderly processes of litigation. Liberty would broaden down from precedent to precedent as the inferior courts followed the decisions of the higher courts.

But these high-court decisions have surprisingly little effect on the actual operations of law and government. Sixteen years after the school desegregation case was decided by the Supreme Court, the public schools in the North are more segregated than before. Children entering kindergarten when the court rendered its decision have long since graduated from all-black or all-white high schools. Public officials openly announce that they will violate the Supreme Court rulings, and they do so with impunity.

On May 15, 1967, the U.S. Supreme Court held in the *Gault* case that children accused of juvenile delinquency are entitled to some of the guarantees of fundamental fairness that are comprised in the phrase "due process of law." The *Gault* decision has been called a revolution. It has been loudly denounced but quietly defied. There has been little meaningful change in the operations of the juvenile courts. The people who are supposed to be protected and benefited by these landmark cases are not deluded. As my clients told me, "It don't do no good to go to court."

Although many of the events described in this book take place in law offices and law courts, the subject is important not just to lawyers and judges, but to everyone, because the operation of law affects everyone. Those who receive due process of law must be concerned with the alienation and hostility of those to whom it is denied. The cases described in this book are neither the best nor the worst. They are not exceptional events, but widely representative examples. They illustrate the effects of the various phases of the second-class justice system on the lives of poor young Americans. These are all actual cases, most of them tried by lawyers in the Office for Juveniles. The names of the judges, policemen, correction officials, and prosecutors are given. The surnames of the children are deleted to spare them further difficulties. (Even in this respect, the law treats the white middle-class child differently from the indigent black. Judge Francis L. Van Dusen once deleted the name of a white law professor's son from an opinion but not the names of poor black students.)

In every nation and in every age, the machinery of government and law enforcement has been utilized to protect and further the interests of a limited segment of the population. Even in nominal democracies like Periclean Athens and Sparta it was understood that slaves and helots were excluded from the rights and benefits of citizenship. Today in some nations apartheid is an explicit policy of government. In other countries masses of people are denied equality of treatment because of ideology, religion, family, race, or property. But the government of the United States is predicated on the rule of law and the belief in the equality of every human being before the law, whether this belief be expressed in the eighteenth-century phrase "unalienable rights" or in the mid-twentieth-century brachylogy "one man, one vote." Our dual justice system was never authorized by law. It evolved gradually in a series of makeshift adaptations, cutting corners and saving money, at the expense of those who have no money and little power. More than 30 percent of Americans are poor, almost half of all Americans are under the age of twenty-five, more than 11 percent of Americans are nonwhite. Today it is not the law of the Constitution that governs their lives, but the fact of apartheid justice.

As a nation, we are committed to resolving public and private disputes in courts of law, not in the forum of the streets or the secret councils of military might or oligarchic power. The functioning of the courts is an integral part of our government. The viability of our government depends on the confidence of the public in its fairness and responsiveness to the needs of all segments of the community. But there is widespread disaffection. Public officials and great foundations are seeking to find the reasons for this loss of faith. The answer is clear. Those who are subjected to the second-class justice system cry out against it. But no one will listen.

Chapter One

WHAT IS A JUVENILE?

When I use a word—it means just what I choose it to mean. . . .
LEWIS CARROLL, *Alice in Wonderland*

"Don't call him a child," the judge snapped.

"But, your honor," I remonstrated, "he is not an adult."

Tyrone is a *juvenile,* a phenomenon of the twentieth century. This makes him a nonperson, neither child nor adult. He is one of several million boys and girls who are deprived of childhood. They do not grow from infancy to childhood to adulthood. Instead they are caught up in the grotesque world of the justice system.

One American boy in nine becomes a juvenile, accused of delinquency. There are special characteristics of this special breed, all carefully catalogued. More than 95 percent of juveniles are poor. Seventy percent of the boys in the inner cities (a polite phrase for the black ghettos) are juveniles. In the big cities of the north, 90 percent of juveniles—male and female—are nonwhite.

Tyrone K. had been arrested by the police on a charge of larceny. He was taken to the juvenile detention center and locked up there to await his trial in juvenile court. Sixteen days later he was taken from the center in handcuffs and placed in a cell in the basement of the courthouse. He waited in the semidarkness for several hours until his number was called. A uniformed armed guard unlocked the cell and sent him into the courtroom, where a judge in black robes was seated on the bench. The room was filled with clerks, tipstaves, uniformed guards, policemen, and the prosecuting attorney. Tyrone stood at the bar of the court. He was ten years old.

The judges of the juvenile court do not like to be reminded that the unending stream of defendants who appear before them are children. They know about the cells and the handcuffs. They know that the institutions to which they send the children are really jails. The solution to this uncomfortable dilemma is semantics. It is easier to change the words than the facts. Every judge was once a child, but he was never a juvenile. When he snitched a pocketknife in the hardware store or took cherries from a peddler's cart or broke a neighbor's window with a baseball, these were just childish pranks. He was not arrested; he was not brought to trial. A juvenile does not engage in childish pranks; he commits acts of delinquency. And he is tried in juvenile court.

March 14, 1968, was a typical day in the Juvenile Court of Philadelphia. Ninety-three cases were listed to be heard by three judges. Assuming each judge sat for six hours, the average time per case, including bringing the defendant into the courtroom and reading his name and address and making a decision, was barely eleven minutes. One boy was eleven years old, one was ten, another only eight. Among the acts of delinquency with which these juveniles were charged were runaway, truancy, incorrigibility, trespass, failure to pay bus fare, and larceny from public telephones. Some juveniles were charged with criminal offenses such as robbery, burglary, assault and battery, and resisting arrest. Two of the children were Puerto Rican, eleven were white. The other eighty were Negro. Six were girls. Five of them were charged with runaway. Only three of the children had private counsel. The others could not afford a lawyer. In courtrooms all over America, similar actions are taking place. The names of the judges and the juveniles are different, but the procedures and results are the same.

This turnstile justice is not what the original proponents of the juvenile court advocated. The movement to provide a separate court for children, different from the impersonal, punitive criminal courts, began in the late nineteenth century. It was part of the awakening conscience of Americans who were concerned about child labor, sweatshops, and the brutal processes of the criminal law and the prisons. The reformers were appalled by the fact that most youngsters who came to court on criminal charges were repeaters. They discovered that the "state criminalized them by the very methods it used in dealing with them," in the words of Judge Julian Mack (23 *Harvard Law Review* 104 [1909]). The first juvenile court was established in Illinois in 1889. Then, as now, most of the defendants were poor. They were the children of immigrants and factory hands. Color was not a problem. Race, as it was then used pejoratively, meant southern and eastern European immigrants.

The criminal law at the turn of the century was far from beneficent. There was no constitutional right to counsel. Few agencies provided legal counsel for indigent defendants. Coerced confessions were admissible. And many confessions were coerced by means of a rubber hose or a nightstick. The appeal *in forma pauperis* (without payment of costs) was rare. Prisons were places of forced labor. There were not only chain gangs of prisoners working on the roads, but prisoners were forced to work in factories and on farms (as are many juveniles today).

The juvenile court movement was launched with high hopes and good intentions. The reformers envisioned a new type of agency, which would not be punitive but would be child- and treatment-oriented. They believed that crime could be abolished by a better social order. No child was born bad; it was only society that made him a lawbreaker and a delinquent. Regular law courts, with their emphasis on facts and rules, could not "help" a child. The juvenile court would not ask, Did the child commit a crime? Instead the question would be, What does this child need? With the help of sociology, psychology, and psychiatry, appropriate individualized treatment would be devised. The judge would not sit on a bench. He would put his arm around the erring lad, and like a wise, kindly father gently lead him into the paths of righteousness.

The Illinois Juvenile Court Act of 1889 provides:

> *This Act shall be liberally construed, to the end, that its purposes may be carried out, to wit: that the care, trust, custody and discipline of a child shall approximate as nearly as may be that which should have been given by its parents and in all cases where it can properly be done, the child placed in an approved family home and become a member of the family by legal adoption or otherwise.*

A good home for every child who does not have the necessary care, guidance, and discipline in his own family is a humane and laudable intent. The legislatures of every state soon enacted similar laws creating juvenile courts with jurisdiction of all charges against children under the age of eighteen, or sixteen in some states. Most of the countries of western Europe, some Latin American nations, Japan, Israel, and Russia have also established juvenile courts. Although these courts were intended to help children, there is no provision for a child to obtain redress for wrongs done to him by his family, strangers, the police, or the schools. The function of the juvenile court from its inception has been to take action *against* children who are alleged to be delinquent, dependent, or neglected. Very soon the courts became overcrowded with the poor, the outcasts, and the problems of society. The child became a juvenile.

The juvenile court is authorized to inquire into the nature of a child's home and the fitness of his parents, to remove a child from his home, to compel him to undergo neuropsychiatric tests, to place him in a mental institution for an indefinite period, and to send him to a correctional institution until the age of twenty-one. These are awesome powers.

The criminal courts also have considerable powers. They can send an adult to jail and, in some states, to the electric chair. Although the Bill of Rights guarantees a person accused of crime the right to trial by jury, fewer than 3 percent of adult defendants can afford to exercise that right. Of 12,308 cases tried in criminal court in Philadelphia in 1966, only 123 were jury trials. But a juvenile does not have even the right to a jury trial. An adult must be accused of a specific crime, a violation of a criminal statute. A juvenile can be brought to court on a charge of being wayward, incorrigible, truant, in need of guidance or care, or likely to lead an idle and dissolute life. A criminal court must find a defendant guilty by proof beyond a reasonable doubt, unless the defendant pleads guilty (as most people do who cannot afford to defend themselves). The United States Supreme Court recently held, by a vote of five to three, *In the Matter of Samuel Winship,* that when a juvenile is accused of an act which if done by an adult would be a crime, the charge must be established by proof beyond a reasonable doubt. But many acts of delinquency are not crimes at all, and children are jailed for being wayward, stubborn, incorrigible, truant, and for a host of other noncriminal acts. An adult is entitled to release on bail pending trial, if he can pay the bail bondsman. A juvenile has no right to bail. The rules of evidence apply to trials in adult court. In juvenile court there are no rules. Hearsay is freely admitted. In all other courts only evidence presented in open court can be considered by the judge and jury. The juvenile court staff investigates the "facts" and reports to the judge without presenting the findings in open court. The Constitution guarantees every person a "speedy public trial." Although in many cities there is a delay of six months to a year or more before an accused is brought to trial, the trial is open to the public. Lawyers, interested friends and relatives, passersby, and the press are present. Juveniles do not get a public trial. Since the abolition of the infamous Star Chamber in 1641, the juvenile court is the only civilian court in Anglo-American law that operates in secret.* The judge of a criminal court cannot impose a sentence greater than the maximum fixed by statute for the offense of which the defendant is found guilty. The juvenile judge has no limitation other than the age of twenty-one, when the defendant ceases to be a juvenile. *The criminal law is predicated upon making the punishment fit the crime. Juvenile jurisprudence seeks to make the punishment fit the child.*

Individualized justice is an appealing and humane idea. The late, distinguished Judge Jerome Frank commended this approach to law enforcement. He described it as

> ... [an] *understanding, sympathy and unvarying resolve to unravel the relentless web of conditions which determine human behavior, whether it be a child's delinquency or a parent's neglect . . . Some lawyers feel that the Children's Courts do not dispense uniform 'justice'. In thinking so, they overlook individual differences among these people and ignore the fact that the court endeavors to deal with these crucial differences rather than search for those similarities which, in other places, call for dispensing what is called 'even handed justice'. . . . Is it not possible that the techniques of the Juvenile Court could desirably, in some measure, be taken over by all our trial courts?* [Courts on Trial *(Princeton, New Jersey: Princeton University Press, 1949) p. 331.*]

Judge Frank was never a juvenile court judge. I do not know whether he observed juvenile courts in action over any long period of time. There can be no doubt that the two approaches are strikingly different.

*New York's Family Court Act prohibits "indiscriminate public inspection" of juvenile court proceedings. This is interpreted to exclude the press. New Jersey opened the juvenile courts to the press in response to critics who accused the courts of being "soft" on juveniles (*The New York Times*, September 12, 1965, p. 123). In Philadelphia, the press is present and reports the names of the children tried in juvenile court. But the child's friends and the public at large are not admitted to the courtroom.

The physical settings of the two courtrooms reflect these differences in function and purpose. In an adult court, the prosecuting attorney sits on one side of the room, the accused and his counsel on the other side at parallel tables. Both are outside the bar of the court. The judge is on a raised platform in the middle, the fulcrum of the scales of justice. He will hear and weigh evidence presented to him alternately. First the state presents the case against the accused; then the defense; rebuttal follows, and surrebuttal. The judge (and jury if there is one) has only two choices: guilty or not guilty. The result is equally clear-cut: freedom or the penalty fixed by statute.

The juvenile court does not have this simplicity, either physically or in the way it functions. The judge sits on a raised dais. At his side is a court representative who has the files and records of each child who comes before him. The prosecuting attorney, the school representative, and various social workers cluster near him. Only the juvenile stands outside the bar of the court, usually alone, without counsel. His parents are seated in the room. In juvenile court, testimony is generally so brief that no chairs are provided for the defendant, witnesses, or defense counsel, if any. People who have to stand are less likely to be long-winded than if they are comfortably seated. So what if defense counsel, with no place to put his papers, forgets a telling question on cross-examination? Things go more quickly. No judge could dispose of thirty to eighty cases in a day if defendants and lawyers were permitted to sit.

A juvenile trial is captioned: *In the Matter of* (the child's name) *Billy Black.* An adult criminal trial is captioned: *State v. John Doe.* The difference is significant. In criminal court it is clearly the state against the accused. The purpose of the trial is to determine guilt or innocence. The purpose of the juvenile hearing is to determine "whether the child is in need of treatment or rehabilitation" (Uniform Juvenile Court Law drafted by the National Conference on Uniform State Laws, Section 29). In criminal court the only consideration is whether the defendant has been proved guilty. In juvenile court the judge is to weigh the interests of the child *and* the state.

Neither the state nor the child has been benefited by the juvenile court. More than 67 percent of all juveniles are arrested again after they are brought to juvenile court. Like the criminal court that it supplanted, the juvenile court has "criminalized [the juveniles] by the very methods it used in dealing with them."

Although the juvenile courts try more than six hundred thousand children each year, it was not until 1966, in *Kent v. United States,* that a case involving the juvenile court was decided by the United States Supreme Court. And the following year the Supreme Court decided the much discussed *Gault* case. Gerald Francis Gault is a white boy living in Gila County, Arizona. Like a boy I defended in Philadelphia, he was charged with making an obscene telephone call. He was sent to a correctional institution by the Arizona juvenile court for an indefinite period, after a sketchy hearing at which there was no credible evidence that he had made the call. The maximum penalty for an adult who makes an obscene phone call in Arizona is a fine of five dollars to fifty dollars or imprisonment for not more than two months. The Supreme Court reversed the order of the Arizona court.

The *Gault* decision did not restore juveniles to the rank of "persons" guaranteed all the protections of the Constitution. Instead, the court limited its decision to four procedural points in delinquency hearings: The child shall have (1) the right to notice of the charges, (2) the right to confront witnesses and the privilege against self-incrimination, (3) the right to appeal, and (4) the right to counsel. To anyone unfamiliar with juvenile court practice these would appear to be inalienable rights. Why, then, did the ruling cause such consternation in the world of the juvenile court bureaucracy? Surely anyone brought to trial should be informed of the offense of which he is accused. No one should be condemned on the word of an unseen informer or on the basis of a coerced confession. Everyone who is deprived of his liberty by a court should have the right to appeal. This is the law with respect to adults. The right to counsel, which has been subject to much criticism, should have been equally clear.

In 1932, in *Powell v. Alabama*, the United States Supreme Court ruled that an adult accused of crime needs "the guiding hand of counsel at every step in the proceedings against him." And in 1963, in *Gideon v. Wainwright*, the court held that the state must provide defense counsel for every defendant who cannot afford to retain a lawyer. A child—with all the disabilities of immaturity, ignorance, and fear in the strange surroundings of a court—would seem to be in greater need of the guiding hand of counsel. The consequences to the child—in loss of liberty, separation from his family, loss of formal education and the opportunity to mingle with young people of the opposite sex and develop the ability to live in society—are often catastrophic and cannot be measured simply in months or years. The twelve months between a boy's sixteenth and seventeenth birthdays may be more meaningful in the influence on his life than the decade between his thirtieth and fortieth birthdays.

A few lawyers had argued this point for years, but without success. The presence of a lawyer is objected to for many reasons. Lawyers take time. They slow the speed of the court in disposing of cases. If lawyers are to be paid by the public, this is deemed an unnecessary expense even though it may save the taxpayers much more money by reducing the number of children who are institutionalized. It is argued that a lawyer may "get the child off" and thus lead him into a life of crime. Counsel for an adult may also get him off, but this does not necessarily lead to crime, because the adult is presumed to be innocent. The effect of an adjudication of delinquency on an innocent child is seldom considered, because a juvenile is not presumed to be innocent.

Counsel is unnecessary, many authorities say, because the court will protect the child. The way in which the juvenile court acts to protect children is clearly revealed in the case of

Thomas Lee B. Tom was brought into the juvenile court of Philadelphia on May 10, 1967, as a witness in a murder case. This was five days before the Supreme Court issued its decision in the *Gault* case. Although counsel for one of the defendants asked the court to advise Tom of his rights before he testified because it was likely that the boy might be charged with delinquency on the basis of his own testimony, Judge Clifford Scott Green refused. He told Tom, "You have an obligation to the court to tell us the truth." Five days later it was the law that Tom did not have to testify at all. The police had questioned Tom about a week before the hearing. The boy told the police he wanted a lawyer, so they got one and brought him into the interrogation room. The lawyer was an assistant district attorney. Tom thought he was a public defender. Shortly after the hearing, Tom was charged with delinquency for "participating in a murder," a vague charge unknown to the criminal law.

In theory, a juvenile court is not a criminal court. The judge is not supposed to function as a judge weighing evidence and applying the law. He is supposed to be a substitute father. The hearing in juvenile court is not supposed to be a trial but a friendly conference with the child, his parents, and the probation officer where all can speak freely. No need for an attorney to be present, either for the prosecution or for the defense. The judge is supposed to find out the background of the child, his deficiencies, and his needs, and to provide a program of care and rehabilitation. Such a procedure, however, requires a great deal of time, patience, understanding, and skill.

In some communities the juvenile court judge sits in chambers and confers with the child and his parents. But few judges have the time for such conferences and few recognize the need for searching inquiry into the facts of the alleged delinquency. Often a judge is expected to dispose of more than fifty cases a day.

The Philadelphia Juvenile Court also had conference-type hearings until the 1950's, when the district attorney's office entered the picture on a regular basis. A dynamic young assistant district attorney fresh out of law school decided that a prosecuting attorney belonged in juvenile court. Under her direction a juvenile division was established. For some fifteen years the court tried cases with counsel for the prosecution present but none for the defense. Such was the practice in many juvenile courts throughout the nation in 1967. It is little wonder that Mr. Justice Abe Fortas found that the child in juvenile court has "the worst of both worlds." In fact, the juvenile is not in the world of the child with its care and protection, or in the world of the adult with its rules and rights. The juvenile is in limbo, that place to which worthless things are relegated.

One reason that juveniles were denied the protection of persons under the Constitution for more than seven decades was the fact that lawyers so seldom appeared in juvenile court. Some courts prohibited lawyers from representing children; others discouraged it. A California study (before the *Gault* decision) disclosed that fewer than 1 percent of the children in juvenile court were represented by counsel. The same situation prevailed in other states. One exception is New York, whose law guardian system does provide lawyers for juveniles. But this differs considerably from the representation given a nonindigent adult. A sample study made by the Office for Juveniles found that fewer than 3 percent of the children in Philadelphia were represented by private counsel. On January 25, 1967, for example, when forty-three children were tried before two judges, only one child had private counsel. Without a lawyer, a child does not know that he has the right to appeal or how to take an appeal. Unless a case is appealed, the higher courts do not know what happens in the trial courts. Without an actual case before them, appellate judges can do little to correct abuses or effectuate reforms. Without appellate opinions printed in the law reports, the law professors and scholars have no convenient material on which to base their studies. Consequently, the juvenile court was largely ignored by the legal profession.

From time to time interested citizens and persons doing research on problems of children and the law spent a few hours or even a few days observing juvenile court. However, a spectator who listens to a trial of ten or fifteen minutes cannot know whether justice is being done. Without investigating the case, he cannot know whether the juvenile is guilty or innocent. This is particularly true when the child has no one to speak for him. Often these youngsters are inarticulate. They cannot explain what they were doing, where they were, or why. They do not know the law. They do not know what constitutes a defense to the charges. Often they do not know what they are accused of. Their silence is presumed to be an admission of guilt.

The first problem in "telling it like it is" is vocabulary. Americans in the 1970's laugh condescendingly at Victorian prudery and the use of a word like "limb" for leg. Latinisms have been abandoned by now in favor of plain Anglo-Saxon four-letter words. But the lexicon of the juvenile justice system is based on the theories of seventy years ago. It has little relation to the facts. In this Wonderland of the juvenile justice system, words take on a life of their own. They have an inner dynamic and keep their vitality long after any connection with objective reality has vanished. The juvenile court bureaucracy is aware of psychological and sociological jargon. A judge "relates" to a juvenile in a five-minute encounter separated by the physical barrier of the bench and by the knowledge that the judge has unfettered power to deprive the juvenile of his liberty. Neuropsychiatric examinations are routinely ordered so that the judge may have scientific advice to decide to which overcrowded custodial institution he shall commit the juvenile for rehabilitation. It is disconcerting when the judge is reminded that the juvenile is really a child. He does not like counsel to put on the record the fact that the juvenile is four feet eleven inches tall and weighs ninety pounds, that his weapon was a ball-point pen. The prosecuting attorney calls the boy Mr. B. The judge calls him a juvenile.

Observing the juvenile court in action is like attending a play given in a foreign language one understands imperfectly. Words have to be translated if one is to comprehend what is happening. Here is a glossary that is indispensable for understanding what actually occurs in the juvenile justice system. It is structured like a French-English dictionary, giving the standard American words and the equivalent term in the strange argot of the juvenile justice system.

LEGAL WORD	JUVENILE COURT WORD
Child A person under the age of twenty-one.	**Juvenile** A nonperson subject to the jurisdiction of the juvenile court.
Criminal Court A court of law bound by rules of evidence and procedure in which a defendant has a right to a speedy public trial, a right to trial by jury, a right to bail, and a presumption of innocence.	**Juvenile Court** A special agency "to determine whether the best interests of a child and the State require the care, guidance and control of such child" (Juvenile Court Law of Pennsylvania). As a result of such determination a child may be incarcerated until the age of twenty-one.
Arrest Taking a suspect into custody. In making an arrest, the police must observe cer-	**Apprehension** Taking a child into custody. Because a juvenile is not "arrested," none of the safe-

LEGAL WORD	JUVENILE COURT WORD

tain well-defined procedures. For example, unless the person is seen committing a crime or the arresting officer has good reason to believe that the person is fleeing from the scene of the crime, it is necessary to have an arrest warrant. The policeman goes before a magistrate and swears that a certain crime has been committed and that he has reason to believe that a specific, named person has committed the crime. He testifies as to the facts giving rise to this belief. If it sounds reasonable, a warrant is issued.

guards or restrictions governing arrests applies. A child may be apprehended by the police without a warrant. He may be apprehended simply for the purpose of interrogation. He may be removed from his home, school, or recreation center without a warrant, days after a crime was allegedly committed.

Preliminary Hearing

A preliminary hearing is held before a judicial officer who determines on the basis of testimony of actual witnesses (not hearsay) whether there is sufficient evidence to hold the accused for a trial.

Intake Interview

A preliminary hearing before a nonjudicial employee who decides on the basis of hearsay evidence, no evidence, or the child's prior record to hold the child for trial on charges of delinquency.

Bill of Indictment

A document charging the defendant with having committed specific violations

Delinquency Petition

A paper charging that a juvenile has committed an act of delinquency, which does

LEGAL WORD	JUVENILE COURT WORD

of the penal code at specified times and places, which is personally served on the defendant or his lawyer.

not specify what act, when, or where. It is not served on the child or his parents and can be obtained by his lawyer usually only after many requests.

Trial

An adult has a trial governed by rules of evidence and procedure, the purpose of which is to determine guilt or innocence of the crime charged.

Hearing

A child has a hearing at which there are no rules whatsoever, the purpose of which is not to determine whether the child committed an illegal act but to decide whether it is in the best interests of the child and the community to deprive him of his liberty.

Judge

A judge of an adult court is a duly elected or appointed official learned in the law, who is charged with the duty of deciding cases on the law and the facts.

Parens Patriae

Parens patriae is an old Latin term misapplied to a juvenile court judge, who may or may not be learned in the law, which gives him the power to send any child in his jurisdiction to a correctional institution (jail). The phrase transforms a judge into a wise kindly father to thousands of boys and girls whom he sees for as little as three, four, or five minutes.

LEGAL WORD

Try Cases

The function of a judge of an adult court is to preside over the trial of cases according to the rules of evidence and the law.

Sentencing

An adult is sentenced to serve a term in jail, with maximum and minimum periods specified by statute.

Peonage

"The practice of holding persons in servitude or partial slavery, as to work off a debt or to serve a penal sentence." Peonage is illegal.

JUVENILE COURT WORD

Dispose of Cases

The function of a juvenile court judge is to dispose of cases. This he does by sloughing them off on "intake," holding preliminary conferences to get admissions and confessions to avoid hearing cases, and by placing juveniles on probation to avoid deciding guilt or innocence.

Commitment

A juvenile is committed to an institution (often the same jail to which adults are sentenced) for an indefinite period for his rehabilitation.

Training

Training in an institution for juveniles is washing the superintendent's car, washing dishes, changing the bedding of incontinent inmates, working in a factory for ten cents an hour, digging potatoes in the fields, and similar learning experiences during commitment.

LEGAL WORD

JUVENILE COURT WORD

Jail

A place in which a prisoner is confined, which he cannot leave without court order. It has bars, walls, locks, and often a "hole," that is, a dark place of solitary confinement. A jail is manned by guards with guns and sticks.

Children's Village, Youth Home, Development Center, Junior Republic, etc., etc.

A place in which a juvenile is confined, which he cannot leave without court order. It has bars, walls, locks, and often a "hole," that is, a place of solitary confinement. A children's village or other place of commitment is manned by counselors and cottage fathers and mothers who are often equipped with guns and sticks.

Convict

A person who has been convicted of a crime. He is subject to recognized civil disabilities that can be removed by obtaining a pardon. Many societies exist to help a convict return to society and obtain employment.

Delinquent

"An adjudication of delinquency shall not be considered a crime or constitute a criminal record" (Model Juvenile Court Law). There is no pardon for delinquency. The record follows the child to school, to the Army, and to his prospective employers. There is no procedure by which one can obtain a pardon for the nonexistent crime of delinquency.

We can now follow the processes of the juvenile justice system.

Chapter Two

THE POLICE AND THE POOR

Walk up to that kind policeman,
The very first one you see,
And simply say, "I've lost my way.
I cannot find my street."

White, middle-class children in the bright cheerful kindergartens of suburbia happily carol the "Songs of Safety." The kind policeman is a familiar figure to them. When a poor black boy sees a policeman, he does not walk up to him; he runs the other way, as fast and as far as he can. The black boy learns to avoid the police at a very early age—and for a very good reason. In the week of January 22, 1968, the Philadelphia police shot and killed four boys at different times and places. Black boys are routinely beaten by the police.

A child's first contact with "the law" is usually the police. "The moment of truth for the law," said Mayor John Lindsay, of New York City, "is on the streets." For some people, the law is lodged in a policeman's nightstick, and from that decision there is no appeal. For others, the police may turn a blind eye to many infractions of the law. A Negro boy in the city has a 90 percent chance of being arrested, according to Dr. Alfred Blumstein, executive secretary of President Johnson's crime commission. This does not mean that criminality is so much higher in the inner city. Ninety percent of college students, in a recent questionnaire, admitted that they had committed at least one act for which they could have been arrested. They had not been arrested, however. It is estimated that one shopper in ten in New York City steals from stores. Few white adult

shoplifters are arrested. This initial decision—to arrest or not
—is a fateful one, for it starts the process that may lead to prison
and a life of crime. The innocent child arrested without cause,
held in a detention center with truly delinquent boys, stigma-
tized by the fact of arrest, may be started on the road to antisocial behavior and real crime. The guilty child who is arrested
while his equally guilty companion is released also becomes
hostile. The policeman on the beat or patrolling in a car has
practically unlimited discretion to arrest juveniles, to release
them after arrest, or to ignore their violations of law. We in the
Office for Juveniles saw how those decisions were made in
scores of cases.

Robert is only nine years old, small, inconspicuous, and
quick. But a youngster four feet seven inches tall cannot outrun
a healthy man of five feet ten on an open sidewalk, and Robert
could not find a hiding place. He was caught and arrested. When
I first saw him, he was in a cell with seven other black boys. They
were sitting in the semidark gloom of the basement cell block
in the juvenile courthouse. The bigger boys were sprawled on
a wooden bench. The open toilet was foul and smelly. Robert,
being the smallest, was on the cement floor, squeezed next to
the toilet. I could scarcely see him in the murky darkness. The
delinquency petition charged Robert with "breaking and entering, robbery, larceny, receiving stolen goods, resisting arrest
and disorderly conduct." It was hard to believe that this small
boy was able to commit all these offenses. Two uniformed police officers had made the arrest—each fully armed with a gun,
a nightstick, a blackjack, and possibly Mace. Could Robert have
resisted them? There was no weapons charge, so the boy must
have been unarmed.

Standing in a corner by a basement window, Robert told
me his story. Eight days before, while he was walking home
from school, two men had run past him carrying several packages. One small bundle had dropped on the sidewalk. Unde-
cided whether to call out to them, Robert finally said nothing

and waited. A few minutes after the men had disappeared around the corner, Robert picked up the bundle. Just then he heard the siren of a police car several blocks away. He tossed the bundle under a parked car and fled. A few minutes later he was seized by the policemen, taken to the police station and then to the detention center. Now he was to be tried. He didn't know what the charges were. He'd told this same story to the policeman and to the intake interviewer. But no one listened. He repeated it to me with weary, hopeless resignation.

Although the boy was charged with larceny, the delinquency petition did not specify what items had been stolen or from where. Fortunately one of the arresting officers happened to be in the courthouse. I learned from him that the bundle contained two clean shirts and had been taken from a laundry. The laundry owner had identified the shirts at the police station by the laundry markings.

Although it was the custom in juvenile court for the policeman to read off the statement of the complainant as the state's evidence, I insisted that the laundry owner testify. This was achieved only after considerable argument. The judge was indignant that I would not stipulate that if the laundry owner were called he would give the same statement as the summary contained in the police report. After all, the judge pointed out, the package didn't belong to Robert. Was I trying to teach this poor boy how to beat the law and set him on a life of crime?

I said No. The boy was presumed to be innocent, and he was entitled to confront his accuser. With much grumbling over the waste of time and the perversion of the juvenile court system, the judge directed the assistant district attorney to produce the laundry owner. The case was continued.

At the next hearing the laundry owner was present and testified. Over two thousand dollars' worth of clothing had been stolen from his shop. Entry had been made through a second-story window. On cross-examination, the owner was asked to describe his premises. When pressed, the man stated that the window in question was very high and access to it from the outside most difficult. He then volunteered his opinion that it must have been a professional job. After looking at Robert, the man acknowledged that such a small child could never have got in or out of the window or carried off the quantity of goods that had been taken.

Robert was put on the witness stand and told his story for the fourth time in his flat, unemotional voice. Judge Charles Wright leaned over the bench to look at the small prisoner standing at the bar of the court.

"You hadn't done anything wrong, Robert. Why did you run when you saw the policeman?"

" 'Cause I knew they wouldn't believe me."

"And they didn't!" Judge Wright laughed.

Robert was released after he had already spent eight days in detention. The policemen walked out, bored and indifferent. The Negro judge did not suggest that the arresting officer might have checked out Robert's story. It is a fact of life that no one, least of all a policeman, ever believes a black boy.

Although a little investigation by the police would have saved Robert from arrest and detention, he was one of the fortunate children because he was released. Many others are less fortunate. After being arrested and held on the flimsiest evidence, they are often considered guilty *because* they were arrested. On a second arrest without probable cause, the fact of the prior baseless arrest is held against a child. And so a record of delinquency is built against a child who may never have committed an offense. Seeing a record of several arrests, a judge may decide to send a boy away for years "for his own good." From there the pattern of delinquency takes over. The origin of this process may be nothing more than a policeman's decision to bring in a suspicious-looking boy.

There is a well-established body of law governing arrests. A policeman and a citizen may arrest a person actually seen committing a crime or fleeing from the scene of a crime.

In all other circumstances, an arrest warrant is required. The policeman must go before a magistrate, present evidence that a specific crime was committed, and further present evidence showing that there are reasonable grounds to believe that the suspect committed the crime. The juvenile, however, is not arrested by the police and taken to jail. He is apprehended by the police and placed in custody—in handcuffs and behind bars.

Some of the children whom we represented were picked up by a policeman who thought these particular children might be guilty of an offense. Others were rounded up after a crime was reported. The police are under pressure to clear a case by arrest. Once an arrest has been made, whether or not it is the right suspect, the police can close their books. If the arrested person is acquitted, the courts are blamed for being "soft" on crime. When the victim of a crime describes the criminal as a teen-aged Negro male, the police frequently go to the areas of high crime rates and look for boys. Some of our clients had been snatched out of bed, out of classrooms, out of recreation centers, and even church youth meetings. In many cases there was no probable cause for their arrest. No magistrate would have issued an arrest warrant. Other boys were simply picked up when strolling along the city streets. But no child represented by the Office for Juveniles was arrested with a warrant.

Often boys are apprehended simply because they are "known gang members." It is not a crime to belong to a gang. However, the juvenile aid policemen in most cities have a list of "known gang members." Gang membership of an individual is never legally proved or established. After a crime, it is a simple matter for the police to round up all the boys on the list of "known gang members" and interrogate them (often with physical coercion) until some clues—both true and false—emerge. All the boys are then charged with delinquency.

Many teen-age black boys and girls have told me that the police frequently apprehend a boy, take him in for questioning, and then, instead of returning him to his home or the place where he was found, take him in the patrol car to the turf (territory) of a rival gang and leave him there. The results, of course, can be violent, and it is reported that some juvenile deaths occurred in this fashion.

It is understandable that the small boys of the ghetto run when they see a policeman. As they get older and bigger, their hatred and fear of the police grow, and with good reason.

Derwen G. is only twelve years old; he is four feet ten inches tall and weighs ninety pounds. On the afternoon of Wednesday, May 22, 1968, when school was over, Derwen walked across the street to a luncheonette where Rudolph Perrone, an off-duty policeman in plain clothes, was standing in the doorway. Derwen said he bumped into Perrone while trying to edge past him and go into the shop. Derwen was arrested on Thursday, the day after the incident, and charged with assault and battery. Upon my request to the court, Derwen was released pending a hearing. On Friday Derwen was rearrested by Perrone. This time he was charged with assault and battery and assault with intent to kill. Officer Perrone is six feet tall and weighs 210 pounds. This is the testimony he gave in juvenile court against Derwen:

> *I was standing on the steps of the steak shop talking to the proprietor of the steak store when the defendant [Derwen] came up the steps. I was standing with my arms crossed in front of me, and he punched me in the chest.* I reacted by pushing him with my right foot. . . . [*Emphasis supplied*]

On cross-examination he gave these replies:

Q. Did you say anything to him [Derwen] at that time?
A. No, I didn't.
Q. Where did you kick him? Where on the boy's body?
A. It was in the upper part of his body.

Perrone testified that after he kicked Derwen, the boy ran to the corner, some thirty feet away, that Derwen then had a knife in his right hand, and that the boy threatened to kill him. Perrone said that Derwen then got on a trolley and rode away. Perrone did not see him again that day. Derwen testified that he had a pen—not a knife—in his hand and that he did not punch Perrone or say anything to him.

Derwen's teachers testified that he was bright and that his reputation for veracity was good.

There was testimony, later stricken by the judge, that Perrone had cuffed another black child in the juvenile detention center.

I requested Judge Frank J. Montemuro to sit as a committing magistrate and hold Officer Perrone on a charge of assault and battery. Even if Derwen had struck the police officer —which a black boy would do only if he were mad or an imbecile —the officer admitted kicking the child. Perrone was not injured. He did not claim self-defense. In his phrase, he "reacted." Kicking a black boy is a common reaction of many policemen. Judge Montemuro discharged (acquitted) Derwen of the offenses, but refused to hold Officer Perrone. Nor did the judge remonstrate or express any disapproval of Perrone's conduct.

Derwen attends a special funded demonstration school for bright under-achieving youngsters. When his principal, Peter Buttenwieser, went to the police station after Derwen's arrest to see if he could get the boy released, the policemen were amazed—why should anyone from the school system interest himself in such a routine occurrence as the arrest of a black boy? I spoke to a judge to obtain the child's release pending trial, and the judge wanted to know what kind of a "kook" that principal was.

Older boys are not simply kicked once and permitted to run away. They are often severely beaten. On May 9, 1967, Ronald H. was in a Western Union office on Market Street in

West Philadelphia. Suddenly Ronald saw a gang of boys outside approach two of his friends, both named Sam, and begin to attack them. He rushed out to their defense. Sam A. had an umbrella case. Sam B. removed his belt to use it as a defensive weapon. Ronald had nothing but his bare hands. A police car driven by Officer Brignola drove up by chance, and the gang fled. Ronald and his two friends started back to the telegraph office. Officer Brignola ordered them over to his car. Sam B. fled. The testimony of what occurred next is confused. Sam A. was seized by Brignola. Officer Brignola testified that when he seized Sam A., Ronald grabbed him in an effort to free Sam. Brignola said he threw Sam into the police car. While kneeling on top of Sam A. and holding Ronald with one hand, he phoned for assistance. At least a dozen police cars and one wagon, which were two blocks away at the scene of a burglary, rushed to Brignola's aid. Brignola admitted that when he grabbed Ronald, the boy was uninjured and not bleeding. Brignola also admitted that he himself was not hurt in the scuffle.

Brignola stated that he first saw the boys about 3 P.M. The hospital records show that Ronald was admitted at 3:35 P.M. on May 9 and that he was brought from the police station at 55th and Pine Streets, charged with "resisting arrest." The clinical notes read in part:

> *17 y.o.N. [year old Negro] beaten on afternoon of admission, 5–10 min. loss of consciousness—Patient has swelling of both eyelids, R & L closure of eyes—gross swelling of o u c bloody ooze from o.s. upperlid swelling o.p. extends to (R) temporal and sufro-orbital area. . . .*

On May 15 Ronald was operated on and a teflon plate was inserted in his cheek where the bone had been crushed. He was not discharged until May 26. At the date of the trial, June 21, he was still being treated, suffering from severe headaches and badly impaired vision.

Officer Brignola explained, "I had to subdue him by using my blackjack and nightstick."

Ronald testified:

*They [the policemen] threw Sam in the wagon and put handcuffs on
me. They handcuffed my hands behind my back and then he [Brig-
nola] took his knee and hit me between the legs and threw me in the
wagon. . . . He [Brignola] brung me in [to the 55th and Pine streets
station]. He took and hit me in the stomach and I fell on the floor.
I was trying, you know, to put my hands up but I had handcuffs on.
So, he took and put one foot on top of me. I moved my head. The next
time he did it, he came down right in my face, and then the colored
officer said, "No you don't," and about six white officers grabbed him
and they were struggling. That's all I remember. The big officer
standing in my face.*

Sam A. testified:

*They walked me and Ronald H. side by side through the door [of the
police station]. As soon as we got through the door, one officer pushed
me and punched me in my mouth. I looked around and I saw Ronald
on the floor, right in the doorway. There were other policemen. He
had Ronald between his legs. He said, "This one is mine," and he
started stomping him in the face. The first time, Ronald moved and
then they started stomping him right in the face.*

Months later Judge Clifford Scott Green finally entered
an order discharging Ronald and Sam of the charges of resisting arrest. No action was taken against Brignola although I
made strong and repeated complaints to the police department,
which promised to investigate.

Almost every day I saw black boys come into the law
office badly bruised and battered, claiming that they had been
beaten by the police. They often brought eyewitnesses. I also
saw many injured children in the detention center and in the

adult jail, where children over the age of sixteen are held awaiting trial. These boys told of being beaten, kicked, and knocked
around by policemen.

My first reaction was incredulity. How could officers
sworn to uphold the law be guilty of such gross violations of
basic rights? I had been practicing law for over a quarter of a
century. I knew many policemen. They were always courteous
and pleasant. In fact, they were often very helpful about giving
information. My sons had grown up knowing the kind policeman who stopped traffic so they could cross the street on their
bicycles. Was this some act that guilty youngsters were putting
on for a naïve middle-aged white lawyer?

I questioned the boys, their neighbors, the storekeepers,
the doctors and interns who patched up their wounds. No matter what misconduct these boys may have committed, it was
clear that they had not inflicted these terrible injuries on themselves. Disbelief gave way to outrage. If the juvenile court would
not protect the children, then these facts had to be brought to
the attention of the bar association. As lawyers we have a duty,
I believe, to see that the law is enforced in a lawful manner. But
I knew that before making charges I must have unimpeachable,
disinterested eyewitness evidence. Corporation lawyers might
not believe statements of ghetto dwellers.

In March, 1967, such a witness unexpectedly appeared.
Nathaniel Saltonstall, headmaster of Chestnut Hill Academy,
called to see if there was any meaningful volunteer work that
high school seniors might perform in our law office. He felt that
the privileged boys of the academy needed to see something of
urban problems and to make a contribution of time and effort
to the community. He sent us three bright, eager boys who were
to be with us for three weeks and to make themselves useful.
When they returned to school, they wrote reports of their experiences. The boys asked if they might go out with the police
to see for themselves what really happens when an arrest is
made. (A similar project, Police Observation Project for Law

Students, was instituted more than a year and a half later by Rutgers University Law School, Newark, New Jersey. See *Student Lawyer Journal*, November, 1968, p. 12.) Police Commissioner Clarence Bell gave permission for the boys to ride in a red car with Juvenile Aid policemen.

James Perloff was one of these boys. In the spring of 1967 he was seventeen years old. He entered Stanford University in the fall. Part of his report for Chestnut Hill Academy describes his experiences with the police. This is what Jimmy wrote:

ONE DAY AT THE JAD
by James Perloff

On Wednesday morning March 15, 1967 I went out on patrol with officers B. and T. of the gang control squad of the Juvenile Aid Division. They are assigned the job of maintaining control over all the gangs in Northwest Philadelphia (Germantown, Roxborough, etc.), an area of sixty-five square miles.

As we started out, T. turned around to me and explained that the gang control officers were the toughest in the JAD.

The first assignment they received was a runaway from YDC. His mother had turned him in by telephone to Mr. Silver at YDC. Silver asked to speak to the boy. He told him that the police were coming to pick him up. By the time we had arrived at the house the boy had fled again. We therefore went out on patrol. We passed two boys (both black) but didn't stop to check them because the officers felt that they were probably "old heads" (gang members over 18).

Within 45 seconds, we came upon 4 red cars at the site of an attempted burglary. The description of the two suspects exactly matched that of the two boys we'd seen, so we proceeded instantly to pick them up. The car we were in (J10) was unmarked and the officers made no attempt to identify themselves when they came upon the two boys. They searched them and pushed them into the car. The suspects however seemed to sense that their apprehenders were policemen. We

took them back to the site of the attempted burglary and obtained
positive identifications from the witnesses.

We then took them to the 39th police district at about 11:00.
They put the boys in a windowless tank. B. told them to remove their
jackets and immediately slapped them hard to show that he wasn't
kidding around.

B. took one of the boys (James W., AKA James Leon G.)* out
of the tank and took him into the JAD office in the building. B.
questioned him a little and proceeded to slap him around violently.
He then turned to me saying, "Do you know the first thing we're
supposed to do?" I hesitated a while and replied something about
warning the defendants of their constitutional rights. He agreed and
turned around and continued the questioning.

I went back to the tank with T., who had wandered in during
the questioning. He asked the boy (Bruce R.) several questions and
not receiving satisfactory answers proceeded to work the boy over
viciously, pounding his head against the wall and kneeing him. Bruce
R. held up well and refused to admit that he had anything to do with
the burglary. T. took him back to the office to join B. and the W. boy.
They continued questioning them, slapping them periodically. T.
turned to me and said, "Juveniles have no rights." He then told R.
that he had a right to silence (that's all he told him) and then told
him that his rights meant nothing to him [T.] and that he'd better
talk. He gave R. fifteen minutes to talk or he'd let B. get violent with
him.

(They later told me that they have a routine where B., a
vicious hulk of a man, was the "baddy" and T. the "goody" [their
words] befriending the boys. They felt that the contrasts and interplay
between the two of them was useful in obtaining the confession.)

For the next fifteen minutes nothing happened as the officers
checked their alibis and did some questioning. They continued questioning the boys for about an hour. T. then took R. out of the room
for no more than 30 seconds. They returned and R. confessed. At

*The report contained the full names of the boys and the policemen.

2:00 P.M., their parents were called, and the boys were taken away. All during the questioning, B. had worn a blackjack sticking out of his pants. He pounded it on the table every so often to add atmosphere to the interrogation.

T. told me that he never uses a blackjack but that B. does sometimes. He said that a blackjack can only be used in real close and that he hesitated to use it there, preferring to use his hands ("no blood"). He said though that he sometimes did use his pistol in lieu of a blackjack.

B. and T. were summoned out of the room once during the questioning. When they returned they were angry. They later told me that the district captain had severely reprimanded them for beating the kids. A sergeant had reported to him that they were beating the kids and they were bleeding (in fact, they did not bleed). They weren't mad at the captain; they felt he was only doing his duty. They were rather angry at the sergeant though for having told the captain.

They finished up their paperwork, on which they had been working all along, at about 3:00 P.M. They spent about two-fifths of their time at the station doing the paperwork on the case. Their load is unbelievably large: short incident report, juvenile contact report, arrest report, description of the suspects, a detailed report of the facts in the case, and juvenile release forms. We spent the rest of the day patrolling around their assigned area. They did all the work because it involved a juvenile, in spite of the fact that it didn't involve gangs.

Here at last was unimpeachable evidence not just of an isolated instance but of a pattern of brutal treatment of young boys by the very policemen specially designated and trained to deal with youngsters. It lent credence to the horrifying evidence that was accumulating in our files.

With the ingrained habits of a lawyer, I naturally proceeded through channels. It did not occur to me that my fellow members of the bar, with whom I had had warm, friendly relations for decades, would not respond to this plea to help protect children.

I worked nights going over the cases with the staff—the lawyers, the secretaries, and the part-time investigator. We didn't want to lose a minute in getting help. We prepared a long, carefully documented report and addressed it to the board of Community Legal Services, the parent agency of the Office for Juveniles. The report contained a copy of James Perloff's paper, and the summaries of typical cases that had come to the office. (In order to protect the youngsters who had reported to us, we did not reveal full names.) Here are a few excerpts from the report:

M. H. was arrested on August 16, 1966. He was beaten and kicked by police officers. Five stitches were taken in his head at Graduate Hospital. At the Juvenile Court hearing, at which M. H. was charged with resisting arrest, the policeman admitted that the boy had not committed any offense. The officer testified that the boy was running away. Two armed policemen, both large and husky, claimed that the boy hurt himself when he fell against the police car.

G. W. was stopped and searched by the police. His wallet with $19.00 was taken from him and later returned with only $4.00. When G. W. asked for the return of the $15.00 he was taken into the police station and beaten.

On December 17, 1966, twelve (12) boys were arrested at the Master Street Recreation Area. At the Juvenile Court hearing all charges against all the boys were dismissed because there was no evidence that anyone had committed an offense. Three of these boys were severely beaten by the policeman who made the arrests. One had his arm broken.

On the evening of March 27, 1967, D. T. was in a White Tower restaurant, 2250 North Broad Street. There was a fracas outside on Broad Street. Two police officers came into the White Tower restaurant, grabbed the boy and said, "Come on." The boy asked,

"What for?" The second officer pulled out a blackjack, hit him on the left side of the face, knocking him off the stool and onto the floor. While he was on the floor, three or four more police officers rushed in and started to beat and kick the boy. After the beating, they dragged him to the wagon. The White Tower waitress stated that the officers had no reason to beat the boy. D.T. was seen by this office the following day when he was in a deplorable condition. His eye was completely closed. He had been taken to the Philadelphia General Hospital that night. Four stitches were necessary to close the wound over his eye. He was groggy from the beating and from loss of blood, and lack of sleep. Pictures were taken at this office to show the serious nature of his wounds. Despite repeated requests for an early listing of this case, it has not been heard. A complaint was filed with the Police Advisory Board. Its activities were enjoined before the complaint could be heard. By the time the case comes up for hearing in the Juvenile Court, the boy's face will have healed and the court will not have the horrifying evidence of police misconduct.

Many mothers have stated that they have heard their children screaming in the police station but have not been permitted to go into the interrogation room.

Every case of police brutality known to this Office involves poor Negro and Puerto Rican boys. Both Negro and white officers participate in these beatings. . . .

The report concluded with a plea for action, for a conference with the police commissioner, for an investigation, for some sign that the legal agency for the poor would take steps to enforce the law for the protection of the poor. The board thanked me for the "excellent report." But no one really listened. No meetings were held. No investigations were made. Nothing happened.

We found the same reaction in other quarters.

Not a single judge in the juvenile court held any policeman on criminal charges, no matter how clear the evidence or how vicious the attack on the children, although we repeatedly made that demand. On one occasion I had to promise the judge not to bring a prosecution against the policeman who had beaten the boy I was representing, before the court would release the child. The police often agree to drop charges against young black boys in return for their agreement not to sue for the beating. If the boy has no counsel, no deal is made and the boy has to stand trial.

Judge J. Skelly Wright finds it ironical that the recent Supreme Court decisions requiring the police to warn suspects of their rights offer little protection to the poor, who are subject to police harassment and brutality unless they are convicted of crime, in which case their convictions *may* be overturned. Of course, at least a year will elapse before the appeal is heard, and during this time the appellant is in jail.

Congressman John J. Conyers of Michigan urged the American Bar Association to recognize the "close relationships in which the prosecuting attorney's office, the police, and the criminal courts are normally found to be working. . . ." The Office for Juveniles found that the judges, with rare exceptions, were committed to protecting the police. No judge ever reprimanded a policeman who admitted striking a child. Some judges brushed aside the request to sit as a committing magistrate and hold a policeman for action by the grand jury. Others denied it indignantly. One or two blandly suggested that the injured child had a remedy by bringing a civil action for damages against the police officer.

Such a right of action is largely illusory. The child can seldom pay the filing fee and costs for service of process on the defendant. The case will not come to trial for at least four to six years. By then the witnesses will have vanished. The plaintiff may be miles away. The child's injuries, one hopes, will have healed. The bruises, lumps, and swellings will be gone. And what is a scar on the face of a poor black boy worth in dollars and cents? Few lawyers will bother to file such actions on a contingent-fee basis—that is, with payment of the lawyer only if a recovery is made. To put the burden of policing the police on the victims of their misconduct is an additional indignity.

For many years I had been a member of the Civil Rights Committee of the Philadelphia Bar Association. It is composed of lawyers who have asked for this assignment because they are interested in civil rights. It is a biracial committee. These lawyers meet regularly and devote a great deal of unpaid time to problems of discrimination and violations of individual liberties. I addressed them and reported the numerous substantiated cases of police beating, injuring, and maiming poor boys. I showed photographs of the boys. I read them excerpts from Jimmy Perloff's paper. The committee sat politely while I spoke, and then adjourned. Did they listen? Nothing happened.

Several radio and TV employees and a white reporter for the Negro newspaper *The Tribune* came to see me. Although there was nothing in the press about my report on police brutality, they had learned of my concern. All of them wanted to give sworn statements that there is a group in the police department known as the Kill a Nigger Club. On careful inquiry, it became evident that each of them was willing to swear to hearsay. The newspaper reporter had been at a party with several cops who, after a few drinks, told him about the club. The radio and TV people were told by other policemen about the Kill a Nigger Club. They gave the names of officers who had bragged about being members. Whether such a club exists or not, I do not know. But there are innumerable people who believe that the Kill a Nigger Club is alive and operative in Philadelphia. This was reported to leaders of the Negro bar. Nothing happened.

It is not only poor black boys who are beaten by the police. Reginald M. is a college student. On September 20, 1967, he was driving a friend's car. The Philadelphia police stopped him—after all, Reginald is black and the presumption is that the car is stolen. Reginald was handcuffed by the police and then beaten.

A Puerto Rican boy wrote about his experience with the police, as follows:

> Last March 1, Antonio V. was stopped at gun point by the Philadelphia police at Spring Garden and 18th Streets . . . I had seen the police car pass me, and suddenly [they] stopped their car. Rushing at me with guns drawn, they demanded that I should not move or I would be shot. Naturally, I was completely bewildered and asked an explanation. Their answer was, "one more move, we shoot!" Then they searched me. Finding nothing, they released me.

Similar conditions prevail in almost every city in the North. Philadelphia is no worse than Detroit or Newark. The Passaic County grand jury charged the Paterson, New Jersey, police with brutality toward Negroes and Puerto Ricans. Los Angeles and Chicago are the same. Small cities and large ones must face the fact that their policemen reflect the general hostility toward people who are poor or nonwhite or who espouse unpopular ideas. The policeman, however, is armed with a nightstick, a blackjack, a gun, and often a can of Mace. This is a formidable arsenal to put in the hands of any man. The danger is multiplied when the policeman knows that he will rarely have to answer to anyone for his actions.

Nor does the policeman protect the poor. The complaints of the ghetto dwellers are ignored. When they are robbed or beaten by criminals, the police often turn a deaf ear.

I first became aware of the black child's continuous state of insecurity and fear when I began to look into the boys' school records. "Leroy," I inquired, "why didn't you go to school for two weeks? Were you sick?"

"No'm. The Morroccos [a large gang], they beat me up 'n I couldn't go across the street."

The phenomenon of violent juvenile gangs is not peculiar to Negro boys. The "skinheads" in England engage in conspicuous brutality. Gang killings in Montreal, Quebec, and

Glasgow, Scotland, are common. Communist East Europe is plagued by similar problems. There, juvenile delinquency is called "hooliganism."

Leroy's mother confirmed the problem with the local gangs. She told me, "I called the police and told them. His new leather jacket was all ripped up and he got a bloody nose. They wouldn't do nothin'. I went to the school. But the guidance counselor—she say it's not a school problem."

I heard this tale of frustration again and again. The black boy walks the street in fear of other boys, the strangers from the next block or the other school. The homicide cases that the Office for Juveniles handled almost always involved poor black boys shooting each other. There is little police protection for them. During the first seven weeks of the year 1969, eight teen-agers were killed in gang fights in Philadelphia alone (*Philadelphia Inquirer,* February 24, 1969, p. 25). The problem again is nationwide.

Those who speak loudest about "controlling crime" are singularly silent about providing more and better policing of the slums.

Most citizens are not really concerned with police incompetence or police misconduct. It does not happen to us. The police are polite and helpful to most white middle-class people. The policeman in suburbia and in the wealthier sections of the city will go out of his way to return a lost child. While waiting in the police station until mama is reached by phone, the little boy or girl is fed ice cream and soda pop by smiling police officers. Grateful parents suitably reward them.

This happy camaraderie of police and citizens continues as the child grows into the adolescent years. Neither liquor laws nor curfew laws are enforced at fraternity parties, proms, and country club dances for teen-agers. Police do not raid debutante parties. When a middle-class teen-ager is picked up for curfew violation or automobile accidents, a call is immediately made to the parents, who hurry down to the police station to reclaim their youngsters and thank the policeman for his help. Most complaints are adjusted right there. The police and the parents find this unofficial arrangement mutually satisfactory. The judges and prosecutors do not want more cases sent to court. The victims are usually reimbursed; everyone is satisfied. No one complains.

The middle-class American adult retains his regard and trust for the police. The only time he is likely to have contact with a policeman is for a traffic violation or when he calls upon the police for his protection. The urban dweller in a high-rise apartment is comforted by the sight of a policeman on the corner when he walks his dog in the evening. He never knows when he may be robbed or mugged. The police are there to protect him and his property.

Since the days of Sir Robert Peel in the early nineteenth century, the policeman has been the friend and protector of the propertied classes against the marauding of thieves, pickpockets, robbers, and other low types. If these ruffians have quarrels with the police, no one cares. Today when the police demand a raise in pay, the good citizen is apt to reflect that the policeman's lot is not a happy one. It is not a career the solid citizen would recommend to his son, but his sympathies are naturally with the police. He shares their hostility to lawbreakers and malcontents who make life difficult and often dangerous for the policeman.

In the early 1960's a few small groups of liberals pressed for the establishment of civilian advisory boards to hear complaints by citizens against the police. None of these proposals included a recommendation that such a board be given disciplinary powers over the police or be authorized to award damages to the victims of police brutality. After the urban riots, the President's Commission on Law Enforcement and Administration of Justice (in its task force report *Juvenile Delinquency and Youth Crime,* 1967) recommended: "Every jurisdiction should provide adequate procedures for full and fair processing of all citizen grievances and complaints about the conduct of any public officer or employee."

Such bodies do not afford the citizen any redress. It is doubtful whether the airing of grievances relieves the tensions and hostilities arising from police abuse. But even such powerless advisory bodies have been abolished in New York and Philadelphia, which were foremost among the few cities that had created such boards.

The vast majority of citizens apparently are satisfied with the conduct of the police, although they read in the daily press that policemen shoot and kill black boys and beat hippies and peace protesters. The district attorney does not prosecute policemen who shoot unarmed civilians. Nothing happens.

There was a brief flare of indignation when the New York City police clubbed white middle-class Columbia University students in the spring of 1968. A high-level investigating committee was promptly convened to inquire into charges of police brutality. Members of the committee, who had been noticeably silent when black boys were beaten in their own hometowns, joined in a careful, restrained report, critical of both the police and the university. It was printed in less than six months. The press and the public, however, lauded the police.

It was not until young white middle-class supporters of Eugene McCarthy were tear-gassed and beaten by the Chicago police before the TV cameras that a sizable segment of the American public and Attorney General Ramsay Clark became aware of the dangers of unrestrained police power. Millions of Americans sat transfixed in horror before their TV sets on August 28, 1968, watching helmeted and booted, fully armed policemen charge unarmed civilians in front of Chicago's Hilton Hotel. I also watched but with a sense of *déjà vu*. The police action was the same as it had been many times before. But this time the boys who were clubbed were not poor, and very few were black. This time it happened on a boulevard in the center of the city, not in the slums. This time some reporters who had

been beaten by the Chicago police and a few senators spoke out.
This time a high-level committee investigated and reported.
Max Frankel, in the introduction to the Walker Report, finds:
"Yet the ultimate value of the Walker Report is its demonstration that the violence of word and deed in Chicago was the
product not only of momentary rage but also of the gradual
conditioning of both the demonstrators and the policemen."
Policemen have been conditioned to believe their function is to
repress with force and with fury those people for whom society
has little regard. The people for whom the public has the least
respect are, of course, the poor, the black, and the young.

   After Chicago, some high-level public spokesmen are
now busy repairing the shattered image of the police. The
suggestions follow a pattern of old solutions that have failed, or
point out problems of such long-range that little immediate
change can be expected: abolish white racism; rebuild the
ghetto; restructure the family; raise the salary of policemen;
professionalize the service; educate the man on the beat. Judge
George C. Edwards, Jr., of the United States Court of Appeals
for the Sixth Circuit and former police commissioner of Detroit, recommends: "Integrate police forces. Improve professional standards. Seek federal assistance, particularly for
college level police training" (*The Police on the Urban Frontier: A
Guide to Community Understanding*, Pamphlet Series No. 9 [Yale
University: Institute of Human Relations Press, 1968].). Some
of these proposals are being adopted. Salaries have been increased in many cities. But a brutal policeman will not become
less brutal just because he gets a raise. Some policemen now
spend hours listening to lectures on anthropology, sociology,
psychology, and intergroup tensions. Authorities on these subjects are being paid to lecture to the police and the police are
paid to listen. One specific recommendation has been widely
adopted, the use of Mace. The Kerner Commission suggested
that Mace was less injurious than bullets. The arsenal of many
policemen now includes a container of Mace—in addition to a

gun, a nightstick, and a blackjack. The International Association of Chiefs of Police reports that four out of five local, county,
and state police agencies have purchased chemical spray weapons, but only one out of three has provided written instructions
to govern the use of these weapons. The instructions rarely
limit their use. Although these chemicals have been used more
than thirty thousand times, there has been no discernible reduction in the use of firearms. I have represented numbers of
black boys who were sprayed with this painful, disabling, and
possibly permanently injurious chemical *after* they were handcuffed and in the police station. (The order of the United States
District Court for the Eastern District of Pennsylvania, in *Bethea
v. Monaghan, et al.* No. 68-2529, sets forth guidelines for the use
of Mace.)

The other recommendations are, of course, desirable.

Policemen should be paid decent salaries and have
professional standards. There should be no racial discrimination in the hiring of policemen. But even if these recommendations were fully effectuated, would the problem of mistreatment
of the poor and the unpopular be any different? Some black
officers are brutal; some white officers are humane. The system
does not punish brutality or reward decency. Often the most
ruthless and cruel rise fastest to positions of power. Burton
Levy, director of the Community Services Division of the Michigan Civil Rights Commission, calls for sweeping changes in the
police system. He writes:

> *During the past five years, millions of dollars have been spent
> by police departments, much of it federally funded, for police-com-
> munity relations programs (really "police-Negro relations"). . . .
> Intensive experience with police in all parts of the nation, combined
> with results of other studies by law enforcement experts, academies
> and civil rights organizations provides convincing evidence that the
> problem of police-Negro relations in the urban centers is one of
> patterns of values and practice within the police* system. *My as-*

sumption now is that the problem is not one of a few "bad eggs" in
a police system that recruits a significant number of bigots, reinforces
the bigotry through the department's value system and socialization
with older officers, and then takes the worst of the officers and puts
them on duty in the ghetto where the opportunity to act out the
prejudice is always available. [*original emphasis*] [*"Cops in the*
Ghetto," 11 American Behavioral Scientist *31 (March-April,*
1968).]

It is easy to avoid reform by recommending changes that
are so sweeping, expensive, and long-range as to be impossible
of fulfillment. White racism and poverty may be responsible for
many ills of the ghetto. But it is not necessary to remake all of
American society to alleviate the problems that the poor suffer
from the police. Policemen could be compelled to obey existing
laws prohibiting assault and battery and homicide. They could
be compelled to make arrests in a lawful manner. They could
also be prosecuted promptly and vigorously when they act law-
lessly.

Programs for education of the police without a change in
community morality may be just another expense for the taxpayers. For the police, like other employees, do what their employers expect of them. The late Thomas Merton, a Trappist
monk, wrote:

Yesterday I offered Mass for the new generation, the new poets, the
fighters for peace and for civil rights, and for my own novices. There
is in many of them a peculiar quality of truth that older squares have
had rinsed out of themselves in hours of secure right-thinking and
non-commitment. May God prevent us from becoming "right-think-
ing men"—that is to say men who agree perfectly with their own
police.

The right-thinking citizens, whether they be on commissions and committees, in city hall, or in large law offices, still

agree very largely with their own police. And the ghetto dweller still must protect himself not only from criminals but also from the police.

Mrs. D. is poor and black. She is a widow who has no pension or insurance. She avoids "the law." In desperation, she came to me to get her son back from the police station where he was held. James is only eleven. The police suspect that he saw a man being killed. The crime took place near James' home. At the time of the crime, fixed by the police, James was home in bed, as Mrs. D. had repeatedly told the policemen. The first time the police came, they questioned James at length in his own home. He was never advised of his constitutional rights, which include the right to remain silent. When he was unable to give them the information they wanted, the police took him to the station house and kept him there all night. A few nights later they returned, dragged the boy out of bed, and again took him to the police station and held him. The next morning Mrs. D. sought a lawyer. Inquiry disclosed that no charges had been placed against James. Finally, after threats of writs and suits for illegal arrest, the boy was released.

Before she left the office, I advised Mrs. D. of her rights. "If the police come back for James, ask to see the warrant for his arrest. If they don't have a warrant, don't let them in the house."

"But," asked Mrs. D., "what do I do when they break down the door?"

I have discussed this question with many lawyers, but I have not found an answer.

Chapter Three

THE DISPOSAL UNIT

disposal, *n.* getting rid of something; a device for grinding up garbage to be washed down the drain

Random House Dictionary of the English Language

Thomas W., Sr., arrived at the detention center at nine fifteen in the morning. In his thin brown hand he carried a small square of paper. It was a printed form with the names typed in.

In the matter of Thomas W., Jr. *To* Thomas W., Sr.: *You are required to be at the Youth Detention Center at 9:30.*

The little square with the word "delinquency" was checked. A purple stamp with a facsimile signature was printed at the bottom. Underneath were the words "Juvenile Court Judge."

Mr. W. went up to the girl at the reception desk and showed her the notice. "A policeman give me this paper last night. He tell me my boy is here. Can I see him now?" he asked. Tommy had not been home the night before, and Mr. W. was worried.

"You want to see 'im now—are you kidding? They'll bring him down when the case is called. Here's your number. Thirty-seven." She dunked her danish in the paper carton of coffee.

Mr. W. sat down to wait for number 37 and whatever was to follow that. No one explained to him that he was awaiting the intake interview of his son. Intake, in the juvenile justice system,

is the step that precedes the actual court hearing. It is supposed
to weed out the unimportant and frivolous charges against children, reserving only the important cases for the juvenile court
judge.

After a child is arrested, and if the charges are not
dropped at the police station, intake is the next step in his
delinquency processing. If the child has well-to-do parents who
can be reached by phone, and who will hurry over to the police
station, the charge will be dropped unless it is a serious crime.
If the child's family has no telephone, if he is ragged, if he is
black—he will very likely be held in detention overnight. Even
if he is released at the police station, the parent must sign a slip
agreeing to present himself or herself and the child at the detention center the next morning for an intake interview.

What occurred at the intake interviews reported in this
chapter is reconstructed from parents' accounts to me, and
from innumerable observations of other intake interviews. No
transcript is made of intake interviews. No judge is ever present, and rarely an attorney or an observer. I do not know of any
researcher in the annals of practices of the juvenile court who
has observed intake interviews and analyzed their procedures
and results.

Mr. W. waited for over two hours to see the intake interviewer. He did not know the charges against his fourteen-year-
old son. He did not know the consequences of the interview. He
did not know that he had a right to counsel. Like most of the
parents of children in juvenile court, he was poor and black. He
was also intensely concerned for the welfare of his child. Mr. W.
was distracted and numb with worry.

When Tommy was arrested, what he had done, where he
had been all the previous day—Mr. W. did not know. And no
one would tell him. The large room was cold. Mr. W. kept his
overcoat on as he sat on a hard wooden bench waiting. Soon the
room began to fill with women and boys. There were only a few
other men and a handful of girls. Many infants and small chil-

dren were lying on the floor, carried or dragged in by their mothers. By ten thirty the arrivals had ceased. There were almost a hundred people in the room, but no one said anything. They simply sat, mute and uncomplaining, as the morning wore on.

From time to time the girl at the reception desk tossed her carefully straightened long bob and called out a number. After she finished her breakfast, she put polish on her fingernails. Mr. W.'s back began to ache. He dozed off and then awakened with a jerk. What if he had missed his number? What was happening to Tommy in those mysterious locked quarters? He could not forget the terrible tales that were told about this place—the girl found hanging from her knotted pajamas, the boy with initials carved into his arm by an older youth, the sexual assaults, the concussions from furniture hurled about, the nameless acts by the guards.

At last the girl called, "Thirty-seven." Stiffly Mr. W. got up and walked to the desk.

"Down the hall to your right. Sit on the bench and wait 'til you're called."

The hall was dim. Squirming kids, irritable mothers, apprehensive as the time drew near; slaps, whimpering, no voices except when the door opened. Finally number 37 was called again.

Mr. W. walked into the room at the end of the hall. He was still wearing his overcoat, carrying his hat, and clutching the piece of paper. As he entered the bright room, Tommy came in through another door.

"Papa, Papa—"

"None of that now. Sit down, W," the large light-skinned woman behind the table rapped out. She turned to Mr. W.

"Are you the father?" He nodded. "Where's the mother?"

"She doesn't live with us," Mr. W. whispered.

"Oh, one of those!" The woman wrote something on the

paper in front of her. She straightened up and said loudly, "In the matter of Thomas W., Jr." She looked at Tommy. "Are you Thomas W., Jr.?"

"Yes."

She then turned to an elderly white man sitting at her right. "What is the case?"

He shuffled through some papers and then read haltingly. A young girl at the left end of the table picked up her pen to take notes on what the man was reading. (I have changed the name and address of the prosecutrix to protect the child.)

"On the night of October seventh, nineteen sixty-seven at eight thirty P.M., Mrs. Frances Bolden, thirty-nine ninety-six North Thirteenth, made a complaint to the twenty-third district charging Thomas W., Junior, Negro male, aged fourteen, with forcible rape on Annetta Bolden, colored female, aged five. Defendant was apprehended at his home at three forty-five P.M., October tenth, nineteen sixty-seven, and denied the charges. Annetta was examined at city hospital, no penetration, inflamed vagina"—he stumbled over the words—"severe leucorrhea. That's all."

"Now W., what do you have to say for yourself?"

"I told them. I don't know nothin' about it. Where's Mis' Bolden? She know I never touch Annetta. Why Mis' Bolden always comin' to our house to get me to baby-sit Annetta?"

No one answered Tommy. The words died away. He looked at his father.

Mr. W. twisted the worn hat. "Tommy's a good boy. We go to church Sundays. He works hard." It was difficult to speak in that room where no one seemed to listen to him. The young girl had stopped writing. She didn't bother to take down what Tommy and Mr. W. said. The white man's eyes were closed. The fat, stern-faced woman looked right through Mr. W.

"Judge, your honor," he begged," please can I take Tommy home?"

"You heard the evidence," she snapped. "Inflamed

vagina, severe leucorrhea! You know what that means?"

Mr. W. shook his head dumbly.

"Young W. has been fooling around with that little girl," the woman told Mr. W. She turned to the young stenographer. "Mark the case 'court in.' Father, your boy's going to stay here and learn that he can't do filthy things like that."

Tommy raised his hand. "Please, can I talk? I didn't do nothin', I'm telling you the truth."

"Next case."

Mr. W. rose slowly. He was bewildered. Was this the trial? That lady didn't pay any attention to him. An armed guard came in and took Tommy out through the same mysterious door through which he had come in. "When can I see him?" Mr. W. asked.

"Visiting day is Wednesday, one to three. Give him a card." Mr. W. took the card and walked out, down the long corridor, down the stairs. There was no one to tell him what had happened or what would become of Tommy.

Not long after this, a woman was called in for an intake interview concerning her three sons. Mrs. D. is a small brown woman, neatly dressed. She was holding three slips of paper like the one Mr. W. had.

The large woman behind the desk turned to the guard. "Bring in Raymond first." In a few minutes a wiry seventeen-year-old boy came in. He stood up straight and defiant. He turned to his mother.

"It'll be all right, Ma."

"Sit down," the interviewer ordered. "Are you Raymond D.?"

"Yes. I didn't do nothin'."

"You keep still now. We'll hear the evidence and then you can talk. Well?" She glared at the elderly white man. He was delaying her. There was a long list. The intake interviewers usually try to get through with these proceedings by noon.

Finally the man found the right piece of paper.

On the previous Tuesday at 9:30 P.M. at the recreation center, seven boys were taken into custody. The police report charged the boys with loud and disorderly conduct and said that Raymond D. had been cursing.

"I did not curse. I was sitting over in the corner with my friend. Where's that cop?"

The intake interviewer told Raymond to keep still. The rest of the police report was read.

The policeman had taken Raymond and his two brothers and four other boys to the police station. They were all charged with resisting arrest, assault and battery, and disorderly conduct.

Raymond was furious. The policeman had broken his pipe and slapped him. The boys who had been making the noise had jumped over the fence and run away when they saw the police car drive up. Raymond had refused to run.

"I ain't done nothin' wrong. Why should I have to run?" he asked me, when I interviewed him in jail. I didn't want to tell him that speed and discretion were better defenses than a lawyer.

The intake interviewer wasn't interested in what Raymond said. Apparently the police report in front of her was more reliable than anything a child might say.

Mrs. D. tried to speak up. Raymond had a job. The family needed his paycheck. If he missed too much work, he might be fired. The other two boys were in school. She wanted them all home, but missing school wasn't nearly so bad as missing work.

Paying no attention to Mrs. D., the interviewer looked at Raymond's file, which had been brought in to her by one of the innumerable clerks.

"You've got quite a record. Assault and battery—nineteen sixty-four."

"That wasn't nothin' but a little fight in school. I didn't go to court on that."

"Nineteen sixty-five—larceny, receiving stolen goods, and conspiracy."

"You mean last summer?"

"Yes."

"Beans took me for a ride in a car. I didn't know it was stolen. Beans told me how he borrowed the car and then took all us kids for a ride. I was let go."

"Last month, another larceny of automobile."

"I ain't had a trial yet. I didn't take no car. And I didn't do nothin' wrong last night. I got a right to sit in the recreation center." Raymond was indignant. "I got a job. You can't hold me. Look." He pulled out his paycheck and showed it to her.

"You've got an answer for everything. You think you're pretty smart just because you've got a check. Well, this is one thing you can't get out of. Hold him for assault, aggravated assault and battery, disorderly conduct, conspiracy." The intake interviewer scratched her head—was she trying to think of another offense to add to the delinquency petition?

"But I didn't do nothin'," he repeated.

"You can tell it all to the judge. This time it's 'court in' for you. Next case."

"Gimme back my check." She handed it to him. "Here, Ma, you go get me a lawyer, now."

The interviewer turned to Mrs. D. "You're on DPA [Department of Public Assistance (relief)], Mother! You've got no money for lawyers. The judge will take care of him. You don't need a lawyer in juvenile court, you understand me? Call Lawrence B."

Raymond D. was taken out of the room by an armed guard, still yelling to his mother, "Get me a lawyer, now. Don't forget."

The day at the detention center continues until all the children are processed. The weary interviewers try to finish by noon. Then the paper work begins. Triplicate, quadruplicate copies to the director of the detention center, the court, the district attorney. Everybody gets a record of the interview except the child and his parents.

Thomas and Raymond were both held in jail as a result of these brief interviews. Both Mr. W. and Mrs. D. thought that the interviewer was a judge and that this was a trial. When it was all over they did not know what crimes their children were charged with or why they were being held in detention.

The intake interviewer never saw the child whom Tommy W. was accused of molesting. She never saw the child's mother. All that was before her was a piece of paper. No one had sworn to the truth of the statements on that paper.

Intake is a hybrid proceeding, the nomenclature and personnel being derived from social work and the atmosphere and function from police courts.

The United States Children's Bureau Standards for Specialized Courts describes intake as follows:

> . . . *the basic function of the intake service is to make "a preliminary inquiry to determine whether the interests of the public or of the child require that further action be taken." Generally most of the facts upon which these determinations are based can be secured from the complainant or can readily be obtained through office or telephone interviews.*

This is a most important function. It takes the place of a preliminary hearing for an adult, in which the magistrate must determine whether there is sufficient evidence, believing everything the prosecution presents, to make out a case against the accused. These preliminary hearings for adults are supposed to weed out false charges. The intake interviewer seldom views his role in such legalistic terms. A California study (*A Study of the Administration of Juvenile Justice in California,* prepared for the Governor's Special Study Commission on Juvenile Justice, 1960) indicates that only 25 percent of the intake interviewers mentioned insufficiency of evidence as the reason for dismissing charges against a child.

Intake is not authorized by statute. It grew up as a convenient way of siphoning cases away from the overworked juvenile court judges. It also provides an easy method of getting information on those cases that do go to court. This material later comes before the judge as the social worker's recommendation for disposition, that is, sentencing. Often the child's statements made at intake are used by the judge at the trial to test his credibility. If there is a discrepancy between the report of what the child said at intake and his testimony under oath in open court, the judge may conclude not that there was an error in the very casual report but that the child is a liar.

The intake interviewer is usually a social worker or probation officer. Like his counterpart in welfare agencies, the interviewer questions the child and other people and then decides what, in his opinion, is best for the child.

The critical importance of intake is recognized by students of the juvenile court system. The Institute of State and Local Government (in its 1957 report, *The Philadelphia Juvenile Court*) found: "The juvenile's first contact with the Court is through intake interviews. This first meeting is crucial to the child, the community and the Court. In brief intensive interviews, delicate judgments must be made whether the case should be adjusted or held for formal court hearing, and whether the child should be held in detention pending hearing. Skilled staff, clear policy, and careful controls are essential." This analysis of "intake" is accurate.

There are three choices—"adjustment," "court out," and "court in." When a case is adjusted, no further action is taken. The child and his parents assume that the charges have been dropped and that the child is exonerated. But the court does not attach this significance to adjustment. It simply means that the intake interviewer has determined that it is in the best interest of the child, whether guilty or not, to take no further action. The charge remains on the child's record. "Court out" is a decision to release the child pending trial and to have a petition of delinquency placed against him. The child will be brought to trial weeks or months later. "Court in" is an order to hold the child in detention (jail) until he has a hearing before the juvenile court. This hearing may be a day or a month later. There is no statutory time in which the child must be brought to court, and few juvenile courts have any fixed rule as to the limit of pretrial detention.

In welfare agencies the intake interviewer screens persons applying for some sort of grant, such as public assistance, medical care, orthopedic appliances, psychiatric help, or family counseling. What the applicant wants costs money, and the interviewer is the guardian of the purse strings who must determine eligibility and need. Often these two criteria merge in a generalized decision as to "worthiness." The interviewer must be wary of lies. If the applicant does not answer the questions or if his answers are unsatisfactory, his request will be denied.

Why should such a procedure be applied in the juvenile justice system? The child at a juvenile intake interview is not asking for anything. He and his parents are compelled to submit to this interview, which may result in loss of freedom for the child.

Intake, like the juvenile court itself, has a crowded schedule. A single interviewer may be expected to process forty or more children in a day. These brief interviews fall far short of the intensive, delicate decision-making proceedings envisioned by the Institute of State and Local Government. Being trained in the social disciplines rather than the formalisms of the law, the interviewer puts aside questions of fact and law such as Did the child do the act? and Is it an offense? Instead he is supposed to establish a rapport with the child and, in less than ten minutes, arrive at a solution to the social problems presented by the whole child that will be conducive to his rehabilitation.

Every day, in every city and county in the United States, intake interviewers are making decisions affecting the liberty of children. In some communities the interviews are longer; in others they are shorter. The structure is the same. An individual who is not a judge makes a decision whether to deprive a child of his liberty on the basis of a hearing at which none of the safeguards of the law is observed. The so-called evidence read from a paper is pure hearsay. The person who gathered the information is not there to be cross-examined. The eyewitnesses from whom the reporter obtained his information are not present to be examined or cross-examined. The facts as reported often indicate that no crime was committed, and yet the child is held for trial. The child does not have a lawyer and is not informed of his right to have counsel or his privilege against self-incrimination. He is not permitted to confront his accuser. Neither the protections of the law nor the supportive aids of social work are possible at such a mongrelized proceeding.

The standard by which the intake officer is guided is whether the best interests of the child *and* the public will be served by detaining or prosecuting the child. Such a standard if applied by a court would be held void for vagueness. Its two criteria present conflicting interests. The probation officer may believe that it is in the best interests of society to lock up a child who has not committed any crime but whose home conditions are such that he *may* get into trouble. If he thinks that the child's home is unsuitable or that the child is lying or unrepentant, he can order him to be held in custody.

Many social workers and judges believe that freeing a child is not fair treatment even when there is insufficient evidence to sustain a conviction. They are concerned that acquittal of a possibly guilty child will lead him to think that crime does pay. The role of the juvenile court, they believe, is to change the attitudes of these children. A child who admits his misconduct and promises to sin no more will often be released, while one who firmly insists upon his innocence will be held for the discipline that will break his unruly spirit and reform his evil heart. For this reason, many children admit offenses that they never committed. Some are released. Others are held in jail until trial.

At the court hearing these confessions are often introduced in evidence.

On the other hand, the intake officer may believe that it is in the best interests of a child who has a good home to release him even though he has committed an offense. The ghetto child runs a high risk of incarceration, while the middle-class white child is seldom deprived of his liberty regardless of the offense. Substitute for the word "poor" the word "black" and for the word "middle-class" the word "white": This is what the children and their parents see at intake. They do not know that they are not in court. The intake interviewer is frequently called judge and rarely disclaims the title.

After being held in the juvenile detention center for more than six weeks, Tommy finally got help because of the interest of an attorney's wife. Tommy had raked leaves and done odd jobs for Mrs. Coleman all summer. In November she decided to have her cellar scrubbed and she stopped at Tommy's house to ask him to come over and work on Saturday. Tommy's sister told her that Tommy was in jail for rape. Mrs. Coleman simply did not believe that this nice youngster who had cut her grass, moved her furniture, and even washed her dishes could have done such a thing. She knew that he needed a lawyer, and so she came to the Office for Juveniles.

Tommy had been deprived of his liberty in an interview of about three minutes. More than eight hours of a lawyer's time and five and one-half hours of the court's time were required to obtain the discharge of a child against whom there was no credible evidence. I kept a time chart of how long it took to get Tommy released and cleared of these charges.

11/3   Went to detention center, refused per-
        mission to see Thomas without written
        request of parent. Letter to father.   1½ hrs.

11/7	Interviewed Thomas at detention center, filed petition for court hearing, subpoena for medical examiner.	1 hr.
11/22	Court hearing. Thomas released.	4 hrs.
12/22	Continued court hearing.	1 hr.
1/22	Continued court hearing. Prosecuting witnesses did not appear. Charges dismissed	½ hr.

Prior to the hearing, I obtained a copy of the report of the medical examination made of the little girl. I was not satisfied with the report and insisted that the doctor be in court to testify. At the first hearing the doctor admitted under cross-examination that there had been no penetration, and that the infection and inflammation could be the result of dirt or masturbation. I moved for dismissal of the charges. The court thereupon reduced the charge to attempted rape.

Little Annetta was not very bright. I demanded that the prosecutor establish her testimonial capacity. On cross-examination, it became clear that she did not know the meaning of truth or falsehood. When asked, "What does it mean to tell a lie?," she shook her head.

The district attorney asked her, "What did Thomas do to you?" Objections to that question were overruled.

She answered, "Something bad."

On cross-examination, she said she didn't know what he did, Mommy said it was bad.

After four hours of futile questioning, the hearing was adjourned, over my protest. I asked that the boy be discharged (acquitted). Instead, the mother was told to take her little girl home and instruct her on the meaning of truth and rape. At the second court hearing the girl was equally unresponsive. Neither the mother nor the girl appeared at the third hearing. The charges were then dismissed.

Because Tommy was released, there is no transcript of these hearings. This report is based on my notes in the file.

Raymond also was released after being in jail four days and losing four days' pay. At his hearing we insisted that the arresting officers testify. From their statements it was clear that none of these boys had committed any offense. At most they had been noisy and possibly rude. But they were in a recreation center.

One beneficial result of Raymond's arrest was that we stopped the practice of having children jailed indefinitely by the decision of an intake interviewer. On Raymond's behalf we filed suit in the federal court against the intake interviewer and other court personnel for loss of wages. We alleged that no one except a judge has the right to deprive anyone—child or adult— of his liberty. It was the interviewer's action that had illegally held Raymond in detention and cost him his wages for four days. We had often complained about intake, and the court had always refused to consider any changes. But the possibility of having to pay damages to the children brought a quick response. After the suit was filed, the juvenile court immediately instituted the practice of having a judge hold detention hearings for every child detained by the intake interviewer.

If Thomas W. had not been a black child but a white adult, a Mr. W., he would not have spent five minutes in jail, much less six weeks. Annetta's mother could not have caused the arrest of any Mr. W. simply by complaining to a policeman. She would be required to swear out a warrant, and allege under oath that a crime had been committed and that she had reason to believe that Mr. W. was the guilty party. If such an oath is taken falsely or maliciously, the accused person has a cause of action against his accusers. While such lawsuits are rare, they do constitute an *in terrorem* restraining force, especially when the accused is financially able to sue.

Before Mr. W. could have been arrested, a magistrate,

justice of the peace, or alderman would have had to issue an
arrest warrant based upon probable cause. If such a warrant had
been issued and Mr. W. had been arrested, he would have had
a preliminary hearing before a judicial officer at which he was
represented by counsel. His counsel would promptly have exposed the incompetence of Annetta and the lack of any substantial evidence. But even if the judicial officer had held Mr. W., he
would have been entitled to be released on bail pending trial.

The prosecutor would have been required to present the
evidence to a grand jury. It is unlikely that a grand jury would
indict on such flimsy evidence. If it did, Mr. W. would be entitled
to a trial by jury. At this trial the judge would be required to
instruct the jury that the burden of proof was on the state, that
Mr. W. was presumed to be innocent until proved guilty, and
that, if there was a reasonable doubt of guilt, the jury must
acquit. If only one of the twelve jurors had such a doubt and
voted for acquittal, Mr. W. would be free. The maximum penalty
for attempted rape in Thomas' state, as in most jurisdictions,
is five years. But as a juvenile Thomas could have been deprived
of his liberty until the age of twenty-one, a period of seven
years.

The task force report, *Juvenile Delinquency and Youth Crime*
(1967), of the President's Commission on Law Enforcement
and Administration of Justice frankly admits that very little is
known about the prejudicial phases of the juvenile justice system. It warns against overreaching and arbitrary actions. But it
also recommends that intake be more systematically employed
and that probation officers enter consent decrees to utilize the
"treating" authority of the juvenile court. A consent decree
requires the child, usually without counsel, to admit guilt. Although he may be released, he then has a court record.

The United States Supreme Court also compounded the
confusion with respect to intake. Although refraining from
passing on the constitutionality of this practice, about which the

court admitted it knew very little, the court nonetheless suggested the use of extrajudicial techniques to "dispose of cases."

Recent new juvenile court laws, such as those of California and Colorado, expressly authorize intake and the detention of a child by a probation officer. The National Commission on Uniform State Laws has drafted a new model juvenile court law, presumably to meet the requirements of the *Gault* case. This draft also sanctions intake and permits a nonjudicial officer to detain (jail) a child pending trial. The commission is a body of great prestige. Its recommendations are accorded respectful attention by the busy members of the fifty state legislatures who have neither the time nor the money to undertake the study of such legislation. It is, of course, difficult to oppose a law that has the imprimatur of the commission. The courts, the students of the court, and the legislators who must provide the funds for the juvenile court are understandably in a quandary. They are reluctant to change well-established patterns and to institute new procedures that may be slow and cumbersome. The bureaucracy is accustomed to intake. Juvenile court judges and probation officers like intake and recommend using it more widely. It relieves the judges of a great deal of work and elevates the role of the probation officer. The lawyers almost never attend intake interviews. No one objects except the juveniles.

Intake is justified as a quick and cheap way to dispose of many cases and save the cost of providing more judges. But even on a dollar-and-cents basis, it is questionable whether intake is cheaper than a proper judicial hearing. The swollen bureaucracy of the intake system rivals that of the courts.

The hidden costs of intake are incalculable. The child loses his liberty and is exposed to delinquent or criminal behavior by other inmates. Thomas missed so much schooling that he had to repeat the entire year. He may never complete high school because of this lost year. Raymond missed four days of work and his salary for those days, which he and his mother sorely needed. Fortunately Raymond's employer was willing to take him back after I phoned him and explained the situation. Many a child loses his job and his chance of getting another one because of detention pending trial. The cost to the community in the child's hostility to law must also be considered. The warden of a jail in which both adults and juveniles are incarcerated pointed this out when he asked me to obtain new trials for several of his young inmates.

"As long as these boys insist that they didn't get a fair trial there is nothing we can do to help change their antisocial attitudes," the warden explained.

The President's Commission reports that the earlier a child comes into contact with the juvenile justice system the more likely he is to have a subsequent criminal career. The child's first, all-important contact with this system is intake.

The Supreme Court has devoted many opinions to specifying in detail the requirements for fairness in arrest procedures for adults. The court has also held that the Constitution requires fundamental fairness in the adjudication phase of the juvenile justice system. Is a denial of fairness in the pre-adjudication phases any less serious? At intake a child may lose his privilege against self-incrimination; he may lose his liberty; he may lose his respect for the legal system.

Intake has an overriding virtue, however. Quickly, quietly, and unobserved, it disposes of hundreds of thousands of juveniles.

Chapter Four

IN THE MATTER OF. . .

The accused is presumed guilty until proved innocent.

The trial of Jean Valjean, VICTOR HUGO, *Les Misérables*

If the charges of delinquency against a child have not been dropped by the police or adjusted by the intake interviewer, the child comes before a judge of the juvenile court. This has been aptly described as "the three-minute children's hour."

Wendell D. is one of the twelve thousand children who have their three-minute day in the Juvenile Court of Philadelphia each year. His case is different only because he was later retried and was able to prove his innocence after spending twenty-two days in jail for a crime he did not commit. Thousands of other innocent boys and girls spend years of their youth in jail.

In 1965, Wendell and eight other boys were accused of making an obscene telephone call to Judge Juanita Kidd Stout. Seven of the boys were tried in the juvenile court by Judge Stout and committed to correctional institutions.

Wendell was then fifteen years old. He was a quiet boy who seldom caused any trouble. Consequently, neither his neighbors nor his teachers paid much attention to him. He sat in school year after year, and , like most slum boys, learned very little. In a suburban school Wendell would have been a devoted water boy for the football team or an assistant stage manager

for the dramatic club. He did not aspire to leadership or noto-
riety.

Nevertheless, Wendell's name and address were bla-
zoned on every newspaper in the city. He was subject to public
condemnation as a juvenile delinquent. Wendell is black and
poor, a resident of the inner city slum.

Fortunately for Wendell, however, Jack Minnis was
among the thousands of people who read *The Philadelphia Inquirer* on March 18, 1965. Jack is a professor of English at
Drexel Institute of Technology. Most of the faculty of Drexel
and the adjacent Ivy League University of Pennsylvania live
miles away from the campus, and do not see or hear the black
city pressing in on them, except when they are making urban
studies. The Minnises chose to live nearby. Their two blond
children play on the street with all the kids. On summer evenings the boys on the block would come and sit on the steps to
talk to Jack Minnis. Slowly and cautiously he began to teach
them to read. He did not have a grant. This was not an antipoverty project or an experiment to be written up for a thesis. He
simply began to help children who desperately needed him.
Wendell was one of these boys.

Refusing to believe that Wendell had made an obscene,
threatening telephone call, Mr. Minnis called the American
Civil Liberties Union. Spencer Coxe, the executive director,
promptly called me as one on the list of volunteer attorneys.
These civil liberties lawyers represent people without fee, when
their constitutional rights appear to have been violated.

Immediately I filed a petition for a rehearing in juvenile
court. The Juvenile Court Act of Pennsylvania provides as a
matter of right that any child may petition for a rehearing within
twenty-one days. The practice of the court is for the same judge
to hear the case over again on the rare occasions when such a
petition is presented. Rather than take an immediate appeal, it
seemed preferable to get a new trial and put some facts favora-

ble to Wendell on the record. Besides, I really had no idea what evidence there was against the boy.

From the court records, I discovered that Wendell was charged with "threats, making obscene phone call, conspiracy." The only offense comprehending obscene telephone calls under the penal code is "malicious use of phone calls," which defines the offense as follows: "whoever anonymously telephones another person repeatedly . . ." The maximum penalty is five hundred dollars and six months in county jail. The charge was not even several calls. Was one phone call a violation of the act? Probably not. With whom was Wendell charged with conspiring—and conspiring to do what? The records did not indicate these necessary elements of the offense. What evidence was there that Wendell had made the phone call? Unless the receiving party's phone is tapped, it is impossible to trace an anonymous phone call. Did the person who received the call recognize the voice? Did he recognize nine voices? Were all the boys together at the time the call was allegedly made?

Neither Wendell nor his mother could answer these questions. Both of them had been in the courtroom at the trial, but neither one knew what the charges against Wendell were or who had testified as to what. They had never been given a written notice of the charges.

Wendell's mother explained to me, "It all happened so fast. I walked into the courtroom. Wendell was standing up there with the other boys. I couldn't even talk to him. Nobody told me nothing. The policemen talked. The judge, she hollered at us. We mothers couldn't say anything. Then they took the boys back to the cells. It was all over in ten minutes."

Juanita Kidd Stout, the trial judge, told me that she could not schedule the rehearing until the notes of testimony were transcribed. This seemed reasonable, and I promptly ordered the notes of testimony. They were not forthcoming. The stenographer first had to get permission from the judge to transcribe the notes. I wrote; I called; I wrote again. Finally the notes were produced.

I read the transcript aloud. It did not take fifteen minutes. An average hearing of less than five minutes is common in juvenile courts throughout the United States, according to the task force report, *Juvenile Delinquency in Youth Crime,* of the President's Commission on Law Enforcement and Administration of Justice, 1967.

Neither Wendell nor the six other boys had counsel. An assistant district attorney was present as prosecutor.

Here are the significant portions of the testimony.

BEFORE: HON. JUANITA KIDD STOUT, J.
(Court Room "A," 1801 Vine Street)
OFFICER WASHINGTON, NO. 6217 (JAD).
Q. Tell her Honor the circumstances.
A. As the result of a complaint received by your Honor that on 3-16-65, at approximately 10:30 A. M., in Court Room D, the sheriff stated there were threats to your Honor. As a result of this, we made an investigation, the other officers and myself. We apprehended Frederick J., age 14; James B., age 13; Wendell D., age 15; Richard C, age 15; Andrew B., age 16; Emanuel L., age 15; James W., age 15; Calvin J., age 18; Herbert B., age 19.

These boys are admitted members of the 36th and Market Street Gang. Frederick J. and his brother, Calvin J., are reported to be the runners.

Upon conducting an investigation, we found four boys had not been to school and were truants that day, James B., Frederick J., James W., and Andrew B. These four boys didn't attend school that day. . . .

Upon questioning these boys, they all denied having or making any telephone calls. The four boys I named were available at that time. The rest of the boys were attending school. [*emphasis supplied*]

OFFICER JACKSON, No. 3093 (Gang Control).
Q. Officer, do you have something to add?
A. Officer Hedgeman and myself, while conducting an investigation on the threats directed to your Honor, and also the obscene telephone calls, we interrogated Richard C. and Andrew B., who informed us of weapons stored in a vacant property at 3651 Cuthbert Street. Officer Hedgeman and I in company with the two offenders went to that location, and found inside an empty room, which was nearest to the bathroom, this .12 gauge Browning semi-automatic shotgun. It was recovered by [Richard] C. They stated that they had knowledge that these guns were stored by the gang in the vacant house, but denied having placed them there.

OFFICER HEDGEMAN: Your Honor, during our investigation, it was learned this young man here, known as Calvin J., is also known as "Sonny." It was reported that Calvin sold the pistol about a week ago for $10.00.
BY THE COURT: (To Calvin J.)
Q. Is that right, Calvin?
A. No.
Q. Did you have one?
A. No. I don't go with these boys.
OFFICER HEDGEMAN: Your Honor, he is a recognized leader, and his brother, Fred. He is known as "Pots and Pans."
BY THE COURT: (To Frederick J.)
Q. Is that your nickname?
A. Yes.
THE COURT: Let us have the school reports on all the juveniles.
MRS. GODMILOW (school system representative): Your Honor, Wendell D. is in the 9th grade at the Sayre Jr. High School. He has been absent 42 days, of which 13 were considered excused. He is failing two subjects. He has normal intelligence. He is not a disciplinary problem in school.

MRS. GODMILOW: . . . Emanuel L., you had him before you on Monday.

THE COURT: Tell me again.

MRS. GODMILOW: Emanuel L. hadn't been absent at all until January, when he started to stay out. He has accumulated 15 days since then. He is passing all subjects. His behavior in school is acceptable. This boy leaves school each day at 11 o'clock for the Youth Conservation Corps.

PROBATION OFFICER PARKER: Your Honor, his mother states he is no disciplinary problem at home.

BY THE COURT: (To Emanuel L.)

Q. How did you get involved with these boys?

A. I am not with the gang. I go with the boys to the gym.

MOTHER OF EMANUEL L.: We used to live around that neighborhood.

BY THE COURT: (To mother of Emanuel L.)

Q. Why does your boy associate with these boys?

A. He is not really a member of the gang. He knows them for years.

Q. I will teach him to have better associates.

THE COURT: He is committed to the Youth Development Center for an indefinite term. Now we will get back and consider Richard C.

BY THE COURT: (To Richard C.)

Q. How old are you?

A. I am 15.

Q. You are committed to Glen Mills. Who are the other members of your gang who are not present today? What are their names?

A. One is "Chuck."

Q. What is his last name?

A. I don't know.

Q. Where does he live?

A. I don't know.

Q. Where can we find him?

A. He would be on 60th Street most of the time.

Q. How old is he?

A. About 15.

Q. Who else is a member of your gang?
A. Some boy named "Cool Breeze."
Q. What is his last name?
A. I don't know.
Q. How old is he?
A. He is 16.
Q. Where does he live?
A. I don't know.
Q. Who else is a member of your gang?
A. "Tenderloin."
OFFICER WASHINGTON: We can get him.
BY THE COURT: (To Richard C.)
Q. Who else?
A. That is all I can remember. The rest are in jail.
Q. Are you sure?
A. Yes.

BY THE COURT: (To mother of Andrew B.)
Q. You are his mother?
A. Yes.
Q. Your son was absent 78 days last year, and 48 days this year.
*A. I had a fire in November, and I lost everything. No one is working.
I support these children myself. I am not on DPA [relief]. I had to
get some clothes.*
Q. I will remove him so he won't give you any trouble.
*A. Could I ask you something? Could you send him to the Youth
Development Center? I don't want him in with the crowd.*
Q. He is too old.
A. (not answered).
*THE COURT: Commit for one year in Pennypack House [adult
prison] for B. He is also a truant.*

BY THE COURT: (To Wendell D.)
Q. You are Wendell D.?
A. Yes.

Q. How old are you?
A. I am 15.
Q. You have been absent 42 days, and only 13 were excused?
A. Yes.
BY THE COURT: (To mother of Wendell D.)
Q. Are you his mother?
A. Yes.
Q. Why was your son with this gang?
A. I don't know anything about it. . . . He was in school the day of this pick up.
THE COURT: He is committed to the Youth Development Center for an indefinite term. [He could have remained until the age of 21.] He is also a truant.

MOTHER OF CALVIN J.: The day the phone call was supposed to have been made my boy was at home.
BY THE COURT: (To mother of Calvin J.)
Q. What about the next day?
A. He was in the detention house.
BY THE COURT: (To Herbert B.)
Q. Who made the phone call?
A. I don't know. I came home on Monday night, and I went to bed. I didn't get up until ten or eleven o'clock the next morning.
Q. Why were you so late in bed? You don't work?
A. No.
BY THE COURT: (To mother of Calvin J.)
Q. Do you work?
A. No.
Q. How is he being supported?
A. I support him.
CALVIN J.: I am going on job training.
BY THE COURT: (To Calvin J.)
Q. You were placed on probation the last time. There is nothing in our record to indicate you are off it.
A. I thought I was off probation.

Q. Judge Hoffman placed you on probation. Your probation is revoked. You are committed to Pennypack House, and furthermore you are held in $2,500.00 good bail on the charges of threats, contributing to the delinquency of a minor, conspiracy, and malicious use of the telephone.

Calvin was then over the age of eighteen and entitled to be tried as an adult. Had he been under eighteen, he would not have been released on bail. At his trial, charges were dismissed for lack of evidence.

Wendell D. was in jail and he remained there for twenty-two days until Judge Stout held a rehearing. The statute requires the child to petition within twenty-one days. It does not require the judge to hold the hearing within any time limit.

Although under the Constitution the burden of proving the commission of a crime and the burden of proving the guilt of the defendant is always on the prosecution, this is not the rule in juvenile court. It is essential to prove an affirmative defense. In any court it is difficult to prove that one did *not* do something without an impregnable alibi. A character witness would at least be of some help. A lawyer is always better able to represent a client whom he knows and understands. Therefore, I called Jack Minnis. I wanted to know what kind of a boy Wendell was, his habits, his strengths and weaknesses, and anything else relevant to Wendell and the case.

On Tuesday, March 16, 1965, Wendell had gone to school. He had attended every class and eaten lunch in the lunchroom. Because it was a nice day, he stayed in the playground after school. There were no after-school sports, no drama club, no music club, nothing but the streets or the playground for the hundreds of students at Sayre Junior High School.

About four o'clock Officer Washington and Officer Hedgeman of gang control drove up to the playground in a police car. Washington is a huge Negro, well over six feet tall.

Hedgeman is a large husky white man. Andrew and James were in the back of the car. They waved to Wendell. The officers asked who that boy was and were informed he was Wendell. The officers told him to get in the car. The boys were taken to the police station. Each one was asked if he had made a telephone call threatening to get Judge Stout. None of them knew Judge Stout. Each said he had not made a phone call. Wendell said he was in school all day and the police verified the fact. No one was advised of any constitutional rights. No parents were called.

Despite their denials, the boys were held at the police station and interrogated repeatedly. They were asked if they belonged to gangs. Wendell said he did not. Then he was beaten by one of the officers for lying. In the gang control book there is a list of names of "gang members." The Reverend Johnson, a white Episcopal priest who works in the ghetto, believes that he inadvertently supplied some of the information for the book when he told the police the names of the boys who came to his youth group.

At some point in the long night, the boys were asked about a gun. Andrew said he had seen a gun and believed it might be in a vacant house. The gun did not belong to him and he had never fired it. About midnight the officers took two of the boys to the vacant house and searched it. They were threatened with more beatings if the gun was not recovered, and the boys were beaten. A gun was found in the house by one of the police officers. The boys were then taken back to the station house. About 4 A.M. those under sixteen were sent to the juvenile detention center and those over sixteen to the adult detention center.

The boys did not see their parents for two days. Neither the parents nor the children were notified of the charges or the right to counsel. The two older boys, being above the juvenile court age, did obtain counsel.

At the trial on March 17, 1965, Emanuel's mother wept

and pleaded for her son. As a result she, too, was committed to jail. What was her offense? No one knows.

On April 7, 1965, a rehearing (a new trial) for Wendell was held. Because Wendell was released, I do not have the transcript of the rehearing. Counsel purchases the transcript—or, in the case of indigents, petitions the court to have the transcript free—only when an appeal is taken. If the client is freed, there is no need for the record of the trial. The first trial of all seven boys had probably not taken more than fifteen minutes; the retrial lasted almost four hours. Wendell had been convicted at the first trial even though there was absolutely no evidence of guilt. At the retrial I would have to prove that Wendell had *not* made the phone call.

I demanded that the person who had received the alleged phone call testify. This was Deputy Sheriff DiMarino, who reportedly answered the telephone for Judge Stout when the alleged threatening call came. He stated that the phone call had come at about 10:30 A.M. He did not recognize the voice. He could not identify it now if he heard it. It was a clear male voice, young, fluent, no distinguishing accents or characteristics. This was the entire evidence with respect to the call. At this point in an adult trial, the defendant would have been acquitted for lack of evidence. In juvenile court it was necessary to present an affirmative evidence of innocence. I proved through public school employees that Wendell had been in school that entire day. He could not have had access to a phone at that hour; he was in a classroom. He was not in the company of the other accused "co-conspirators."

Judge Stout then tried to commit him as a truant. But the evidence showed that Wendell had been seriously ill, that when he was absent from school he was sick or he was in danger of being beaten by hoodlums. His mother had repeatedly asked the police for protection but none was provided for him. After four hours of testimony and twenty-two days in jail, this innocent boy was finally released.

I was then faced with the problems of the six other under-age boys. Certainly there was no evidence that any of them had made the alleged obscene phone call. Why should they remain in jail? Several of them, moreover, were not receiving much, if any, schooling in prison. Months of their lives were being wasted.

Petitions for rehearing were filed on behalf of several of the others and rehearings were held. Judge Stout refused to release them. I then filed a petition for writ of habeas corpus in the Court of Common Pleas, the court of general jurisdiction that is authorized to issue such writs. (Habeas corpus, known as the great writ, is a court order to the jailer to bring the prisoner to court for a hearing on the legality of his detention.) My petition alleged that there was no evidence in the record that these boys had committed any offense. District Attorney Thomas Reed, a Negro, now a judge, filed an answer admitting that the boys were not guilty of any offense. The answer further avers:

> The purpose of a hearing [sic] Juvenile Court is to determine how best to serve the interests of the particular child brought before the Court. There is no "complainant." The Commonwealth believes and therefore avers that that which transpired before Judge Stout fully warranted the action Her Honor took.

Judge Charles Guerin denied the petition from the bench and advised counsel to return to Judge Stout for any relief.

An appeal to the superior court was filed immediately. That court avoided deciding the case. Instead of holding a hearing and rendering a much needed decision with respect to the authority to issue writs of habeas corpus for juveniles and jurisdiction to deprive innocent children of their liberty, the superior court called Adrian Bonnelly, President Judge of the County Court, which includes the Juvenile Court as one division. Judge Bonnelly ordered the boys released that day.

Judge Stout has not sat regularly in juvenile court since this series of cases. She has, however, received innumerable plaques and awards for her contributions to law enforcement, a profile in *Life* magazine, and more favorable publicity than any other judge in the jurisdiction. She received the highest number of votes as being a qualified judge among those up for reelection. Of course, very few attorneys represent poor children, and many members of the bar feel that they are being liberal by voting for a judge who is both black and female.

Judge Bonnelly, on the other hand, has been repeatedly under fire from the district attorney and the press for releasing "dangerous criminals."

The incarceration by a court of nine innocent black boys did not noticeably disturb the public, the bench, or the bar, although it was widely reported in the press. Nor were the high-handed and flagrantly unjust juvenile court proceedings of any concern to the organized bar, the law schools, or the crime prevention societies. Wendell and the other boys went home and were soon forgotten.

This series of cases first revealed to me how the juvenile court tries cases of poor children who do not have private counsel. In the succeeding years we in the Office for Juveniles saw many more such cases in which a juvenile court judge made a decision to incarcerate one or more children after a hasty three- to ten-minute hearing in which there was little legally admissible evidence of guilt, no cross-examination, and no evidence submitted on behalf of the child.

For a judge in adult court to determine whether John Doe killed Richard Roe may take two or three weeks. It is not easy to analyze conflicting testimony of eyewitnesses and opinions of experts, and to draw inferences and conclusions from the circumstances surrounding the death. To determine whether Billy Black is in need of treatment or care is much more difficult. The factors leading to such a conclusion are numerous and amorphous. The process has been described as follows:

A combination of impoverished economic position, a marginal scholastic record, a particular kind of disrupted family situation, a current infraction of burglary, and two past citations for auto theft yields a disposition. What disposition? If we ask court agents, they will honestly and appropriately answer that it depends. On what does it depend? It depends on other factors. On what other factors? Well, perhaps a diagnosis of the child's personality, but that too depends. On what does that depend? Ultimately on the needs of the child . . . [emphasis supplied] [David Matza, Delinquency and Drift *(New York: John Wiley and Sons, 1964) p. 115. This study of juvenile delinquency and the court was supported by the Ford Foundation.]*

Most juvenile court judges do not know whether to adhere to the rules of evidence and decide the case on the facts as presented in court or to look at "the whole child" and do what is best for him. It is not easy to take an all or nothing position. Few juvenile court judges have arrived at a conscious philosophical or juridical choice. They hear lectures, they try to keep up with mountains of literature. None of this gives much guidance to the person on the bench who sees scores, indeed hundreds, of poor black children from deprived environments who may have done something contrary to law. A parent who has known his own child from the moment of birth, who understands his personality, his family conflicts, his strengths and weaknesses, his loves and hates, his joys and sorrows—frequently does not know what is best for his own child. The juvenile court judge, who is often not a parent and who is unaware that middle-class adolescents behave much like alleged delinquents, is expected to make such determinations twenty-five, thirty, or even seventy or eighty times a day.

Faced with the dilemma between a strict due-process trial and doing what is best for the child, many judges try to do a little of both. If there is some evidence that the child may have committed a crime, they look at his record. If that indicates that he has been in court before or is having trouble in school, the judge will probably decide that this is a child in need of treatment or rehabilitation.

How does the endless process of making such decisions actually operate? The techniques of the juvenile court were graphically described by Francis J. Morrissey, Jr. Morrissey is a member of the Philadelphia bar who from time to time volunteered his services to represent indigent children in Philadelphia Juvenile Court after the court decided that it should attempt to give token compliance with the *Gault* decision. Significantly, no one has publicly disputed the accuracy of his observations. Morrissey begins a day in juvenile court:

> *At 9:00 o'clock on the morning appointed, the attorney checked himself in for case No. 12 with an outside man, who also noted on his sheet the timely presence of the defendant,* John Doe, John's mother, Mrs. Doe, and the shoemaker who was the prosecuting witness. Thirty-eight other cases were listed for that court. Upon inquiry, the outside man conceded that the co-defendant, Richard Roe, had not checked in. Had Richard Roe been served, the attorney asked anxiously. The outside man said he couldn't tell yet; the sheriff's returns had not yet come in. . . .*
>
> *. . . The attorney went into the courtroom and made himself comfortable. 9:15. A parade of people—inside man, outside man, and various other attachés—was speeding in and out of the little anteroom behind the bench.*
>
> *. . . At 10:05 the judge ascended the bench. He apologized for the delay, ascribing it tactfully to technical difficulties in listing.*
>
> *"No. 15," roared the inside man. Three juveniles and three adults entered the courtroom and were swiftly sorted out by an attaché. "Sit down in the first row," he shouted at the adults. They half-sat. "Leave your hats, coats and handbags and come up here,"*

---

*A juvenile brought to judgment is not properly called a defendant but a child. In these tales, however, it has been found more convenient to use the terms defendant and codefendant.

the inside man roared at them. Hastily they obeyed, dropping their apparel in haphazard piles. As they peered up expectantly at the judge, the inside man addressed the court: there were three juveniles involved, he stated, only one of whom was represented by counsel today; by some oversight the lawyers of the other two had not been notified. The trial could not go on, and, accordingly, the judge announced a continuance, explaining courteously to the six present why the case had to be relisted for another day.

While they were retrieving their belongings, the attaché shouted, "Everybody out the rear door." Disoriented, some started for the door through which they had entered, others shuffled uncertainly. They bumped and milled briefly. "Out the rear door," shouted the attaché, herding them in that direction. He was a long-suffering man, and his rolling eye besought the spectators to witness his grievous immolation. The six straggled out, faces expressionless. "Man, we're cattle," muttered one of the adults. "No. 17," roared the inside man. . . .

It was 10:30. The attorney checked with the outside man. No Richard Roe. He returned to the courtroom. . . .

The attorney found Mrs. Doe. No, she had not seen Richard Roe. She had to be out of there by eleven, she complained, or she'd lose her job. . . .

When the juvenile hearing actually takes place, it is often equally chaotic. Delay and the passage of time obviously dim the memories of the witnesses. Many of them have disappeared. The prosecutor, of course, produces some evidence, if only a written report by the arresting policemen. It is easy for the prosecutor to obtain such reports and to compel the witnesses to appear, if he thinks their presence is necessary. The child has little opportunity to locate witnesses to exonerate him. Even if he knows who they are and where they live, he does not know how to get a subpoena and serve it. He certainly does not have the money to pay the witness fees. If the witness is not paid fees and carfare, he does not have to honor the subpoena. Certainly the child does not know how to obtain expert witnesses, nor can he pay them for their time. These are just a few of the disadvantages a poor child faces in defending himself against an accusation that may be false.

In the Office for Juveniles we discovered that more than two-thirds of the children whom we represented were innocent of the crimes and offenses with which they were charged. We did not simply take the word of the child, but we did proceed on the presumption that the accused is innocent until proved guilty. By forcing the state to prove the case against the child and, where possible, by making a reasonable investigation, we were often able to establish innocence.

Louie M. is one of the many innocent children saved from jail by the obvious device of insisting upon accepted legal procedures. He was brought into court on a purse-snatching charge. He had been in jail more than a week since his arrest. Judge John Meade suggested that the prosecution show the attorney the police report and see if counsel couldn't save time by a guilty plea. This was a first offense. This judge is a very kind man and I was reasonably sure that Louie would be placed on probation.

The report stated that a woman had hailed a passing police car at 10:30 P.M. and said her purse had just been snatched by a young Negro male who ran west. The policemen drove slowly west and two blocks later found Louie sitting on his own doorstep with the complainant's pocketbook. All her possessions were there. The money (about two and one-half dollars) was missing. Louie denied that he had snatched the purse. He told the policemen that a boy had run past a few minutes before and dropped the pocketbook. Louie was on his way home from visiting friends. He picked up the pocketbook and sat down on the step, where the light from the street lights was good, to examine the pocketbook.

Louie had no witnesses. He insisted that his statement to the police was true and he said he did not want to plead guilty.

I demanded that the commonwealth prove its case. The court employees shrugged in annoyance. This was the kind of pettifogging that lawyers caused when they were permitted in juvenile court. There couldn't be a clearer case.

The arresting officer read from his report. On cross-examination he admitted that Louie's clothes had been searched at the police station and that he had only thirty-two cents. There was no explanation of what had happened to the victim's two and one-half dollars.

The next witness was the owner of the purse. She identified the purse. On cross-examination she stated that she had about two and one-half dollars. She knew she had two one-dollar bills and some change. She positively identified Louie. There was no doubt in her mind that he was the boy. On cross-examination she described the place where the purse-snatching occurred. It was in the middle of the block. The streetlight was at the corner. How could she be sure Louie was the boy? "Well," she replied, "he's wearing the same red shirt he had on at the police station."

Of course it was the same red shirt; he had been in jail ever since. She admitted that the boy in the red shirt was the only one she had been shown at the police station. I asked her what was in her pocketbook. Would she please examine it on the stand and make sure all the items were in it? She pulled out the usual assortment of things—handkerchief, comb, a small bottle that she identified as containing her medicine. On further questioning she said the medicine was eye drops. She had very bad cataracts on both eyes. Louie was discharged. (Because the boy was acquitted, there is no record of this case. The lawyer's file contains the substance of what is related here.)

The case of Charles W. illustrates the dilemma of the juvenile judge who does not follow the rules of practice and who is not compelled to do so by counsel for the child. It, too, is an ordinary, run-of-the-mill case. The only difference is that the Civil Liberties Union of Lancaster, Pennsylvania, became interested in Charles and took an appeal. Charles W., a fifteen-year-old Negro, was arrested in an interracial fracas in Lancaster, Pennsylvania. All of the persons arrested were black. All of the state's witnesses were white. The trial was held on July 24, 1968. No witnesses were called on Charles' behalf. I have read the entire transcript of the trial—thirty-eight pages—many times and I cannot figure out who did what. Apparently the judge was not too sure either.

The principal witness against Charles was a Mr. Reed. He testified that he is six feet five inches tall and weighs about 230 pounds. Another prosecution witness was Mr. Miller, over six feet tall. These two adults and a third white man had come into a Negro neighborhood to play basketball. After they left the basketball court and went out on the street, a fist fight occurred. Several black boys over the age of eighteen were arrested. They were subsequently tried in adult court and placed on probation. Charles was the only juvenile arrested.

Williams, a white male adult, testified, for the prosecution, as follows:

> *Q. Will you state to the court the extent with which you saw Mr. W. [Charles] participating in this matter at all?*
> *A. Well, I was standing up on the hill and they were down at the parking-lot* and I didn't see him hit Mel—I don't know whether he hit Mel or not but I saw him swinging at Andy. *I don't know if he hit him because I was up on the hill but I did see him swinging at Andy. [emphasis supplied]*

This was the substance of the evidence of delinquency.

Charles was put on the stand to testify in his own behalf. He said:

> *A. He [Reed] was talking—he was just fat-mouthing the whole time —then somebody hit him through the window.*
> *Q. They hit him?*

A. Yes.

Q. When they hit him then what happened?

A. Then he got—then somebody jumped in on him with a stick, then he jumped out the side. I was standing over on the other side of the car.

Q. Were you standing on the side he jumped out of the car?

A. Yes.

Q. What happened then?

A. He just got out and started swinging. Then I started swinging.

Q. You started swinging?

A. Yeah. And then he started backing up and then I kicked him and he fell down.

Q. He started swinging at you?

A. Yes.

Q. Did he hit you?

A. Yes.

Q. And did you swing back at him?

A. Yes.

Q. Did you hit him?

A. Yes.

Q. You hit him where?

A. In his face.

The defender stated to the court:

> *. . . I think it is obvious from his testimony that this is not one of the leaders in whatever this gang consisted of, or what occurred here, and I don't even believe he was one of the main perpetrators. I think he was perhaps along with them, and as his own testimony was, he admitted that he did participate in the fracas.*

Charles testified that he did not strike until after he had been hit. He acted in self-defense. In adult court this would constitute a plea of not guilty.

Judge Joseph B. Wissler apparently attempted to look at

the whole child and do what he considered was in Charles' best interests. Judge Wissler did not make a finding as to whether Charles committed an offense in violation of the penal code. Following are the complete remarks and the order of the judge:

> THE COURT: *Well, of course he has been in trouble before. In 1965 he was charged with burglary and placed on probation.* [*Of course, there is no way of knowing whether in fact Charles was guilty of this offense.*] *You also have some trouble in going to school, don't you?*
> DEFENDANT: *Yes, sir.*
> THE COURT: *Were you suspended from school, also? You seem to be in need of some stricter discipline. Isn't that about right?*
> DEFENDANT: *I don't know.*
> THE COURT: *You don't know. Well, if you don't know, the court so finds from the testimony in this case and from your prior conduct.*
> *The court adjudges Charles a delinquent and commits him to the State Correctional Institution at Camp Hill, Pennsylvania.* [*Under this order he must remain in jail until the age of twenty-one unless released by the court.*]

Camp Hill is also the prison for adult males under the age of twenty-five who are convicted in criminal court. (The daily routine at Camp Hill is described in Chapter 7.) The maximum penalty for assault and battery is two years' imprisonment.

Putting aside questions of the Constitution and procedure, one must ask the basic questions upon which the juvenile court law is premised. Is it better for Charles to be in jail than to be at liberty? Is it in the best interests of Charles or of society to keep him under lock and key during the years when he should be growing into responsible adulthood? Professor Monrad Paulsen answers these questions with a resounding No. He writes:

A contact with the Juvenile Court not only is unlikely to assist a youngster to become a better citizen but, according to respectable theory today, it is likely to lead him into further "delinquency." [*"Children's Court: Gateway or Last Resort,"* Case & Comment, *No. 6, p. 3 (1967)*]

The court's decision was made in a half hour at most, on the scantiest of information. Few people would invest four thousand dollars on the basis of the information available to Judge Wissler. Almost anyone would take more time and trouble and make a better investigation of the prospects of a return on the investment before making a decision involving only this sum of money. The cost of maintaining Charles in jail is almost four thousand dollars a year. His mother was assessed five dollars a week toward his maintenance. The public by this hasty decision is forced to expend almost twenty thousand dollars in the vague expectation that jail will be beneficial to Charles and to society.

The hearing did not determine guilt or innocence. Nor did it provide any substantial basis for a determination that Charles was "in need of treatment or rehabilitation." Attempting to fulfill the functions of criminal court and of juvenile welfare, the hearing, *In the Matter of Charles* . . . , did neither.

Chapter Five

TEMPORARY DETENTION

For him there is no tomorrow.

JOSÉ DE ESPRONCEDA, *El Diablo Mundo*

The case of John R. had been before the juvenile court more than twenty times. Each time, a clerk entered it on the day's list. Each time, the social workers and Mr. and Mrs. P. were notified. Each time, arrangements were made to bring John from the detention center to the courtroom. An army of file clerks gathered the ever-growing folder with John's case history and had it in the courtroom for the judge to see at the appropriate moment. Some twenty times the court crier called out "John R."

John, nine years old, stood alone before the bar of the court. The judge leaned over to peer down at the small solitary figure.

"How are you, John?"

The boy did not answer.

"I guess you're kind of disgusted. Well, I don't blame you. Mrs. Mundy, what are we going to do with John R.?"

Judge Joseph L. McGlynn, Jr., leafed through a file several inches high while Mrs. Mundy lumbered up to the bar of the court. She is a senior social worker for the Department of Welfare, a large black woman. "Your honor, the diagnostic center hasn't completed its studies. We won't be able to make a suitable plan until we get their report."

"I ordered those studies three months ago," the judge complained.

"We sent in the request promptly. But they didn't see him until five weeks ago."

"Five weeks to write up a report! What do they do over there, anyway?"

"You know how it is," Mrs. Mundy replied.

The judge and the social worker shrugged their shoulders over the inscrutable ways of the psychiatric evaluation center. This highly professional organization is paid a large sum on a contract basis to do neuropsychiatric studies for the juvenile court.

"List John R. before me in thirty days," the judge said to the court representative. "No, make it sixty days so we surely have a report and let them know I want it."

The court crier stood up. "The case of Willie S., Raymond T., Samuel Y. Boys stand up, mothers sit in the first row. No talking."

As the next group filed in, the crier noticed John R. standing silently at the bar of the court. "C'mon, John. Out you go." John turned and walked back to the door from which he entered.

A nice looking middle-aged woman, sitting next to a man in a dark suit, stood up and began to cry.

"Can't I have him back, Judge? Please, we want him."

The judge, who was already reading the files of the next three boys, looked up, startled.

"Who is this woman?"

The social worker came up to the bar of the court.

"Your honor, Mrs. P. was the foster mother."

"This is not your child, is it?" the judge asked. "You're not related to the boy?"

"No, sir. But I've had him since he was eight days old. He's just like my child. I want him back."

The judge was reading again. "You've been here before. You know we're trying to find a place for him. Come back in sixty days."

Mrs. P. sat down sobbing quietly. Her husband took her hand.

The crier stood up again. "All parties on the case of John R. out the back door. No talking."

As Mr. and Mrs. P. left the courtroom, they saw a joyful reunion of mother and son. Mrs. P. knew the mother and congratulated her. "How did you get Cochise out of the center?" she asked. And then she learned that there was something new —a lawyer for poor children.

The receptionist for the Office for Juveniles was young and pretty. All day she listened to weeping mothers and hostile kids. Her typing was a bit smudgy but she had an unerring ability to get to the core of a problem. Often I asked her to talk to a child who found it difficult to tell his story to a white middle-aged attorney.

She came in to see me, her eyes wide with indignation. "John has been in the Youth Study Center for twenty-seven months. Mr. and Mrs. P. are three dollars over the eligibility. We can't send them away."

"No. We can't send them away," I agreed. "Please ask Mr. and Mrs. P. to come in."

The eligibility rule had to be strictly observed lest the bar association complain that the poverty office was taking clients away from lawyers. Of course, no private lawyer would take any of these cases. A couple with eighty-eight dollars a week total income can scarcely pay a nominal fee, much less an adequate fee for the hours of work that each case required.* Since we represented John, an orphan, the financial status of Mrs. P. was no bar to our taking the case.

Mr. and Mrs. P. came in to talk to me. John R.'s story was

*Private counsel could, however, represent associations of poor people. If each family contributed one or two dollars, these groups could retain their own lawyer and direct their own destinies. OEO legal services, however, engage in creating such community action groups, incorporating them, and representing them in a wide variety of matters.

quickly told. Nine years ago a little black boy, probably less than a day old, was found in a paper box. He was promptly rushed to the city hospital and the Department of Welfare was notified. There was no identification on the box. The infant was wrapped in a towel from Woolworth's. A search of all hospital records in the city was made, but all boys born on the previous day were accounted for. There appeared to be no way to trace the parentage of this foundling. The department made up a name for him. His birth certificate lists the boy as Negro male, parents unknown, religion Catholic. The department alternates between Protestant and Catholic in assigning a religion to its wards. The baby abandoned just before John was designated Protestant, so John became a Catholic. When he was eight days old, the department turned him over to Mrs. P. The department liked Mrs. P. She never asked for extra money and she seldom complained. The caseworker could check on Mrs. P. by telephone instead of making the tiresome quarterly visit to her home.

Everything was fine for six years. John called Mr. and Mrs. P. "Mom" and "Pop." Even they sometimes forgot that he was a foster child. Once or twice they thought of adopting John. The social worker told them it cost more than two hundred dollars for an adoption, so they dropped the notion. In fact, the court costs for adoption are ten and one-half dollars. And by petitioning for leave to file *in forma pauperis,* Mr. and Mrs. P. could probably have had the court costs waived. But the caseworker from the Department of Welfare either did not know of these procedures or did not think it worth the trouble to regularize the status of a poor black child.

In September of John's sixth year, Mrs. P. registered him at the nearest elementary school. She was required to bring his birth certificate, and John was enrolled as John R. In deference to Mrs. P.'s request, the teacher called him Johnny P. First grade presented only the usual problems. It was not easy for Johnny to sit still in a room with thirty-eight other squirming kids.

Sometimes when Johnny had a nickel, a bigger boy would steal it. He learned not to tell and not to complain. Johnny had to share a book with two other children. Soon he could say, "I see Dick. I see Jane." But he was not too sure about some of the letters—*p* and *g* and *q*, which looked alike to Johnny. He wanted a book of his own. Mrs. P. asked the caseworker if there was an allotment for school books. There wasn't. But Mr. P. bought Johnny a book at the ten-cent store.

Mrs. P. remembered the last summer she had Johnny. She cried a little while telling me what a good boy Johnny was. He went to the recreation center every day. There he made a little basket for Mom. Once a week they took him to the swimming pool. The department didn't give an allotment for bathing trunks, but Mrs. P. bought him a pair—red. They were stolen, but by then the summer was almost over.

The second grade teacher didn't have enough books to go around either. Johnny had forgotten all the letters. He ran around the room. The teacher shouted, "John R., sit down." But Johnny preferred to keep talking to his friend Gary. Besides, that wasn't his name. He was Johnny P., not John R.

Johnny didn't like second grade. The teacher hollered at him. He didn't have a book. He couldn't remember all those little letters. He didn't like to sit still. At home he could get up whenever he wanted. Johnny would take his plate and sit on the floor in front of the TV. He didn't have to sit on a chair at the table. When he wanted to talk, he talked. Mrs. P. didn't care. Sometimes she'd say, "Hush your mouth, Johnny, you gives me a sick head talkin' so much." But Mrs. P. never hit him. And Johnny went on talking or singing in a funny little chant.

"I been to that school more'n six times," Mrs. P. told me. "The counselor lady, she say Johnny just can't keep still; he bother the other kids. I says 'I knows he cain't keep still.' Then she tells me to talk to my caseworker and have her take Johnny to the Youth Study Center to have him studied and see why he cain't keep still."

She began to cry again. She had taken Johnny to the center more than two years ago, and now they won't give him back to her. Visiting day is Wednesday from one to three in the afternoon. It's a long way to the center. Sometimes she didn't have the carfare, so she couldn't go and see Johnny. Mrs. P. liked to bring Johnny something when she visited. But "they" took the candy away from him. The last time she was there, Johnny didn't talk. He just sat on the floor in that noisy room full of kids and mothers.

"Did you sign a paper when you brought Johnny to the center?" Mrs. P. doesn't remember.

A check of the court records was made. Johnny had been brought into court on a delinquency petition. The caseworker was listed as the complainant who charged Johnny with being incorrigible. The petition was signed and sworn by a court employee who had never seen John. The caseworker had no personal knowledge of Johnny's incorrigibility. Mrs. P. did not know the meaning of the word and stoutly maintained that Johnny was always a good boy. At the first hearing in juvenile court, there was no testimony other than that of the caseworker, who reported what she had been told by Mrs. P. about Johnny's troubles at school. Mr. and Mrs. P. and Johnny were present. The judge told Mrs. P. that Johnny would be examined by some doctors who would help him. No one told them that Johnny could have a lawyer. No one told them that Johnny had been adjudicated a juvenile delinquent.

Johnny was seen and evaluated by psychiatrists and psychologists. The first report states: normal intelligence, passive aggressive personality, abnormal affect, anxiety; recommendation: structured environment. The psychiatrists months afterward found that "psychiatric intervention would not curtail delinquency pattern." But John was not delinquent in a legal sense when he was first petitioned into court. John had never violated any law. He did not customarily and habitually disobey his foster parents. It was thought that he needed psychiatric help to adjust to the requirements of a classroom of thirty-eight children where silence was demanded. Twenty-seven months later, the finding was that psychiatry would not help the delinquent—that is, criminal—behavior pattern of a child who had never committed a crime.

John has been seen, tested, evaluated, and screened by batteries of high-priced professionals employed by the court system. He has never been treated. I do not know whether Johnny has really developed such pronounced antisocial tendencies that he should be incarcerated with delinquents (who include killers, rapists, and muggers) or whether there is simply no space in any psychiatric institution, and this is just a way of getting a problem child placed in an institution that does have an empty bed. Often if the institution that the child needs is not available, the child is altered to fit the institution that does have room.

Although the lawyers employed by most legal agencies serving the poor usually do not see the client until the day of the trial, the Office for Juveniles attempted to have the lawyer who tried the case know the child and his parents, consult the school records, and find friends who could serve as character witnesses. On occasion, I would persuade a private psychiatrist to see a child as a special favor to me. Before deciding on strategy this time, I wanted to see John.

It wasn't easy. I went to the Youth Study Center and spoke to the receptionist barricaded behind a glass window like the ticket seller at a movie theater. "Visiting day is Wednesday, one to three, parents only," she snapped. I showed my attorney's card and the warrant of attorney from Mrs. P. Lawyers are not permitted to see children, the receptionist said. I asked to see the director.

Robert Perkins, the director of the Youth Study Center, saw no reason for letting a juvenile consult with counsel. Children are different, he explained; the center is not a jail but a shelter for temporary lodging of unfortunate youngsters awaiting trial or suitable placement. But I simply refused to leave without seeing Johnny. After a few awkward minutes during which we politely chatted about legal rights, the Supreme Court, and other areas about which the director was uninformed, he capitulated. It would be ridiculous to call a policeman to remove a lawyer for trespassing in a public building. It was easier to permit me to see John than to make a fuss. Many small victories are won on this principle alone.

Mr. Perkins called for a matron to conduct me from his office to the main part of the center. We walked down a corridor to a locked and bolted fire door. This was carefully unlocked, and the matron and I entered a passageway. The fire door was locked and bolted behind us. At the end of the passage there is another heavy metal door, also locked and barred. This was unlocked and then also carefully locked behind me. Every time I cross over this passage from the free portion of the center to the jail section, I think of Dante's inscription over the portal of the Inferno, Abandon Hope All Ye Who Enter Here. A young Negro attorney with the Office for Juveniles who had once been locked in the center told me his sensations of horror when the guard thought he might be an inmate and had at first refused to permit him to leave.

Two large uniformed guards with guns in holsters loll behind a desk strategically situated between the boys' wing and the girls' wing. There is a large window overlooking a basketball court and a grassy lawn surrounded by a high smooth stone wall. The sun was shining on this day, but there were no children outside. The windows were tightly shut, and the place was hot and stuffy. The guards laughed and joked while drinking Cokes. Not a child was visible inside or outside.

I was ushered into a cheerful but stifling room to wait for John. In a few minutes a silent little dark brown boy appeared with a matron.

I explained to John that Mrs. P. loved him and had talked to me. I would try to get Johnny out of the center and back home.

"Would you like that, Johnny?"

The boy nodded. His eyes filled with tears, but he did not speak.

"What do you do here all day?" I asked Johnny. "Do you have school?"

"Sometime."

The matron interrupted. "He is a very disturbed child. Some days he can't be contained in a classroom."

Both the public schools and the institutions use this telling term—"contained." The child either can or cannot be "contained." Evidently containment of people, be it an individual child or a hostile nation, is not an effective measure.

"What does he do?" I wanted to know.

"He won't sit still. He used to talk a lot in class and interrupt the teacher. I understand he's better now, quieter."

"Can you read, Johnny?" I asked.

"No'm."

"What do you do when you're not in school?"

There was no answer.

The following week Johnny and Mr. and Mrs. P. were back in court. I went into the bond room where the children in custody wait just before their cases are called. Johnny was down in the cellblock in the basement. The guard sent him upstairs. When he saw me, he smiled in amazement. Clearly Johnny had not believed or not understood what I had told him about a hearing in court and going home to Mr. and Mrs. P. Johnny took his place on the bench with the other children waiting for their cases to be called.

"Sixty-nine cases today." The court crier showed me the list. "Don't take too long. We'll never get out of here." It was ten o'clock. The court employees were frantically checking and phoning, trying to get the necessary parties and witnesses together, so that the judge could start on the list of cases. The social worker was finally located and John's case was called.

Mr. and Mrs. P. filed into the courtroom and sat in the front row.

The assistant district attorney stepped up. "May it please the court, I have been requested by the Department of Public Welfare to oppose the instant petition for release of John R. on two grounds. First, John is a ward of the department and as such is represented by their counsel. The attorney has no standing. Second, the department opposes the release of this minor. He is simply awaiting suitable placement. The department will request his release as soon as a suitable place is found. We ask that the petition be dismissed." (The arguments of counsel and statements of the court are reconstructed from my notes.)

The judge leaned back and sighed. Clearly it was going to be a long day. A legal argument would simply set the whole schedule back at least a half hour and accomplish nothing. The assistant district attorney sat down, his duty done. I had been standing at the bar of the court next to John. (There are no chairs or table for counsel in juvenile court.) I began my argument.

"John is entitled to representation against his guardian, the ubiquitous Department of Public Welfare. Just as a child is entitled to have counsel to represent him against a natural parent who mistreats him and as an alleged mentally ill person is entitled to counsel in an action to obtain his release from an institution even though he may technically be a ward of the institution. Moreover, the department uniformly fails to provide counsel for its wards. When a child who is on aid or relief is arrested, the department refuses to provide counsel for him. The department . . ."

Judge McGlynn evidently wanted to avoid this tangle.

"Proceed. We agree that you may represent this juvenile. Are you seriously suggesting that we release him? Have you read the recommendations?"

"Yes, your honor. I have not only read the record, I have been to the Youth Study Center and seen this child. This child has not committed any offense known to the law. A social worker made an unsworn statement, based on hearsay, that John was incorrigible, whatever that means. As a result of this petition, defective on its face, this child has been deprived of his liberty for twenty-seven months. He has also been deprived of his right to schooling, and to the love and affection of the only parents he has ever known."

The judge cut off argument by agreeing that John should not be in the center. But his problem was where to put the boy. He ran through a list of mental hospitals and training schools for delinquents, all of which had refused to take John. The hospitals said he wasn't sick enough. One state-supported institution was doing research and would accept only children who could be tested in that program, and John didn't have that particular mental disorder.

I pleaded and argued that the boy should be returned to Mr. and Mrs. P., who love him and want him.

The judge searched through the files.

"It was Mrs. P. who made the complaint against the boy. What makes her think she can handle him now if she couldn't handle him then?"

Mrs. P. was put on the witness stand and under questioning by counsel explained that she hadn't intended to make a complaint. The school had told her Johnny needed help, and she had brought him to the Youth Study Center with her caseworker so that he could be studied and helped. She had never said he was bad or disobedient.

Mrs. P. stated that she would take Johnny at her own expense and adopt him legally if the court would just let him come home. She didn't want the department allotment.

Judge McGlynn continued the case for two weeks and ordered the department to find a suitable placement before the next hearing. The judge refused to release John pending hearing.

We then filed a petition for writ of habeas corpus in the court of general jurisdiction. It was refused. That judge said the juvenile court would have to clean its own house. He would not get involved.

At the next hearing in juvenile court the judge was annoyed. Why had I filed petitions? There were enough other cases for me to handle instead of making so much fuss about John. The court was there to protect the boy. The judge called for the social worker, who asked for a continuance so that the department could complete its plans for John. Again, I moved that John be released to Mrs. P.

The judge then questioned the social worker about the department's views on Mrs. P. The social worker said that the department found that Mrs. P. is not a fit foster mother for John.

I asked for the right to cross-examine the social worker. After a verbal hassle, it was reluctantly granted. The social worker admitted that Mrs. P. had been on the approved foster mother list for over fifteen years. She grudgingly conceded that she had offered Mr. P. another child. What had changed her mind? A caseworker interviewed Mrs. P. and reported that Mrs. P. was not suitable. I moved that the social worker's testimony be stricken as hearsay and the caseworker be produced. Pending such hearing, I again moved for the release of John to Mrs. P.

The social worker and the district attorney opposed the motion. What if the boy gets into trouble? What if he injures someone? It is the responsibility of the court to protect John and society.

John was finally committed to an institution in New Jersey. Mr. and Mrs. P. cannot visit him very often, because it is a long and expensive trip.

What relief does the law provide? An application for a writ of habeas corpus had been denied. There is a right of appeal. Such an appeal, however, might not be heard for five months. A special application for leave to file and proceed *in forma pauperis* is required, because neither John nor our office had money to pay for printing a brief and record. The judge who refused to grant the writ would not hear testimony. The appellate court at best would remand the case for a hearing to determine the facts.

I might have tried to appeal the juvenile court judge's order remanding Johnny to the center. But this is an interlocutory order and generally not appealable. The litigant is supposed to wait until the trial court has made a final disposition of the case. The appellate court will then consider all the errors, such as the hearsay testimony of the social worker, and the failure to call the caseworker. It may finally get to the real question, May a child who has not committed a crime be deprived of his liberty under the guise of treatment for mental disturbance and be held in a jail for twenty-seven months without any treatment? An appeal before final decision would probably just cause further delay. The appeal could not be heard for four or five months, and then the court would probably dismiss it as premature.

Although the Bill of Rights specifies that the writ of habeas corpus shall not be impaired, Congress has limited the jurisdiction of federal courts. The federal court will hear a petition for habeas corpus only *after* the petitioner has exhausted all the remedies in state courts. John was nine when he was put in detention. He was twelve when I first saw him. He would be at least thirteen or fourteen before an appeal to the Superior Court on the writ of habeas corpus could be heard. That court could easily take more than six months to reach a decision. On remand to the trial court, another half-year would likely pass before another hearing was held and the court reached a decision. John would then be fifteen years old. If the superior court decision is against him, it will be another year until his appeal reaches the State Supreme Court. That court has held that a child has no right to liberty. The only right of a child in this state, as in most jurisdictions, is the right to custody. The juvenile court as a wise, kindly father will protect him from his own

evil ways and gently guide him into the right paths. If the State
Supreme Court decides against him, John may be sixteen or
seventeen before his case can even get into federal court. His
entire youth will pass in jail while courts and bureaucrats follow
procedures.

Is the case of John R. anomalous? Unfortunately not.
There are juvenile detention centers all over the nation. These
quaintly named jails are filled to overflowing with children
awaiting trial and awaiting "suitable placement." There is no
time limit on the period a child may be held in jail awaiting trial.
Although the Constitution guarantees the accused a "speedy
public trial," a juvenile is not considered an accused person. An
adult is entitled to be released on bail pending trial except for
very serious crimes. There is no bail at all for juveniles in most
states. Of course, because approximately 90 percent of the children charged with delinquency are poor, bail would not provide
a meaningful remedy.

Neither the Standard Juvenile Court Law promulgated
by the National Probation and Parole Association in cooperation with the Council of Juvenile Court Judges, nor the proposed updated law prepared after the *Gault* decision places any
limitation on the time a child may be held in detention after trial
pending placement (that is, the choice of a permanent jail or
foster home). Nor do the present juvenile court laws of the
several states. The United States Supreme Court has not considered this question, although it was presented on appeal. (See
Chapter 15, "When the Battle's Lost and Won.") The only
prohibition or restriction on the confinement of children under
state law is that a child shall not be placed in the same jail as an
adult. And that limitation is generally ignored.

The National Council on Crime and Delinquency, in its
Standards and Guides for the Detention of Children and Youth, recommends that detention not exceed two weeks. If the child is innocent, two weeks in jail, two weeks of schooling missed, two
weeks of association with dangerous and criminal children, is

far too long. In fact, "temporary" detention before trial and while awaiting placement stretches out for weeks, months, and even years as the bureaucracy of the courts and welfare administration moves ever more slowly.

The statistics tell a grim tale. In March, 1967, there were 186 boys and 64 girls in the Philadelphia Juvenile Detention Center. In March, 1968, there were 176 boys and 63 girls. These were not unusual months. As of March 27, 1967, 33 boys had been in the center more than 100 days, some as long as 650 days, awaiting suitable placement. Only 29 had been there for less than a week. Nevertheless, the fiction is maintained that this is a temporary detention facility. The official view is that children are not held more than three days pending trial. The files of the center show that some children are held a month and longer before trial and that few are released within three days. This situation prevails in almost every state and city in America.

But the numerous research projects on juvenile court problems fail to reveal these obvious facts. Harvard Law School students made a study of juvenile court procedures under the sponsorship of the Walter E. Meyer Foundation. The report states: "In Philadelphia, if a child is held [in custody pending trial] he goes to the judge within 72 hours" (79 *Harvard Law Review* 792 [1966]). The authority cited is an interview with the director of the juvenile court probation office. In fact, many children are held for weeks pending trial. In a survey of one hundred consecutive cases, our office found that the average time of detention pending trial was sixteen days. The Harvard study makes no mention of this lengthy incarceration pending suitable placement. A similar study under the same auspices was reported in the *Columbia Law Review*. The authors of this report note that if the case is not dismissed on the merits, the first duty of the judge "is to determine that the youth 'requires supervision, treatment, or confinement'" (67 *Columbia Law Review* 340 [1967]). The plight of the child who needs treatment that is not available is totally ignored.

This is the standard description of juvenile detention:

For however short a time the detention home cares for a child it must not deny these basic rights. It must provide the best substitutes for the love and guidance of parents, for the mutual respect of the family; it must guarantee a clean, safe, protecting dwelling, health care, protection from evil influence and from mistreatment, education and training through a wide variety of media. There are at present children who remain in detention homes for months, denied every one of these things. What right have we to say that the child's parents have failed if, when authority steps in and removes him from his home to await court action, his basic rights are denied? [*Herbert A. Bloch and F. T. Flynn,* Delinquency: The Juvenile Offender in America Today *(New York: Random House, 1956), p. 296.*]

John was not being punished. Everything that happened to this boy was done for his good. The juvenile court law so specifies. As the Supreme Court of Pennsylvania declared in 1954 in the *Holmes* case: "The state is not seeking to punish an offender but to salvage a boy who may be in danger of becoming one, and to safeguard his adolescent life."

Who is responsible for the thousands of children in detention? The taxpayers, of course, are paying for these temporary jails. In many communities it costs thirty dollars a day per child. An enormous staff or guards, matrons, janitors, and clerks are employed in each detention center to keep a couple of hundred children locked up and isolated as if they were moral lepers or wild beasts.

The Philadelphia center was specially designed as a temporary shelter for children. Its management is confided to a citizen board of trustees, several of whom are octogenarians. All of the board members are distinguished citizens. It is deemed an honor to be named to a nonpaying position on a public board. Of course, it is understood that the board members are purely decorative. Some of them have never been inside the building. The real decisions concerning its management and operations are made by the director. His office is bright and cheerful with pictures of snow-capped mountains and wide open spaces. His window is open and the sunshine streams in. It is the only open window I have ever seen during my many visits to the center. This clean-cut young man came to the city highly recommended as having successfully managed a juvenile correctional institution. But he can do nothing about admitting or removing the children. He must accept every child who is sent there by the police, the juvenile court, or even parents who simply file petitions against their children and abandon them to the system. He cannot insist upon the removal of a child even though the child may be mentally ill or innocent of any crime.

Perkins and I had several conferences. He was polite but wary. Besides parents, there are few, if any, visitors to the center. Those who do come make ceremonial tours carefully conducted by the staff. Lawyers are not among the customary visitors. There are no conventions or guidelines for dealing with a lawyer in a juvenile institution. A lawyer's position in a prison, however, is accepted. He is the intermediary for his client with the prison authorities and the outside world. His visits are a constitutionally protected right. The lawyer submits to a search upon entry and exit. But no guard may be present or eavesdrop on these conferences, and the prison authorities do not place obstacles in the way of a lawyer visiting his client.

In one of my meetings with Perkins, I asked him why there were no children out on the playground. Was the inmate population so reduced?

The director laughed bitterly at such a thought. He explained that the previous night, like most nights, sixty-eight children slept on the floor. "They" just keep putting the children in. And "they" never remove them. The daily press prints with monotonous regularity pictures of children sleeping on the floor in the overcrowded Youth Study Center. Edward Eisen of *The Philadelphia Inquirer* in March, 1967, reported:

> *Friday night, in stifling temperatures, with the putrid smell of unwashed bodies in the air, 60 boys lay on that floor [the gym of*

the Youth Study Center]. They lay there, feet dangling on the hard floor three to a mat. There were all kind there, too. From murder suspects to petty larceny cases. Assistant director Ralph Liming said with an all-knowing sigh: "There'll be more by the time the night's over." Yes, there'll be more. The problem is and has been since this magnificent structure was built 15 years ago, there's no room. The Center was built to accommodate a total of 175 youth, 123 boys, 52 girls who are awaiting criminal hearings. Instead the population has run as high as 248. That's why they're sleeping on the floor . . .

The March 1967 grand jury lashed out at the priority and funds going to such projects as the sports stadium and the Delaware Expressway "while our children are being burned and destroyed." The report to Judge Theodore B. Smith stated: "If there is such a thing as 'first things first,' then why cannot these children, our future adults, be allocated the necessary attention and facilities now?"

On March 1, 1968, Judge Joseph Bruno visited the center and found "wall to wall carpeting of kids." Nothing has changed. Citizens, judges, and lawyers protest. But no one will listen.

There are scores of children all over America like John R., who spend the days, months, and years of their youth behind walls awaiting suitable placement. Mr. Perkins would like to have these unhappy children removed from the Youth Study Center. But he has no authority to move them. There is no place to which to move them. We both knew that. I was concerned about what happens to the children while they are incarcerated in the Youth Study Center. And I pressed him on several matters.

Why, I again asked Mr. Perkins, were no children outside on such a beautiful afternoon? The director explained that the temperature was below 40°. Children are not permitted outside in such weather. They might catch cold. Besides, there isn't enough warm clothing for all of them. More than half the year in Philadelphia the temperature is below 40°.

I wanted to know why John didn't go to school. The director explained unhappily that the Board of Education sends only a few teachers to the center. There is little that they can do with the vast numbers of children. It is a shifting population.

No one knows how long or short a time a child will remain in the center. It is impossible to plan a program of any sort. Many of the children are emotionally disturbed and can't function in a classroom. They become upset. They scream; they cry; they throw things, anything that comes to hand.

Chemistry makes things easier for the administrators of these juvenile warehouses. Thorazine calms children; it also depresses their spirits. But it is cheap and convenient. It may dull the mind after prolonged use. But in many institutions it is commonly and indiscriminately given to children.

The problems and needs of children in detention are extremely varied. There were six boys in the center awaiting trial for murder. Some are there because they ran away from home. Many have been there more than a year. Some will remain only a week or a month. Many of these children sit in idleness. In the adult jails where the older children are placed, there is little schooling. Most of them wash dishes or do other menial tasks.

The percentage of arrested girls who are committed to institutions is higher than that of the boys. In a sample examination of the records of 103 children, 79 were released immediately to their parents. Although only 16 girls were included, 5 of them were held in custody before trial. Four of these girls remained in custody a total of 61 days. The fifth girl was held in "temporary" detention for 150 days. Detention center statistics reveal that 40 percent of the girls arrested are held in custody pending trial.

The girls are usually charged with incorrigibility, truancy, and runaway, none of which is a crime. They often run away from home to avoid sexual molestation by roomers or by members of the household. In such a situation, the girl is confined in the center while her attacker—an adult, entitled to release on bail, jury trial, and the panoply of constitutional protection—is free. The girl may remain in detention until the man is tried.

Girls who for any reason are held in custody are subjected to peculiarly repulsive indignities. It was from Mary Ann S. that I first learned that every girl in the Youth Study Center is required to submit to an internal vaginal examination. Many other girls later complained of these examinations. Denise M., a thirteen-year-old black girl, was examined internally, and she also complained that a middle-aged white matron went into the shower with her and patted her breasts. Denise cried and shuddered while she told me these things.

A girl named Patricia was also examined internally while she was in the center for four days awaiting trial. The doctor reported that Patricia O. was not a virgin and that she was promiscuous. She did not have venereal disease. This report was sent to Patricia's parochial school.

Patricia came back to see me several weeks after I had obtained her discharge from the court. She told me about the report of the medical examination at the Youth Study Center. She had objected to the examination but was told that she had to submit. She was not told of the results or that this report would be transmitted to anyone. Patricia was in anguish. "I'm a virgin. I've never had anything to do with boys—anything like that. You do believe me. Now the nuns want me to leave school before graduation. Can't you help me?"

Again I had to call on a friend. All of us in the office were shameless. When one of "our children" needed help, we would plead with any friend or acquaintance and beg for free services. A gynecologist agreed to see Patricia without fee. He reported that there was no evidence that she was not a virgin. Fortified with this information, I called Judge Frank J. Montemuro, who was most sympathetic. He ordered Patricia's "record" expunged. I also wrote to the school. Patricia graduated with her class.

Mary Ann was the only girl among our clients who re-

sisted the internal examination. She had been arrested for
throwing a snowball at an elderly neighbor, and was taken to the
Youth Study Center. There a check of her school record was
made, and the charge of truancy was added to assault and battery with a snowball. She adamantly refused to submit to the
examination. The Youth Study Center just as adamantly refused
to release Mary Ann until she permitted the examination. After
days of tears and defiance, Mary Ann's mother came to the
office to see if the law would protect the privacy of a thirteen-
year-old girl's body.

For two weeks Mary Ann was kept locked alone in a
room. The authorities insisted that this was not solitary confinement. She was deprived of her clothing, permitted only a pair
of pajamas, while she defied the power of the state to thrust its
hands into the private parts of her body. I visited this frantic
hysterical child between trips to the court. Petitions were presented and denied. Some courts refused to docket them. Others
received the petition but refused to act. No court would grant
a protective order. No court would issue an order of mandamus
to compel another judge who was considering the question to
act upon the matter.

I argued in vain that the right of privacy extends to the
integrity of one's own body. In 1890 Samuel D. Warren and
Louis D. Brandeis found tucked away in the Bill of Rights an
additional right never mentioned by Jefferson, Madison, or
Hamilton: the right of privacy. The succeeding half century has
seen the blossoming of this concept. It protects a man's papers
from government law-enforcement agencies. It protects the
marital relationship from the enforcement of laws banning ar-
tificial contraceptives; it protects the middle-class man who in-
dulges his taste for pornography in his own home. It protects
the man accused of illegal use of drugs from having his stomach
pumped to obtain the evidence of his crime. It may even protect
the middle-class college student from prosecution for the use
of marijuana and LSD. (The American Civil Liberties Union

believes that the right of privacy of the mind prohibits the state from interfering with these experiments, pleasures, and experiences.) But the right of privacy did not protect Mary Ann and thousands of other girls from forcible vaginal examination by the state. The merry-go-round of legal process was played to an inconclusive end. While the lawyers argued and the judges delayed, Mary Ann's strength gave out. The matrons held her legs and the doctor made the examination.

The boys in temporary detention also have a miserable time. Most of them do not belong in a jail. We discovered by checking the records that fifteen of the thirty-three boys in custody more than one hundred days in March, 1967, were not even charged with any criminal offense. They were listed as runaway, incorrigible, medical examination, unsatisfactory probation, or "report on adjustment."

Alvin B., like John R., was in the center awaiting placement. His offense also was incorrigibility. This is not a crime for which an adult could be jailed. Incorrigibility is a legally useful phrase that permits parents to relieve themselves of a child and the state to take control over his destinies. Upon the continued supply of youngsters such as John R. and Alvin B. an enormous bureaucracy depends. When I last checked the records Alvin had been in the center 628 days. He was then only twelve years old. He had been before three different judges, fifteen times. Each time he was brought into court for not more than five minutes and then returned to the center. He has been studied and evaluated again and again. At each hearing he was ordered held in custody awaiting a plan to be submitted by the Department of Public Welfare.

On November 22, 1965, the court ordered that the boy might be placed in a foster home pending placement arrangements. No foster home was found. The record stated as of March 18, 1966: "Copy of summary [from psychiatric evaluation] received. Admission to a state school and hospital where boy can receive psychotherapy, appropriate schooling, and help with prepubertal phase of development which is in his immediate future was recommended." A year later Alvin B. was still in the Youth Study Center. He had not been before the court for eleven months. The judges have forgotten him. The department has no plan. The hospital to which he was referred has no room.

No one knows what thoughts come to him in his dark cell in the basement of the courthouse, or as he lies on the floor in the detention center, wearily waiting, waiting for the inscrutable, unknowable order that will release him.

No one judge is responsible for any specific child. The ever-growing files move from courtroom to courtroom while the child waits for someone to help him. The consequences of this system of irresponsibility are often tragic. *The New York Times* reported the case of Roxanne Felumero, a three-year-old girl, who was killed, allegedly by her stepfather. The case of this child was before the Family Court of New York many times. It came before several judges. According to the *Times*, "the Citizens Committee for Children believes that if Roxanne's case had been handled by the same judge each time, that judge would have realized that it was dangerous to leave her in her stepfather's home."

These children are forgotten in detention centers or left in dangerous homes because there is no place for them. Miss M. MacNeely, director of New York City's public adoption agency, considers a two-year-old child too old for adoption. There are few institutions for noncriminal children who are homeless. Society vainly hopes that citizens will "open their hearts and their homes to children other than their own." This is the plea of the Foster Home Educational Program, a United Fund agency that publishes attractive and expensive brochures advertising the need for foster homes. Because foster parents, unlike social workers in agencies, are not paid for a twenty-four-hour-a-day 365-days-a-year job caring for an unwanted and

often difficult child, the shortage of foster parents is understandable.

On March 3, 1970, the Appellate Division of the New
York State Supreme Court revoked the order of the Family
Court committing a fifteen-year-old boy to a state training
school (correctional institution) simply because his home was
unsuitable. Justice Aron Steuer, writing for the court, said,
"The court obviously cannot provide a facility where none exists." The boy was sent to another institution to await another
hearing.

Children in all parts of the country sit behind bars because there is no other place provided for them.

Two little brothers aged eight and ten were placed in the
Youth Study Center charged with "arson, assault with intent to
kill and conspiracy." More than thirty months later I saw them.
Aubrey H., the elder, had a large purple lump in the center of
his forehead. His brother, Anthony, explained that Aubrey
banged his head against the wall at night before he went to
sleep. Aubrey did not speak much. He had forgotten how to
read, although when he was placed in the center he was doing
well in school.

The true facts of the heinous crime for which these children have been deprived of their liberty will never be known.
There was never a trial on the factual question of whether the
boys were guilty of arson. The court records show that the new
"husband" of the boys' mother made a complaint to the court.
There was a fire in the house when neither of the adults was
home. It would appear that the criminally negligent person was
the mother who left these little children alone. She, of course,
was not prosecuted. She is free.

Was the fire an accident—or a deliberate attempt by the
boys to burn down the house and kill their baby sister, Clarissa,
as Mr. L. contended? The court never made a finding on this
crucial question. Mrs. H. was at the hearing. So were the boys.
The only attorney present was the assistant district attorney. He

presented a report from the fire department. No witness appeared. There was no defense attorney for the boys to demand that a witness be produced and be cross-examined about the evidence of the origin of the fire. There was no evidence as to the intentions of the boys, their intelligence, or their understanding of the dangers of fire. Clarissa was, in fact, unharmed. A neighbor carried her out of the burning apartment. She also led the boys out. This neighbor was not called as a witness. The "husband" was never produced in court for examination. Did he like the boys? Were they a nuisance? Was this episode a convenient excuse to rid himself of these two children who were not his own and who were an expense and a nuisance? There was no one to ask these questions on behalf of the boys. The judge, as a wise kindly father of the boys, did not make such inquiries.

I visited the boys at the center. Aubrey said he didn't want to talk about the fire. Anthony said Aubrey tried to iron Clarissa's dress and the iron caught fire. It happened so long ago that Anthony had forgotten almost everything. It was then thirty months since Aubrey and Anthony had been in the center. Aubrey asked me if he could see Clarissa. But it is against the rules for children to visit the center. Aubrey did not know whether Clarissa was dead or alive. He did not trust his mother, who told him Clarissa was fine. He did not trust me, a strange lawyer. His fears grew and tormented him. Aubrey had been tested, examined, and evaluated many times during these two and one-half years. The reports do not indicate this obsessive anxiety, which is revealed so quickly in a short conversation, and which would be so easy to allay simply by bringing Clarissa to the center so Aubrey could look out of a window and see her. The psychiatrists' recommendation for Aubrey was a mental hospital and separation from his brother, his only friend.

And what did Aubrey do all day in the center? He did not go to classes; he was too disturbed.

After some urging Aubrey went to his quarters and

brought back a neatly painted picture of Jesus. The colors were brilliant. Jesus had bright yellow hair and a gleaming halo. It was a canvas with the outlines drawn and numbered for the colors to be painted in. Aubrey had spent weeks painstakingly filling in the spaces. This was his only activity day after day as the tedious months of his childhood were counted out behind walls and bars.

The Office for Juveniles filed petitions on behalf of these two boys and of other boys and girls who had been waiting months and years for "suitable placement." The juvenile court rejected the argument that a child has a "right to treatment." The court also acted to cut off these embarrassing and time-consuming actions brought on behalf of the children. Orders were given that the monthly population records of the center were not to be given to the Office for Juveniles; no attorney was to be admitted except upon written authorization of the natural parent.

Efforts to get these unfortunate children out of "temporary detention" and to give them treatment or simply return them to life by the judicial process were halted. Those children who obtained release from the center succeeded in getting their freedom only after petitions were filed with the juvenile court by counsel acting on behalf of each child. Once a judge orders a child placed—even temporarily—the matter may never be brought to his attention again. There are more cases every day. Who will speak for this helpless child walled off from life and family? Certainly he cannot speak for himself. The wise, kindly father figure of the juvenile court judge cannot remember all of these children.

Despite a study by the Fels Institute of the University of Pennsylvania recommending against enlarging the center, several million dollars have been allocated for this purpose. No new facility or addition has been constructed. None is even on the drawing boards. The citizens who see this place are appalled by the conditions and urge that more jail space be provided so that each unfortunate child will have his own cot. A bed of one's own in jail is certainly not the best answer society can provide.

The overcrowded dockets of the courts list the same cases month after month. January 25, 1968, was, if anything, a light day in juvenile court. Of the thirty-two cases listed for one of three courtrooms, twenty-five had previously been before the court and were continued for one reason or another; many had been continued more than three times. As the children in detention grow older, one by one they are slowly siphoned out of the center into overcrowded mental institutions. For a child who has endured twenty or thirty months in the center, a mental institution may well be society's last refuge. It is chilling to recall that the psychiatric evaluation of John R. at age nine was that "psychiatric intervention would not curtail delinquency pattern." What is a suitable placement for these juvenile delinquents who have never committed a crime, these emotionally disturbed children whom psychiatry rejects?

Many of the children held in temporary detention are neither dangerously psychotic nor seriously criminal. Some are not even charged with a crime. On July 8, 1969, I sat in juvenile court waiting for the case to be called of a child whom I was representing. In less than ten minutes, five detention hearings were held. Lee D. had been in temporary detention for two weeks on a charge of stealing a TV set. Not only did he admit having stolen the set, but he and his parents had returned it to the owner. The court ordered him back in temporary detention pending trial. Angela Y. is thirteen years old and very pretty. Her parents, middle-European immigrants, asked that she be held in detention because she does not keep her room clean. She was continued in custody pending a trial. A little black girl was held in custody on a charge of shoplifting—she had taken a blouse that probably was not worth five dollars. Daniel S. and Ronald H., both sixteen, were held in custody because the defender was not aware of their cases. Calvin J. is a dirty, ragged little black boy eleven years old. He had been in temporary detention for five weeks while the court issued bench warrants for his family, who had evidently disappeared. There was no return of service, and so Calvin remained in jail. His crime? Missing parents. This was the third time he had been brought before the court. Prosecuting Attorney Louis Mitrano was so dismayed by this child's appearance that he asked the court to take cognizance of the boy's clothing. The judge lifted his eyes from the file, looked at Calvin, and said, "You are the worst-looking child that's come before me."

More than a year after the *Gault* decision, these children were temporarily in jail, without meaningful counsel, without notice of the charges, without ever seeing an accuser, and without access to appeal an order of temporary detention.

The National Council of Juvenile Court Judges held a summer college in 1967 to train judges appointed or elected to the bench since 1965 (reported by Judge Orman W. Ketcham, "Summer College for Juvenile Court Judges," *Judicature,* The Journal of the American Judicature Society, April 1968, p. 330). The cost of this program was covered by a grant from the National Institute of Mental Health. The judges met for four weeks in the idyllic setting of Boulder, Colorado. The fourth and final week of the program considered such issues as the proper use of detention, probation, institutional programs, and alternatives to commitment. The problem is nationwide. Every judge of every juvenile court has encountered a John, an Aubrey, an Alvin, a Calvin. What instructions did they receive at the college to enable them to order a "suitable placement" for these children?

As the judges confer, the reporters expose, and the children remain in custody, I think of a poem by James Dickey, "The Eye-Beaters." It is accompanied by this explanation: "A man visits a Home for Children in Indiana, some of whom have gone blind there . . . A therapist explains why the children strike their eyes."

Chapter Six

TESTING, TESTING . . .

$$IQ = \frac{MA}{CA} \times 100$$

The basic principle underlying all psychological tests is simple: an individual's behavior in one situation *may* be a function of the same individual's behavior in another situation. [emphasis supplied]

HOWARD H. KENDLER, *Basic Psychology*

Tests have two basic functions—The first function is discrimination among individuals. . . . The second is the determination of whether an individual has changed in some measurable respect as a function of time or some other independent variable.

DOUGLAS K. CANDLAND, *Psychology: The Experimental Approach*

Hector M., ten years old, was about to be committed to an institution. After he was adjudged delinquent, the judge had ordered neuropsychiatric tests—a standard practice in juvenile court. Judges depend heavily on such tests in deciding to which institution a child should be sent. After the tests the child is brought back to court and the judge makes the order of commitment. Like most of the children, Hector had no lawyer. Because my case was coming up next, I was standing nearby and heard this exchange.

Judge Charles Wright, skimming through Hector's lengthy record, muttered to himself, "Hard to place this one. IQ sixty-seven, definitely retarded."

A little brown hand shot up and a soprano voice loudly announced, "I ain't retarded, Judge."

Startled, the judge asked me to look into Hector's case. He had been in detention for several weeks after an adjudica-

TESTING, TESTING . . . **135**

tion of larceny. Hector was the oldest of seven children. I learned that he acted as interpreter for his mother, who could not speak a word of English. Hector dealt with the public assistance authorities, he did the family purchasing, and he somehow got his sick little sister to the clinic. Hector was released. He went home to continue to be the head of the family.

Thomas F., according to the court records, had an IQ of 86. He was about to be committed to an institution for mental defectives for the crime of larceny. He had admitted the offense at the intake interview. When I saw him, I asked what he had stolen. He told me it was a book, *Manchild in the Promised Land.* He had finished reading the book and was willing to return it. Counsel's offer of restitution was accepted. Thomas was sent back to school in tenth grade, where he was passing most of his subjects. We did not hear from him again. He was not rearrested, and he will probably graduate from high school.

These boys, like most of the children whom we represented, seemed to us to be normal. Many were functional illiterates, but they were not retarded or defective despite their IQ scores. As Lawrence G.'s mother told me, "We're ignorant. But we ain't stupid." Most of the boys and girls were far from stupid.

One of the very few boys who clearly seemed psychotic was Wiley. He was charged with the murder of his father. His mental state was obvious the first time I saw him, which was in a jail cell.

I walked through the dim cellar lined with cells. The guard called out, "Wiley W." A small dark hand clutched my sleeve.

"Are you Wiley W.?"

"No."

"Who are you?"

"One of your clients."

In every jail and detention center, the children asked for us. But Wiley did not greet me. He did not want to see me. It was a most unsatisfactory interview. The boy was so disinterested as not to be aware of where he was. He kept repeating tonelessly that he had killed his father, he was glad he had done it. And the tears dripped unheeded down his cheeks.

I requested a psychiatric examination. Wiley was charged with murder, and the state was asking that he be tried as an adult. Doubtless the death penalty would be sought even though Wiley was only fifteen. If he were treated as a juvenile, the maximum penalty would be incarceration until the age of twenty-one. Then, unless the court made a finding that at the time of the act Wiley did not have the mental capacity for criminal intent, he might find himself facing a murder indictment at age twenty-one. There is no statute of limitations on a murder charge. I expected that the psychiatrist would find three things: that this child was so disturbed that he did not know the nature and quality of his act; that he could not cooperate with counsel to prepare for his defense; and that his mental ability was less than that of a fourteen-year-old and he lacked the capacity for criminal intent.

We hoped that if Wiley could go to a mental hospital and receive intensive therapy, he could be restored to a normal life. The judge immediately ordered a complete neuropsychiatric examination. Wiley was led in and out of the courtroom in the same dazed, detached condition in which I had seen him. His weeping mother was in the courtroom, but he did not notice her.

More than a month later, I received the court psychiatrist's report. I was aghast. He found Wiley competent to stand trial and to cooperate in his defense, and he also reported that at the time of the act Wiley knew the difference between right and wrong and the nature and quality of his act.

During this interval the Office for Juveniles had been making its own investigation of the death. Mrs. W. had been in another room at the time. She heard a commotion and then a gunshot. When she came into the room, Mrs. W. promptly fainted. There was little information she could give. Mrs. W. vacillated between tears and hysteria. I went back to the court for an order to obtain the medical examiner's report. The juvenile court usually treats such motions as a nuisance. Mr. W. was dead. Wiley admitted he had killed his father. Why was counsel putting everyone to so much time and trouble over technicalities? I persisted. The court directed the prosecutor to make the report available.

The medical examiner is generally very thorough. Not only does he measure and describe the body in detail, but also the place in which it is found. From his report we learned that Mr. W. was six feet tall and weighed over two hundred pounds. He was shot in the heart at very close range. The body was found on the floor of the living room. Chairs and a table were overturned, and there were other signs of a prolonged scuffle or fight. The gun bore the fingerprints of Wiley *and* Mr. W. This gave a completely different picture. Wiley weighed about 110 pounds. He told me that his father had got down on his knees and begged Wiley not to shoot. But Wiley had laughed and shot him right in the heart. Wiley never mentioned a fight. A two hundred-pound man could easily have wrested a gun from this child.

The neighbors were questioned. They had all detested the late Mr. W., a brute who beat his wife and children. Wiley was the youngest child. Now that all the older ones had left home, Wiley bore the brunt of his father's temper.

Another psychiatric opinion was needed. In our customary way we began shamelessly canvassing our friends and acquaintances for free services. Dr. James Nelson, a distinguished Negro psychiatrist, agreed to examine Wiley. He found that the boy was seriously brain-damaged. It was his opinion that Wiley had suffered so badly from his father's brutality that it was essential to Wiley to believe that he had bested his father. Dr. Nelson said that his questioning of the boy indicated that Wiley had pleaded with his father not to beat him and then had shot his father in self-defense. But Wiley had at first claimed that it was his father who had begged for mercy. The boy would rather go to the electric chair, Dr. Nelson said, than admit to himself his weakness before his father.

The case was discussed with the district attorney's office, which refused to withdraw its motion for a certification to adult court. A hearing was held on this issue. (This case was tried before Judge Clifford Scott Green, who ordered the record impounded. The testimony is reconstructed from my notes made at the trial.)

A psychiatrist who had been on the staff of the court for more than ten years testified. He repeated Wiley's version of the killing. But he included a detail that Wiley had not mentioned to me. Wiley told the doctor that first he was just going to shoot his father in the legs to scare him but he didn't want to damage his mother's new sofa. So instead he shot his father in the heart. The psychiatrist concluded his direct testimony by giving his opinion that Wiley knew the nature and quality of his act and was able to cooperate intelligently with counsel in his defense.

On cross-examination, the court psychiatrist was asked whether he had checked Wiley's story with objective facts. The psychiatrist said there was no reason to, because Wiley was in touch with reality. The doctor further stated that if he had known the height and weight of Wiley's deceased father it would not have altered his opinion. He was asked whether there was anything in Wiley's demeanor or behavior that was odd or unusual. He said, "No." The court psychiatrist was then asked whether he had observed the behavior and demeanor of Wiley during his testimony. He replied, "No." He was then asked to look at Wiley and give his opinion as to whether his demeanor appeared to be abnormal. Wiley had been sitting beside counsel with his head down silently weeping throughout the testimony. Again, the court psychiatrist found nothing worthy of note in this behavior. He was asked whether there was anything he observed that indicated the desirability of an electroencephalogram. He replied, "What's an electroencephalogram to me? A bunch of lines on a graph."

Dr. Nelson produced the tapes of the electroencephalogram and explained the abnormalities of pattern indicating severe brain damage. He pointed out that Wiley's thumbs were not the same size, which is further evidence of brain damage. He eloquently described the plight of a seriously mentally ill child who, in order to gain some feeling of manhood and dignity, would go to the electric chair rather than admit that his father had beaten him. Wiley refused to acknowledge that it was he who pleaded for life and mercy, not his father.

We asked that Wiley be committed to a mental hospital. We further requested the court to refuse to certify the case for trial in criminal court. Both requests were denied. Wiley remained in jail awaiting trial. These orders are interlocutory and not appealable.

A lawyer who knows that his young client is mentally ill and in jail opens the morning paper with trepidation. At least one disturbed youngster hanged himself in jail while awaiting trial. Another boy injured himself so seriously that he died in adult jail before he could be tried. Other mysterious injuries and ailments continue to happen to children in custody.

Some few children, like Wiley, clearly need psychiatric diagnosis and help. But what of the vast proportion of children, who are brought to court on such trivial charges as truancy and petty larceny? Any middle-class parent knows that such acts are commonplace and do not necessarily indicate emotional disturbance. Nevertheless the courts overburden the diagnostic services and needlessly subject countless children to testing, often holding them in detention for several weeks for an examination that could be completed in less than a day.

Four little boys who were jailed for the purpose of testing had "jumped" a newsboy, just about their size, and taken two dollars away from him. That evening one of the boys, Chuckie J., had a twinge of conscience. He told his father what he had done. Chuckie and his father went to the three companions. They gathered up the two dollars in nickels and dimes and returned the money to the newsboy. When this heinous crime came up for trial, the court ordered the boys held in custody for neuropsychiatric examinations.

So many children are sent for psychiatric studies that the doctors rush through the examinations. And in some cases they report to the court without making any examination.

Michael D. was a problem from the age of nine. The first time he came to court, Judge Hazel Brown placed him on neuropsychiatric probation. He was examined, evaluated, and treated by batteries of psychiatrists in several clinics until the age of fourteen. At that time Michael told the psychiatrist he did not think he needed any more help, and he stopped coming to the clinic. A year later the clerical system of the court caught up with Michael's file. A letter was sent to the psychiatrist asking him for a progress report. The treating psychiatrist informed the court that Michael had not been seen for more than a year. The court psychiatrist, without ever seeing Michael or getting in touch with his parents, petitioned the juvenile court for the boy's discharge from probation. Judge J. Sydney Hoffman (since elevated to the superior court) entered an order discharging him from probation. Michael was not seen by the judge. His parents were not notified. The court simply removed his name from the list of those on probation without making an inquiry into Michael's condition or behavior. At that very time Michael was in trouble. He was later arrested by the police for causing a disturbance in a restaurant. The policemen noted that his behavior was peculiar. The intake interviewer "adjusted" the matter. Had Michael been on probation, someone might have been notified. By the age of twenty-two Michael had killed an innocent stranger.

Allen T., on the other hand, was held in a prison for mental defectives for years without ever being examined by any doctor. Allen's aunt asked for help in obtaining his release. The boy had been sent away by the juvenile court in one of the many speedy hearings of which it was impossible to find any notes. What evidence there was against this boy, no one knows now. Allen was brought to court by his mother at the age of eleven on a charge of incorrigibility. Mr. and Mrs. T. were separated. Neither one wanted the boy. The court was a convenient dumping ground. Evidently there was a vacancy in Pennhurst, an institution for mental defectives. Allen stayed there until February 8, 1965, when Judge Juanita Kidd Stout ordered him committed to Dallas, a state prison for mental defectives with "criminal tendencies." Allen had been in a mental institution for five years and could not read or write.

For an inmate to be transferred from a mental hospital to a prison for mental defectives "with criminal tendencies," a petition for commitment must be filed requesting the court to appoint two physicians to examine the person. These physicians are required to make an examination and certify that the person is indeed a mental defective with criminal tendencies. Our brief in the superior court (which had remanded the case to the juvenile court for a hearing) sets forth the facts as they appeared from the record:

> On March 21, 1967, a Xerox copy, Form JBC-303 entitled *Defective Delinquent Commitment*, Commonwealth of Pennsylvania, Department of Justice, Bureau of Correction, was supplied by the District Attorney's Office to counsel for appellant.
>
> However, even a cursory examination of this form which includes the psychiatric and psychological reports of February 4, 1965, reveals that these reports were made only in token compliance with the commitment requirements of the Defective Delinquent Act and are a totally inadequate basis for appellant's present confinement.
>
> The "Defective Delinquent Commitment" form contains a printed petition, an order, and small blank spaces for the so-called psychiatric and psychological reports. The petition which prays for

the required mental examinations was signed by the Superintendent at Pennhurst, and dated February 4, 1965. The affidavit for petition for commitment is dated February 5, 1965. The order appointing Benton H. Marshall, M.D. and James C. Hirst, Ph.D. to examine appellant, is not dated. The report of Marshall and Hirst is dated February 4, 1965. All of these petitions, affidavits and orders are on a single sheet of paper which is part of the aforesaid printed form.

This same form includes a blank space denominated "Criminal Record." The report, as filled in, includes "arrests for burglary and disorderly conduct in 1960." Significantly, at the time of these so-called arrests, appellant was 11 years old. There is no indication that appellant was arrested with a warrant or had a due process hearing on these crimnal charges. On the contrary, it appears that he was confined at the Youth Study Center pursuant to an order of the Juvenile Court and transferred to the Youth Development Center in Philadelphia and later transferred, apparently without a court order, to Pennhurst State School and Hospital.

The next blank space in the form is denominated "Brief Description of Present Crime." This summary includes items described as "conduct excitations" some of which are described as "defiant and threatening conduct," "resistance to disciplinary measures," and "damaging influence." It appears that since his confinement in Pennhurst at the age of 14, appellant has been introduced to homosexual practices and has contracted gonorrhea. It is unnecessary to point out that with respect to what is denominated "present crime" there has been no hearing to determine whether this child is guilty of any crime. The description of these alleged present crimes does not accord with criminal acts cognizable under the Criminal Code of Pennsylvania. The "report" of the psychiatrist and psychologist constitute three paragraphs, 11, 12, and 13 of said form. Paragraph 13, entitled "Sources of Information" reveals that the psychiatric and psychological reports were based exclusively on inadmissible hearsay evidence, such as social service reports, clinical histories, reports from other agencies, and institutional histories from appellant's stay at Pennhurst. From the sources of information listed, and from the psychological and psychiatric reports themselves, one must infer that appellant was never personally examined by either of these doctors at the time these reports were made and was not even seen by them.

The blank entitled "Psychiatric History and Present Examination: (Significant Findings Only)" reads as follows:

"Staff evaluations have diagnosed patient as 'mental deficiency, mild' with anti-social reaction. The latter is characterized by the aforesaid abusive, destructive, unstructured, and abnormal sexual behavior. Orientation is normal, and affect is satisfactory; however, poor judgment, inadequate knowledge, and a generally hostile and aggressive attitude toward authority and rules and routines of any kind impair this boy's ability for adjusting to any normal or residential institutional setting. There has been no evidence of psychosis. This pattern is primarily indicative of a developing sociopathic personality which, for patient's age, has already reached a surprisingly advanced stage of expression. It is impossible to predict this patient's behavior from moment to moment, and to plan for protecting others against the consequences."

An ordinary reading of the English language in the reports fails to disclose that appellant is of "criminal tendency," which is a necessary finding in order to meet the requirements of the Defective Delinquent Act. This finding of criminal tendencies which appears in the printed paragraph C is part of the printed form.

The blank entitled "Psychological Report: (Include Results of Standard Psychometric, Projective, Personality, and Aptitude Tests Given)" reads as follows:

"Psychometric examinations have consistently yielded a mental status at the mild level. Most recent I.Q.'s obtained (10–26–64) were WISC: Verbal 75, Performance 68, and Full Scale 69. These measures are probably suppressed by cultural deprivation factors such as the lack of early schooling and emotional insecurity in childhood. Projective Measures of personality organization included the Pender-Gestalt, Draw-A-Person and Rorschach Technique. These revealed an arrested emotional development, possible sub-clinical brain dam-

age, and a marked inability to control his urges and impulses."

It is a necessary precondition under the Defective Delinquent Act to find that the person to be committed is "mentally defective." Clearly, the psychological report indicates that this appellant is not mentally defective. His full scale I.Q. is 69. The report indicates that the results are "probably suppressed by cultural deprivation factors such as the lack of early schooling . . ." Significantly, Allen, who is now only 16½ years old, has had no schooling since his first contact with the court in 1961 at the age of 11. He is illiterate. For these crucial 5 years, 11 through 16, this child has been deprived not only of his liberties but of his right to an education, and of any human or familial contacts which would permit him to develop normal intellectual, emotional and behavioral patterns.

On the basis of this document, which on its face bears these inconsistencies, and without permitting Allen or any relatives or friend to appear on his behalf, this child was committed to Dallas on February 8, 1965, by the Order of the Honorable Juanita Kidd Stout, to be detained there until further order of the Court.

The district attorney opposed the release of the boy, who was supposed to be a dangerous criminal. A full-scale hearing was held. (Judge Adrian Bonnelly presided. Because Allen was released, the notes of testimony were never transcribed. The testimony is reconstructed from the attorney's file.)

Allen is a slim, sensitive boy. He has a gentle smile. When he was brought into the courtroom, he kissed his aunt gratefully. Allen's parents, who were notified to appear, were present. His father is a handsome noncommissioned army officer. His mother is a flashy, young, pretty, and very stylishly dressed woman. They did not speak to each other or to Allen.

In order to prove Allen's criminal tendencies, the state produced the matron of Allen's unit to testify about his behavior. This middle-aged semiliterate white woman had her daily reports with her and the official records of the institution. They were barely decipherable. Spelling was a matter of intuition.

It was obvious that she disliked the Negro boys in her charge. These were the serious criminal offenses that Allen had committed and the penalties that were imposed on him:

> *May 3, 1965– disturbing cellblock by loud and boistrerous [sic] talking—five days in seclusion.*
>
> *May 17, 1965– disturbing cellblock, insolence—indefinite segregation.*
>
> *June 15, 1965– disobedience of a direct order—segregation for 10 days.*
>
> *July 12, 1965– disturbing the cellblock—seclusion for five days.*
>
> *Aug. 2, 1965– disturbing the cellblock—seclusion for five days.*
>
> *Nov. 24, 1965– being in another inmate's cell—indefinite segregation.*
>
> *Mar. 14, 1966– disturbing the cellblock—loss of privileges for 10 days.*
>
> *April 6, 1966– threatening bodily harm to another inmate—indefinite segregation.*
>
> *Dec. 12, 1966– disturbing cellblock by whistling—loss of all privileges for seven days.*

It is interesting to note that the attendants rightly refer to cellblocks. "Seclusion" is a polite word for solitary confinement in a cell furnished with only a mattress on the floor. The cell is pitch black because the only window has been painted over. There is nothing to do. Segregation is another polite word. It means that the boy cannot talk to anyone, cannot be with the other inmates at mealtimes. For an illiterate, there is probably no more dreadful experience than being all alone with nothing to do for these long periods. That Allen did not become psychotic from such mistreatment is remarkable.

These eight offenses were all that could be found in the records of Pennhurst against Allen.

The doctors were called to testify. Because I had

photocopies of the petition for examination and the report, I was delighted that the state had brought these men many miles to testify. To have subpoenas served and witnesses produced from other counties is a formidable and expensive task. Both the petition for examination and the report were signed and notarized on the same date. The court that issued the order allowing the examination was in a different county from the institution. It would have taken at least a day for the petition to reach the court. Assuming the improbable—that the judge signed the order the minute it was received—it would have taken at least another day for the doctors to receive the order. Clearly there was a question about when the examination had been made. On cross-examination, the doctors admitted that neither of them had seen Allen. They had filled out the forms on the basis of reports in the file.

Allen T. was a valuable inmate. He spent his days and nights changing the bedding of the incontinent, truly defective inmates. No wonder that no one ever asked for his discharge.

As a result of the hearing, Allen was released. When he and his aunt came to say good-bye and thank you, Allen told me he wanted to go to school. He said he would like to study to be a therapist. At seventeen, Allen has much to learn. He does not know how to read or write. He has never been in a store or a restaurant. He has never seen a movie. He has never seen a river or a mountain. He barely knows the name of his state. From a prison, Allen stepped into a world of computers, exploration of outer space and ocean depths. Educators say that slum children must start at three years of age to have a head start on the difficult task of learning to live in our times. At seventeen, Allen is at least fourteen years behind.

Ikey F., at seventeen, had already spent some three years in various jails. Now he was charged with murder. The legal definition of murder is "the unlawful killing of a human being with malice aforethought." There was no malice in Ikey. And he

seldom had any thought about what he did, much less any fore-
thought.

I first saw Ikey when he was brought in on a gang fight.
Although he was tall and at first glance looked his age, there was
something childlike and fragile about him. Mrs. F. had four
sons. Ikey was her oldest and dearest. The other boys seemed
to be able to take care of themselves. When Ikey was released
on the gang fight arrest, I implored Mrs. F. to send Ikey to live
in the country. We often advised ghetto mothers to send their
boys to live with relatives in the South. If a black boy is not
militant or aggressive, life is much easier for him in the South
than in the northern city slums. In the South the police leave the
Negro boys alone so long as they stay in their part of town.
Schools are less rigid. Somehow the children learn more easily
in the segregated schools of the South than in the all-black
schools of the North. Unfortunately, Mr. and Mrs. F. didn't have
any relatives left in Georgia. They were all in Philadelphia.
There was no place for Ikey to go but back to the street where
trouble was inevitable. Three years in correctional institutions
had not taught him to read or write or how to take care of
himself on the street or in school.

Mrs. F. sat in the office and cried. Like every mother she
wondered what she had done wrong. Where had she failed Ikey?
She and Mr. F. always had a decent home, enough to eat. They
were never on assistance, she told me with pride. Ikey had been
a pretty child, a good child. Just playful and silly. When he was
twelve he had had a hemorrhage from his penis. He was sent
home from school. She took him to the hospital. He had had an
operation. Mrs. F. wasn't sure just what they did to him. Then
he had got in a fight and was sent away to a correctional institution. Now murder! She wept. Mr. F. sat in silent misery.

Ikey was terribly vague about what had happened. From
the other children I managed to piece together the story. Like
all the other disasters, this one started aimlessly. The boys were
looking for something to do. School was over at two thirty.
They wandered here and there. They heard about a street fair

and walked for blocks and blocks only to find that it was sched-
uled for the following week. Suddenly someone remembered
that there was a gun hidden in a vacant lot. They all went to look
for the gun, and unfortunately they found it. It was getting late,
so they stopped and ate pizzas. Somewhere in their wanderings
they encountered Juanita and Sylvia. The girls giggled and
laughed and teased. Ikey became interested in Juanita. But she
didn't want him.

At some point "Pots and Pans," one of Ikey's friends,
also got friendly with Juanita. She taunted Ikey. "You thinks
you're Mr. Big. Well, you ain't. You ain't nobody and you ain't
nothin.' "

Ikey picked up the gun. And to show how brave and
important he was, Ikey fired. The bullet struck and killed a boy.
Ikey had not aimed at him. He didn't intend to kill anyone.

Was there a solution for Ikey—was there any hope or
cure? He faced the electric chair or a life sentence, which usually
means twenty years in jail. Assuming the most optimistic prog-
nostication, he would serve twenty years without being killed,
maimed, or dying in prison. How could he possibly live in the
world at age thirty-seven if he could not manage now?

A possibility of help came from an unexpected source. A
psychiatrist at a dinner party I attended was telling about his
huge grant to make a study of violence. He had decided theories
about criminal types and criminal behavior. I asked him how he
accounted for the accidental, senseless, unplanned killings, the
stupid things my clients did. His eyes lit up. "You mean you
know a person who has killed someone? I'd like to meet and talk
to a killer. Could you arrange it?"

It seemed odd to me that an authority on violence did not
know people who committed violent acts. Perhaps, I thought, he
might find some mental illness or defect in Ikey. The first step
in helping the boy, I believed, would be to have him tested and
examined. I hoped that a doctor would discover his malady and
recommend therapy instead of jail. Jail had done him no good
before. He needed help. I arranged for the psychiatrist to inter-

view Ikey in prison. He was a little irked that Ikey couldn't come to his office, but I explained that persons accused of murder don't go to doctors' offices.

Months later, the psychiatrist upbraided me for wasting his time visiting that "dumb animal." He can't even read or write, the doctor expostulated. He had not heard about Ikey's medical history, Juanita's taunts, or life in a correctional institution. He had tested and examined Ikey. His scientific conclusion was that prison was the only place for that "dumb animal."

Sammy F., age fifteen, was also tested. The psychiatrist reported "problems of adolescent adjustment; passive aggressive personality." These phrases appear on hundreds of reports by court psychiatrists and psychologists. They offer little guidance to a harried judge trying to do what is right for a child whom he sees for all of ten or fifteen minutes. I talked to Sammy for several hours. I read his school records. I discussed his problems with his mother and his uncle. This report was of no help to me or his parents. We knew that Sammy just didn't think or react like other boys his age.

Of the many clients, both children and adults, I have represented who shot, killed, and stabbed, he is the only one who appeared to be utterly without remorse or even regret. He simply was unaware of the enormity of what he had done. Most people who have committed such an act at least try to find an excuse for themselves. Mike, for example, said, "If he hadn't touched me, I wouldn't have stabbed him. I just can't stand to have people touch me. It was his fault." Not Sammy. He smiled cheerfully in recounting the incident.

Mrs. F., Sammy's mother, came to the office alone. Like so many mothers, she was distraught. Her boy was in jail. She wanted him home. Like most of the mothers, Mrs. F. was bringing up her boy alone, without a father. But unlike many other cases, Mrs. F. had not deserted her husband or been deserted. Mr. F. had died—killed in an auto accident by an uninsured driver. Mr. F. had no insurance, no pension, no property, although he had had a good job. Mrs. F. is small, slim, neat, and speaks correct English. This is not unusual. Of some three thousand mothers of our clients, only one was illiterate and she was a white woman. The black mothers read, write, spell, and speak standard English whether they were reared on a plantation in Georgia where they attended a segregated school for only three years or were brought up in Philadelphia. Their sons, born and schooled in Philadelphia, are often totally illiterate and speak a patois unintelligible to most white people. Often in interviewing boys in jail, the Negro guard would helpfully interpret and explain to me what the boy was trying to say.

The police report charged Sammy with assault with deadly weapon. No one was reported injured. Such a charge might be referring to a fistfight plus a stick or baseball bat. It did not seem particularly serious. I got Sammy released in the custody of his mother pending trial. (Sammy's case was not appealed. No transcript was made of the trial. The case is reported from my notes.)

Although Sammy was only fifteen, he was almost six feet tall, strong, muscular, and dark. He wore his hair "processed," a sort of shiny reddish straight bang hanging in his eyes. His white pants were skintight, his shirt shone with a phosphorescent glow. I could not understand a word he said. The school records showed IQ 142. My usual rule of thumb was to add 15 points for cultural difference. A ghetto child doesn't know that "a stitch in time saves nine" or "a penny saved is a penny earned." The old adages probably aren't true in an affluent society. What does the knowledge of middle-class clichés test other than the knowledge of middle-class clichés? In standard tests the child is required to fill in the last word of such maxims. Such questions appear on IQ tests given in a public school system where more than 50 percent of the students are poor and black.

There was no question that Sammy was smart. He was also sullen and hostile. His mother was afraid of him and afraid for him. I told Sammy to come back to see me again when he was ready to talk to me. I also told him that he was smart and handsome, but that he was concealing these qualities pretty effectively by his style of dress and manner of speech.

A week later Sammy came back to the office with his uncle, a high school teacher. I did not recognize Sammy. He wore inconspicuous clothes. His hair was black and curly. It sprang up from his head, revealing what a Victorian novelist would have described as a noble brow. Sammy laughed gleefully at my bewilderment. This time he spoke standard English.

We were ready to talk about his case. It was simple; it was inexplicable. Sammy and his friend "Blue" were walking down the street when a "cat" in a white Pontiac slowed down and called out to the boys. Sammy walked over to the curb to see what the man wanted. Blue, a fifteen-year-old illiterate (IQ 83), yelled, for no apparent reason, "Sammy. Cap 'im." And Sammy did. Sammy pulled his gun out of his pocket and shot the driver of the Pontiac. By some mechanical defect, the gun did not shoot straight and the bullet, aimed at the driver's heart, struck his arm. Neither boy had ever seen the driver of the Pontiac before.

Sammy had no explanation. He normally carried a gun. His mother did not know this. He was adept in concealing much of his life from her. His uncle was completely bewildered.

We requested a psychiatric test, in the hope that we would learn what was wrong with this boy. Perhaps the psychiatrist would recommend some form of therapy. When I saw the diagnosis—"problems of adolescent adjustment; passive aggressive personality"—I was dismayed. Sammy was, I believed, the most dangerous client I had ever seen. This was no common garden variety of runaway. Sammy, his mother, and I agreed that we would ask that Sammy be sent to a mental hospital.

The court, as usual, followed the recommendations of the court psychiatrist. Sammy was sent to a correctional institution for boys under the age of sixteen. At this place there is no psychotherapy. The waiting list for mental hospitals was so long as to make admission improbable. Because the psychiatric report did not recommend hospitalization, Sammy would always be at the bottom of the list awaiting admission.

I asked the court to note his conduct on the report sent to the institution. Sammy is too young for a prison. The institution to which he was sent is a relatively mild place in the country. The boys sleep in dormitories of twenty. At night the guard locks the door and stays outside of the room.

What will Sammy do when he is locked in the dormitory with nineteen other boys—many of them much smaller, younger, and much less intelligent than he? What will he do in the empty hours of the long day? Unless Sammy commits some crime in the institution and is caught, he will probably be released in less than two years and return to his frightened mother and the life of the streets. There is no alternative.

Every day, in the more enlightened and better staffed juvenile courts, tests are ordered for children accused of everything from truancy to homicide. The behavior of some children as described by eyewitnesses is so bizarre as to amaze even the weary court criers. Others seem to be as normal as apple pie. All these children are run through the same mill of the juvenile court. They are given the same tests. They get the same answers. And they are sent to the same institutions.

It is seriously proposed that children be tested at the ages of six, seven, and eight to predict their "potential criminality." The experts who conduct batteries of tests and interviews now apparently cannot discriminate between children who have engaged in normal, petty misconduct and those who have already committed dangerous and violent crimes.* Any predictive testing will simply use the apparatus of scientific techniques to reinforce the expected conclusion: those who are poor and disadvantaged are potential criminals.

*Significantly, Dr. D. J. West finds little difference in the test results of habitual criminals and nonhabitual criminals. Many habitual criminals had no history of juvenile delinquency. (West, *The Habitual Prisoner*, Cambridge Studies in Criminology, London: Macmillan, 1963.)

Chapter Seven

THE MYTH OF TREATMENT

Regardless of the statutory authority, involuntary confinement without treatment is shocking.

JUDGE DAVID BAZELON

Eighty-five percent of juvenile reformatory inmates go on to commit crimes, according to a report in *The New York Times Magazine* (November 21, 1965). Does this mean that all these children are evil—hardened and unregenerate criminals? Or is something wrong with our correctional institutions?

Myrl E. Alexander, director of the Federal Bureau of Prisons, paints a bleak picture of the nation's prison system: "... As a means of punishment and as an instrument with which to change behavior, imprisonment is still a failure." If our adult prisons constitute a national disaster, failure in juvenile correctional institutions is even more serious. It involves enormous numbers of our children. The average *daily* number of inmates in juvenile institutions in 1965 was 62,773 (President's Commission on Law Enforcement and Administration of Justice, *The Challenge of Crime in a Free Society,* 1967, p. 172). More than one hundred thousand children each year are kept in jails or jaillike institutions. The cost is staggering. On a dollars-and-cents basis, it costs from three thousand dollars to forty-five hundred dollars a year to maintain a child in most state institutions. (This was the cost for Pennsylvania juvenile institutions in 1965.) Some states pay private jaillike institutions as much as ten thousand dollars a year to incarcerate a child. It would be cheaper to send a boy to Harvard than to jail. On a human and societal basis, we cannot even estimate the cost. Detention of a child in a correctional institution apparently leads to further delinquency and adult crime. The younger a prisoner is when first arrested, the more likely he is to return to prison, the President's Task Force on Juvenile Crime and Delinquency has found. Almost 50 percent of those arrested by age fourteen are imprisoned in later life.

Regardless of whether adult prison sentences are justified as deterrent, punitive, or rehabilitative, the purpose of the juvenile court commitments is to provide for "the best interests and welfare of the child and the state." This statement of policy is part of the Juvenile Court Law of Pennsylvania. Similar declarations are found in all of the juvenile court acts.

United States Circuit Judge David Bazelon says that "the central justification for assuming jurisdiction over a child in an informal, non-advisory proceeding is the promise to treat him according to his needs." To date, this promise has been a cruel hoax. Time after time I have heard a judge reassure a tearful mother that her child was going to a wonderful school where he would get an education and therapy. In fact, these children either were unpaid menials or spent their days in enforced idleness. Thirteen-year-old Jesse Gene Elmore described the Juvenile Receiving Home in Washington, D.C., as a "terrible jail." In his petition for release he stated that he was kept under lock and key, behind bars, and in occasional solitary confinement, that there were no doctors or psychiatrists and no school. The boy was released, but the federal court did not pass on the constitutionality of such imprisonment of a child.

Few people, aside from the children and the institutional employees, really know what happens in these innumerable far-flung training schools, children's villages, detention centers, and institutions. Occasionally the public gets a horrifying glimpse into the alien world of correctional institutions when the press reports that a seventeen-year-old boy, whose only crime was running away from home, was raped by another inmate in a prison. Homosexual assaults by inmates and guards have occurred in Washington, D.C., and Chicago prisons, as well as in Philadelphia, the *Wall Street Journal* reported on February 25, 1969. E. Preston Sharp, secretary of the American Correctional Association, finds it a common practice. He says, "It's a result of warehousing a hodge-podge of prisoners in antiquated prisons where they have little or nothing to do." In Texas a probe disclosed that many boys had been badly beaten while in jail. In Minnesota a thirteen-year-old Indian boy, who had been in solitary confinement for forty-one days awaiting a hearing, hanged himself. And a seventeen-year-old boy hanged himself after two days in a juvenile detention cell in Rochester, Minnesota. Representative Bertram L. Podell described the New York penal institutions as hellholes that "would make a criminal out of a saint." In a Delaware prison a seventeen-year-old black boy was shackled to his cot for seven days as a disciplinary procedure. The list of such cases is endless. Similar barbarities occur with horrifying frequency in almost every community.

Few citizens ever visit these institutions for children. Those who do go are usually given a conducted tour that does not include "the hole," the children kept in pajamas all day, the children working in the fields, washing the dishes or the superintendent's car. The New York Joint Legislative Commission on Penal Institutions, however, did carefully investigate the New York City Youth House. In a scathing report the commission recited shocking mistreatment of children:

> *Testimony before the Committee disclosed that the ages of the residents of Youth House ranged from eight to eighteen, with a group of approximately 50 children between the ages of eight to ten, committed to Youth House generally for truancy. The evidence before the Committee developed the fact that these younger children were indiscriminately mixed with older residents charged with narcotics addiction, prostitution, and with acts of criminal violence.*
>
> *Evidence presented by former residents of Youth House and by former employees of the institution revealed the existence at the*

institution of cadres of "councilors" selected from among the older residents to assist the employed staff members in maintaining order and discipline at Youth House. Given some responsibility over the younger residents, these "councilors" enforced discipline by systematic beatings of the youngsters entrusted in their charge. This testimony was coupled with other evidence disclosing occasional beatings administered by staff employees, who were dismissed for such infractions. Testimony was further offered respecting the existence of homosexual practices at Youth House. . . .

The Board of Education maintains a Public School for Youth House children. However, space at the school is so limited in relation to Youth House occupancy, that approximately half the children at Youth House cannot be admitted to the school. Many of the children at Youth House are from broken homes, where they have not experienced the daily discipline of a father going to work every morning and consequently have not developed the disciplinary habit which deters truancy. It is indeed ironic that many of those in Youth House for truancy are obliged to continue playing the truant while at Youth House because of inadequate facilities.

. . . [The Committee found] physical beatings of children, inadequate separation of children by age groups and by offenses, inadequate medical and professional staffing, homosexual practices, and other serious inadequacies at Youth House. . . .

The staff of the Office for Juveniles visited many institutions for children; we spoke to administrators; we walked through spotlessly clean corridors and depressing dormitories. We seldom saw children at play or studying. We did see young boys and girls scrubbing floors, sitting idly, and staring vacantly. Many of the boys who came to the office told us that they had been assaulted by other inmates and abused by guards. Several girls told us that matrons had made advances to them. Even girls in late pregnancy were subjected to these abuses. Such charges, of course, are difficult to prove. It is the word of the child against the adult. No administrator or trustee of these institutions wants to open up such a difficult and distressing subject. The employees, often civil servants, have rights. They will retain counsel. The mere allegation of such misconduct discredits the administrator and the board. There is no one to speak for the abused child.

Even if the juvenile court was more careful in its commitment of children to institutions, there would always be some irreducible number of children who should not remain at home for their own safety and welfare and for the safety of society. Often the parent recognizes his child's need for treatment. The difficulty, we discovered, was to find the help. If a child was physically dangerous, we were reasonably sure that he would be locked up somewhere. But if his behavior was not bizarre or troublesome, if his mother was not an alcoholic or a prostitute, the court did not concern itself with him. There were more pressing cases, and an avalanche of backlog.

Ross C. was one of these children who was not bad or dangerous. He simply needed help. He is a beautiful child of eleven, with silky curls. Huge hazel eyes are rimmed with long, thick lashes. His nose is thin and straight. His skin is tawny. Only the deeply bitten fingernails indicate his extreme distress. Ross's mother, father, and probation officer accompanied him. Mrs. C. is thin and nervous. Although she is not much more than thirty, her hair is gray and her face lined. Mr. C. is much older. He walks with difficulty. The probation officer helped him to his seat. (Because Ross was released, no transcript was made of this hearing.)

We had a sidebar conference with Judge Clifford Scott Green. The arresting officer was not present. The judge ordered the assistant district attorney to show me the police report. Ross and several other youngsters were arrested while stealing candy from a street stand. It was Ross's first arrest. The young assistant district attorney suggested that if we waived testimony, he would recommend probation. Obviously, no one would think of sending this child to jail. Ross admitted that he was trying to steal some candy. In fact, he didn't get any.

I asked the probation officer to tell the judge the family history. Mr. C. had been injured in an industrial accident. He is practically a vegetable. His claim had not been settled and Mrs. C. was the sole support of the family. She had been in a mental institution as a result of all this trouble and had only recently been released. The family was forced to move from a pleasant neighborhood with a good school to a slum. The older brother promptly got into trouble. Thanks to his probation officer he had obtained a job after school and was learning to cope with the neighborhood. The probation officer took an interest in Ross, too, and came to court on his account even though this boy was not on probation and not his responsibility. (William Massey is one of the rare dedicated probation officers. He is a gentle, educated Negro, who cares for his boys. Often he braves the wrath of the court to speak up for one of his probationers. He was invaluable in helping counsel.)

Ross was his mother's baby. He was deeply disturbed by her illness, her nervous hovering over him, and the long hours when she was at work. It was June and school was closing. The probation officer feared what might happen to Ross if he spent the long empty summer days on the street where he lived. The other boys are tough and wary. They can protect themselves from older hoodlums and old winos who prey on young boys. When the police red cars answer a call, these boys know how to vanish. They have their haunts, their friends, their means of filling up the idle hours. Ross had not learned the ways of the ghetto. He ran to his mother for help and he fled from her querulous worries. The probation officer feared that Ross would not be able to make it through the summer.

I asked the judge to find a summer camp, a children's home, an orphanage—any place to shelter this vulnerable child for three months. The judge had the court representative check a few possibilities. Every place was filled. We implored him to enter an order placing Ross in a shelter. A court order must be obeyed. The judge refused to make such an order and suggested that maybe some friend would take Ross for the summer. He knew there was no friend and so did I. The court cut off further discussion. There were dozens of other cases still to be heard.

Ross and his mother each took one of Mr. C.'s hands and slowly dragged him out of the courtroom. They went haltingly down the hot, dusty street back to their two stifling rooms in "the jungle," as the North Philadelphia ghetto is appropriately called. In early September the three of them were back—Ross had been arrested again. There was an ugly gash on his cheek and his lips twitched when he spoke to me. Does Ross now need therapy?

If Ross had been sent to a correctional institution—the only agencies that will always make room for another child—it is doubtful that he would have received any guidance or therapy. We talked to many of our young clients about their lives in these correctional institutions. Camp Hill, a prison under the jurisdiction of the Bureau of Corrections, is for males from the ages of sixteen to twenty-five. Younger boys are frequently sent there. Camp Hill is surrounded by high walls. It has armed guards, a "hole" (dark solitary confinement cell), and all the other accouterments of a modern penal institution. Stephen Y. was confined at Camp Hill for more than two years. He was in ninth grade when he entered. He was in ninth grade when he left. He had not had one day of schooling, one meeting with a psychologist, psychiatrist, or therapist of any sort. He worked in a factory for fifteen cents an hour. Michael McC. spent most of his time at Camp Hill washing dishes. Washing dishes and doing a routine job in a factory are not the kind of learning experiences that would help these boys. Most of them are at least two or three years below grade level in school. Many of them are dropouts.

Frequently, it was the poor school record and a habit of truancy that influenced the juvenile court judge to order the child committed to an institution. The most urgent need of almost every child was remedial education. None of the children represented by the Office for Juveniles had completed high school. If the child was to be deprived of his liberty, the most important compensating factor should have been compulsory remedial education. Instead of providing an education for the child, however, the institution would frequently use him as unpaid labor. Peonage was outlawed by the Thirteenth Amendment to the Constitution in 1865. More than a century later, countless children are employed in meaningless labor in institutions for their rehabilitation. Occasionally a court will rule that a child in a detention home or correctional institution must receive training. This occurred in Illinois after a deaf mute child was in detention for a year "awaiting placement." There were no facilities for teaching a child with this handicap. (See *In the Matter of Adolph Harris,* Juvenile Divison, Circuit Court, Cook County, Ill., No. 665 0 7222, December 22, 1967.)

It is easy for the institution to describe the children's activities as "educational" when, in fact, they are not. Many children in institutions do grubby, unpleasant, boring work, which does not educate or train them. The children are a cheap and indispensable source of labor necessary to maintain the institution. After the Office for Juveniles had obtained the release of many children and slowed the numbers being committed, there were complaints from the superintendents of these institutions that they did not have enough inmates to do the work in the institution. In response to some mad variant of Parkinson's Law, the institutions created to help children cannot survive without the unpaid labor of other children.

The youth development centers are special institutions for teen-agers who have been adjudicated delinquent on charges of less serious crimes. Kenneth Y. was in one of the centers for almost six months. At my request, Kenneth kept a diary of the center routine that he gave me. Here is the record of his life, day after day, in his sixteenth year:

> 7:00 A.M.   *Dressed—go salute the flag—raise the flag.*
> 8:00   *Go to breakfast—come back to the back of the buildings and clean up.*

9:00 Go to recreation room to play records—books or magazines to read.

12:00 Noon Lunch—chicken salad, mashed potatoes, milk.

12:30 P.M. Come back to the barracks—back in recreation room play cards—read.

5:00 Dinner—rice, stew beef, dessert, and milk.

5:30 Back to recreation room and watch TV.

11:00 Bedtime.

Saturday:

7:00 A.M. Get dressed—breakfast—bacon and eggs.

8:00 Clean up barracks—wax and polish floor—make beds.

9:30 Back in recreation room or go outdoors with other boys —basketball—baseball.

12:00 Noon Lunch—meat, mashed potatoes, milk, fruits.

12:30 P.M. Boys go in League Island to play ball.

4:00 Back into barracks.

5:00 Dinner—mashed potatoes with gravy, meat.

5:30 Back in barracks—watch TV—read—play cards.

11:00 Lights out—bedtime.

Sunday:

7:00 A.M. Wash up—make beds—go to breakfast.

8:00 Breakfast—bacon, eggs, milk, toast.

8:30 Back in recreation room—play cards—go outside.

12:00 Noon Dinner—ham, vegetable, bread and butter, potatoes, coffee if you want it.

12:30 P.M. Back in the barracks.

1:00 Visitation with parents—visitors go into the barracks with boys.

4:30 Visitation—otherwise boys can play cards—read—go out in yard, etc.

5:00 Supper—vegetables, carrots, milk, bread—boys work in cafe voluntarily.

5:30 Back to barracks—watch TV.

11:00 Lights out.

Kenneth did not have one minute of schooling, training, or rehabilitative therapy. The voluntary work in the "cafe" can scarcely be considered educational. A life of playing ball and watching TV constitutes neither care nor treatment. After a year in one of these "development" centers, it is more difficult than ever for a boy to study and learn. Many of the boys who ran away from the centers told us that the boredom of caged idleness was intolerable.

Kenneth had no gross psychiatric problems. He was big and healthy and was able to protect himself from attacks by other boys and guards. He was in good physical condition when I finally obtained his release. What his attitude was, I do not know. He politely thanked me for my efforts. He wanted to know about school, working papers, and a social security number. Kenneth had been in the middle of tenth grade (really functioning at not more than an eighth-grade level) when he went to the development center. What he needed was an intensive course in reading, arithmetic, and current events—a kind of ghetto finishing school to enable him to move into the labor force and assume his responsibilities as a citizen. The public schools—locked into rigid courses, credits, semesters, and vacations—cannot accommodate the enormously varied needs of children who move in and out of school on irregular days, who have no intention of graduating or even finishing a term. These children have no regular academic program, no course of studies leading to a future of higher education or of skilled employment.

Before sending a child to an institution, the juvenile court frequently ordered psychological and neuropsychiatric tests. When a vacancy became available in an institution, regardless of the child's needs, he was sent there. After a period of from one to five years, he was released. The boy was just brought back and returned to his mother. There was no service to help him return to school, find employment, adjust to the freedom of the streets. The Office for Juveniles had no social worker or counselor. We did, however, arrange for our clients to get back into public school. We told them how to get a social security number. If the boy was under seventeen, we told him how to get a work permit.

The deeper effects on a young boy of incarceration for a crime of which he may have been innocent are difficult to assess. Kenneth's mother told me that he had had many homosexual experiences. This worried her greatly. The only subject Kenneth discussed with me after his release was his desire to get a job in an auto repair shop.

Verniel W., one of the few "lucky" boys who got his high school diploma while he was in jail, was much more talkative. His mother and father had found a job for him in a factory. Verniel was glad to earn the money but was determined to go on to college and become a lawyer. He wanted to be able to defend the countless black boys who had been jailed, like him, without a real trial. Verniel was a very bright boy, a senior in high school who did well academically. He had a loving mother and father.

I do not know what occurred at Verniel's juvenile court hearing. There was no transcript. His parents did not come to me until he had been in jail for over two years. Verniel told me that on the night of the "crime," he had gone to look for his brother and got caught up in a melee of thirty or forty youths who were fighting with everything from car aerials to guns. Verniel was attacked and injured. He stabbed an unknown assailant in the stomach. This person was never located. Another boy died. Among his multiple injuries was a stab wound in the chest, but death may have resulted from other causes and injuries. Verniel was accused of murder. There was no evidence that Verniel had stabbed the dead boy. Verniel was sent to the state correctional institution. He finished high school in jail. At the time of the "incident," Verniel had been only a semester from graduation. The greater part of his two years in jail was not spent in studies but in working in the paint shop. He learned nothing from these two years of routine drudgery. The supervisor of the prison wrote me that they considered Verniel "one of our most trusted boys."

Was he rehabilitated? I do not know. There is no evidence that he needed rehabilitation. Verniel has a burning sense of injustice. He lost two and one-half years of freedom and two years of schooling. Like all other boys released from institutions, he has a great deal of lost living to make up.

Dean Joseph Lohman of the School of Criminology, University of California, finds:

> *The failure of the juvenile court to fulfill its rehabilitative and preventive promise stems in important measure from a grossly overoptimistic view of what is known about the phenomena of juvenile criminality and what even a fully equipped juvenile court could do about it. Experts in the field agree that it is extremely difficult to develop successful methods for preventing serious delinquent acts through rehabilitative programs for the child . . .* [Juvenile Delinquency and Youth Crime, *p. 8*].

He further suggests that delinquency is "well beyond the reach of the actions of any judge, probation officer, correctional counselor, or psychiatrist."

Dr. Lionel Rosen told the American Medical Conference of State Mental Health Representatives in April, 1970, that "medicine, and especially psychiatry, has oversold itself when it implied vaguely that it could cope with the horrible social ills of our country." He suggested that psychiatrists open their ears to hear what the poor are saying. But who will listen?

I do not know whether the social sciences really cannot offer guidance and rehabilitation to children who are disturbed or have committed offenses. Are psychologists, psychiatrists, therapists, and counselors all going through a meaningless and costly routine? I do not think so. If individual care and guidance were actually given to a child in a nonpunitive setting, he might respond. But the juvenile court system has never really tried this type of treatment for the "delinquent." Instead the courts send children to overcrowded human warehouses. When they are released and commit more antisocial acts, society wonders why. The children, however, know very well why the recidivism rate is so high.

In the spring of 1969 I spoke to the children of Gillespie Junior High School, an all-black school in North Philadelphia, who wanted to know about their legal rights. I asked ninety children if they knew anyone who had been in a correctional institution. Every child raised his hand. My next question was, Are the children better, worse, or the same after they have been sent away? Again the answer was unanimous: They are worse.

Parents also know the effect of these "rehabilitation" institutions on their children. Mrs. B. came to us to get Curtis released. He was a big boy, adept with his fists. Mrs. B. was not worried about physical abuse, which is often a real danger to smaller boys. She had a greater worry. "If Curtis stays there behind bars," she said, "he'll get a don't-care mind."

Although more than 85 percent of juvenile offenses are committed by boys, there is a sizable number of girls who are arrested and incarcerated. They are treated with exceptional harshness. Although girls very rarely commit crimes of violence, 40 percent of the girls arrested are held in detention pending trial. And many of them are sent to correctional institutions, not because they are dangerous but because society wants to keep down the birth rate among poor black girls. Although no judge ever articulated this reason for an order of commitment, we learned in many cases that this was the only possible ground for imprisoning young girls and women.

Lorraine D. came into the office with her mother and her sister Cora. Lorraine was dressed in a skintight black gown that clearly was not bought for her. She wore bright vermilion lipstick. Two front teeth were missing. She was at least forty pounds overweight. Despite her dull gray skin, she was pretty. She was also very nervous. Her large eyes widened as she looked about the strange office in obvious fear.

Lorraine was twenty-four years old. This was the first time Lorraine had visited her family in ten years. She did not know how to behave. She was barely articulate. When I saw her,

I explained that the Office for Juveniles was limited to representing children and Lorraine was an adult under the law.

Cora was the spokesman. She is slim and stylish. Her husband is a truck driver in the sanitation department. Mrs. D. looks young and attractive. She has been employed in the same blouse factory for seventeen years. Her husband had been dead for many years. Her youngest son is in the military service. The other children are married. Lorraine has no money at all. When Mrs. D. looked at Lorraine, her lips quivered.

Cora told me that ten years ago Lorraine was sent to Laurelton State Village by the juvenile court. Laurelton is described by statute as an institution for feeble-minded women of childbearing age. Lorraine was out on a pass. It was a Friday afternoon. On Sunday a matron would come and take her back. Couldn't something be done, Cora asked.

The jurisdiction of the juvenile court terminates when a child reaches the age of twenty-one. By what authority was she being held? This was a question that I wanted answered. Clearly there was no legal right to keep this girl locked up on an order of the juvenile court.

Immediately I placed a call for Judge Hazel Brown. It is difficult to claim one's constitutional rights over the weekend. Judges do not like to be disturbed. The clerk's office is closed. While a justice of the United States Supreme Court will enter an order of the court over the telephone, most lower court judges will not even read a petition that has not been filed and docketed. Unless some court order were obtained, Cora and her mother would meekly and regretfully deliver Lorraine back to the institution. I was continually amazed by the essentially law-abiding nature of the poor. It would not have occurred to these people to hide Lorraine and place the burden on the institution to get a court order for Lorraine's return.

The story was slowly pieced together over a period of hours. In 1957, Lorraine D. was an overweight, sluggish, black fourteen-year-old. It was her first year in junior high school and it was a disaster. In elementary school, the teacher usually put

Lorraine in the front row where she could be watched. Whenever Lorraine would begin to doze off or just stare into space,
the teacher called out, "Lorraine, no daydreaming!" Lorraine
reluctantly turned to her book and the day was not a total loss.

There were 2,300 children in junior high. The bell rang
at the end of a forty-two-minute period. This signaled bedlam
as the children dashed through the corridors, went to the
lavatories, looked for their books, rushed to the candy ma-
chines, made dates for after school, sneaked out on the fire
escape for a smoke. Five minutes later another bell rang. The
children were supposed to have arrived at the next class, be
seated at the proper desks with the right books, and be ready
to start another period. Lorraine could never quite get to the
right class at the right time with the right books.

A guidance counselor called Mrs. D., who gave up a day
of work and went to school. She knew Lorraine was having
trouble and that something was wrong. Lorraine's brothers and
sisters managed to get through junior high. Cora was going to
graduate from senior high school and become a nurse.

The counselor told Mrs. D. they just couldn't keep Lorraine in school, that she needed special help. There was a wonderful school for slow girls like Lorraine. The juvenile court
would send her there and the state would pay for it. All that was
required was that Mrs. D. sign a paper. She did so, believing
what the school counselor told her. Also Mrs. D. did not know
what she would do with Lorraine when she was put out of
school. She couldn't leave a fourteen-year-old girl alone all day.

She pleaded with the counselor. Then she was referred
to the school psychiatrist who told Mrs. D. that the school could
not "contain" Lorraine. There was no alternative. At the hearing, the juvenile court judge assured Mrs. D. that this was a
lovely boarding school and that Lorraine would be taught by
special teachers. Reluctantly, Mrs. D. kissed Lorraine good-bye.
Cora, sixteen, told Lorraine to study hard and come home
soon.

Cora did not see her sister again for ten years, not until

Lorraine came home that morning on her first visiting pass. She did not want to go back to Laurelton State Village.

"Lorraine, tell the lawyer what you do all day at the village," Cora encouraged her.

"I works in the fields—dig potatoes."

"What happens when it rains or snows?"

"We works every day. Matron, she sit in car, smoke cigarettes. I digs."

Her hands are rough and scarred; her feet squeezed into high-heeled shoes are splayed.

I took over the questioning.

"Lorraine, do they have a TV set at the village?"

"Yup, for matrons. We not 'lowed to look."

"Can you remember, when you first went to the village, did you go to school?"

"Never go to school. Just work in fields."

Cora explained that when Lorraine was sent to the village she knew how to read and write but that she has forgotten now. After the first two years she stopped writing letters. She was no longer able to write. Mrs. D. visited once or twice a year. Several times she was not permitted to see Lorraine because Lorraine had misbehaved.

"What did you do?"

"I run away three times. They came after me in jeep with dogs."

"Were you punished?"

"Tie me to bed springs with wet sheets."

"Where was the mattress?"

"No mattress."

Cora says that the sheets were dipped in the toilet bowl. Lorraine nods her head.

"Did anyone else try to run away?"

"Billy Mae run away, Clorina run away." She remembers several other names.

"Who works in the fields? Everybody?"

"No. Work in kitchen, scrub floors. Some old ladies, white hair in fields. Little girls, tiny kids."

Cora explained that Lorraine is so fat because she never gets meat or fruit, seldom any green vegetables.

"What do you do in the evenings?"

"Go to bed. Sunday night movie, if good."

"Did they ever take you to church?"

"No."

Mrs. D. explained that she had been to the court many times asking that Lorraine come home. She had never seen the judge again. The lady at the court told her that Lorraine is very bad. The village can't release her. If she continues to misbehave she will be sent to another place. A year ago, Mrs. D. saw Lorraine and pleaded with her not to run away, to behave so she could come home. And now at last she was released on a four-day pass.

I checked the court records and found that Lorraine was committed by the juvenile court in 1957 on a petition signed by Mrs. D. The petition, which is a printed form, has typed in the averment that Lorraine is habitually wayward and incorrigible. It is the practice of the probation officer to type up the petitions *after* they are signed. The file shows fourteen visits by Mrs. D. to the court. Each time she pleaded with a court employee to get Lorraine released. Mrs. D. never saw a judge. No one suggested that she get an attorney. The court itself never reviewed the file. Laurelton never asked that Lorraine be released or that her case be reconsidered.

Lorraine's public school records list an IQ of 93 in fourth grade, 94 in fifth grade, 90 in sixth grade, and 88 in seventh grade. A score of 90 is considered the cutoff for normal intelligence. There is no record of a psychological or psychiatric evaluation. In seventh grade, Lorraine read at fifth-grade level.

Judge Brown returned the call. She was sympathetic and explained that the commitment was only for Lorraine's protection. After all, if she were at home she might become pregnant.

I volunteered to take Lorraine to Planned Parenthood and also suggested that we might petition for a writ of habeas corpus if the commitment were not terminated. Judge Brown suggested that she call the probation officer and extend the pass for thirty days. This would save Lorraine from returning to the institution. In the meantime, a proper hearing could be held to determine Lorraine's rights and what care would be appropriate for her. I readily agreed. All month, I attempted to get a hearing for Lorraine. The judge who had signed the original commitment could not remember Lorraine. He was not astonished that she was still at Laurelton. After all, she would be of childbearing age for many more years. The pass was extended again. Finally, without a hearing, the court ordered that Lorraine be discharged.

Lorraine is working as a countergirl in a hamburger place. She has a social security number. She is self-supporting.

Cora took Lorraine to a public health clinic where she was diagnosed as hypothyroid. She was given medication and has lost more than twenty pounds. Lorraine is learning to read again. Her skin is now a warm brown and she smiles gaily. Mrs. D. says she still screams in her sleep, dreaming that she is in the village. But Lorraine has a boyfriend and Mrs. D. is planning a wedding.

There are many Lorraines at Laurelton State Village. Unless friends or relatives want to take responsibility for them, retain legal counsel, and expend a great deal of time and money, these girls and women will remain incarcerated until menopause. In most states there are villages, homes, and farms in which poor females are incarcerated to prevent procreation.

The United States Supreme Court gave its blessing to the sterilization of "mental defectives." This opinion was written by Justice Oliver Wendell Holmes, the great liberal. Nazi Germany killed "undesirable" citizens or put them in concentration camps. But the United States will not execute a murderer if he is insane or so mentally defective as not to know

right from wrong. Lorraine was not in a concentration camp or
a jail. She was in a shelter to protect her from having sexual
relations and to protect the taxpayers from having to support
the progeny. It is assumed that any offspring of Lorraine would
be a mental defective. Fashions in genetics also change. A non-
scientist can only wonder what the evidence is for this belief.

Babies are an expense and a nuisance whether they are
human or animal. Pet owners have their female dogs and cats
spayed. Female human beings are jailed for the long years from
thirteen to the mid-fifties.

From time to time I read glowing reports about experimental centers for the rehabilitation of children—job corps
centers and day-care centers: new jails with new names. Some
of these institutions provide care for twenty-four girls or fifty
boys. But the sad fact is that almost all the more than one
hundred thousand children in the correctional institutions of
America each year are in human warehouses. New York Supreme Court Justice Daniel G. Albert declared, "Our procedures for the wayward minors and youthful offenders are not
only anachronistic and unjust, but they are based on facilities
which are inadequate if they are not wholly absent."

Because there is so little likelihood of care, therapy, education, or training being available in institutions for children,
the myth of treatment should be exploded. The options available to the juvenile court judge are no different from the options available to the judge of criminal court: (1) freedom, (2)
freedom under surveillance, known as probation, and (3) jail.
Until there is treatment we do not need the expensive time-
consuming farce of diagnosis and evaluation. For the child like
Ross, who is not a criminal, there is no help; society will not
provide a shelter for him until it puts him in jail. For the sick
child there is only jail. For the mentally retarded there is only
jail. And for the bad child there is also jail.

Chapter Eight

THE ALTERNATIVE OF PROBATION

Parole and probation services should be available in all jurisdictions for felons, juveniles, and those adult misdemeanants
who need or can profit from community treatment.

*Recommendation of President's Commission on
Law Enforcement and Administration of Justice*

The juvenile court judge has three choices in dealing
with a delinquent child: (1) discharge (acquit) the child and turn
him over to his parents, (2) commit the child to an institution,
or (3) place him on probation. In making his decision the judge
is supposed to determine what is "best suited to his [the child's]
treatment, rehabilitation and welfare" (Uniform Juvenile Court
Act, Paragraph 31). The Pennsylvania Juvenile Court Act provides that the judge shall make such order as shall be consistent
"with the needs of the child *and* the community."

In more than half of the cases, juvenile court judges
choose probation. Sixty percent of the delinquents brought
before the New York Family Court in 1964 were placed on
probation, according to *The New York Times* (September 12,
1965, p. 123). This accords with the records of the Philadelphia
Office for Juveniles.

Probation, this most popular of the three choices, is an
anomalous status—not jail but not quite freedom either. The
probationer is left in the community, but he must report to his
probation officer. If he violates the rules, he may be jailed without the formalities of a full-scale trial. Many acts that are not
crimes in themselves, constitute violations of probation.

Few complaints are heard about probation, except perhaps from some of the children themselves. Probation is in great favor—and its prestige seems to be increasing—as a humane approach to the problems of delinquency. And yet, in actual practice, probation is beset by grave inconsistencies and conducted under often mysterious circumstances. What help probation gives a child or what protection it provides for the community, no one knows.

There are, of course, many reasons for favoring the alternative of probation. It does not appear to be harsh on the child, particularly when viewed in the context of the special standards of the juvenile justice system. Because juveniles may be jailed for acts of delinquency that are not crimes, and because they are not accorded all of the protections of a criminal trial, probation does not seem to impose much of a legal burden on a child. The probationer is at home, so neither he nor his family is likely to complain about this surveillance—even when the child has not been found delinquent. (Often a judge may feel that there is no real evidence against a child, but out of caution, lest someone guilty go free, he places the child on probation.)

Probation, always popular with scholars and writers, has become the panacea of penologists. They have two main reasons for favoring it: to keep the child out of correctional institutions and to keep the child out of the juvenile court system.

It is not difficult to understand why probation should be preferred to institutionalization. First, there simply aren't enough institutions to "contain" all these children. Second, juvenile probation—although its costs run to more than ninety-three million dollars a year—is cheaper than incarceration. Even though children get very little attention in these institutions, there is almost a one-to-one ratio of employees to inmates. (There are 162 employees in the Youth Study Center in Philadelphia, which has a stated capacity of 175 inmates. Of course there are often more than 250 children in the center.)

Employees work only eight hours a day; there must be three shifts of guards. Then there are janitors, cooks, laundresses, gardeners, a nurse, a teacher, hordes of clerks and record keepers and administrators. A third reason for preferring probation is that parents might appeal an order committing a child to an institution. No judge likes to have his handiwork reviewed by another court, which will leisurely pick out the flaws in his hasty off-the-cuff comments. And finally, institutions can do great harm to a child. He may be subjected to homosexual abuses and so may she; he may be beaten by guards; he may lose all ties with his family. Often he becomes unfit to live in an open society.

Official disenchantment with the juvenile justice system has also served to cast probation in a more favorable light. It is now widely recognized that contact with the juvenile court system is followed by more alleged delinquencies. The task force report, *Juvenile Delinquency and Youth Crime,* presented by the President's Commission on Law Enforcement and Administration of Justice, finds:

> *Given the absence of evidence of the beneficial effects of official [court] contact, as well as the potentially harmful consequences of such contact, the burden of proof must be on the side of those who believe that official intervention is clearly necessary for the safety of the community and welfare of the juvenile.*

In simple English this means that, because there is no evidence that the juvenile court proceedings do a child any good and because there is much evidence that it may do him harm, the child should not be brought to court unless it is absolutely necessary for the safety of the community or his own welfare. But this begs the question, When is the safety of the community endangered and when does a child need help?

Their recommendations to avoid using the juvenile court are as follows:

Recommendations to improve our system of planned nonjudicial handling for reputed [sic] delinquents fall into three categories: First is the further limitation of referrals into the juvenile court system and the ability of that system to accept such referrals. Second is the creation and the strengthening of alternative agencies and organizations to deal with putative delinquents. Third is the development of an improved capacity on the part of the police and juvenile court system to make appropriate dispositions and refer putative delinquents to alternative agencies and organizations.

These suggestions to keep the child out of the courts simply return to the old cycle. The child was taken out of the criminal courts and placed in the juvenile court because "he was criminalized" by the judicial process. For some sixty-five years informal, essentially nonjudicial procedures were used in the juvenile courts for the welfare of the child. With the *Gault* decision it was suddenly discovered that these informal procedures did not rehabilitate the child or decrease crime. Therefore the juvenile courts have been ordered to function like courts, to determine guilt or innocence on the basis of evidence, and not to place innocent children in institutions in the mistaken belief that this is for their own good. Now it is recommended that the child be removed from the due process proceedings of the juvenile court and be referred to "other agencies" not subject to legal restrictions. If these proposals are followed, *Gault* would indeed be a Pyrrhic victory for the rights of the child.

The second suggestion—to keep the child in the community—is sound. Probation is the highly touted form of "community-based correction." Keep the erring member of society in society and teach him how to cope with its problems. This is the theory. It is reasonable.

Before raising the hope that probation is the panacea for juvenile delinquency, it is well to remember that probably two-thirds of the juvenile repeaters have been on probation for a

year or more. It is time to take a careful look at probation to see
what it may realistically be expected to accomplish.

Any valid study of the methods and accomplishments of
the juvenile probation system must focus on the probation
officer—but this is precisely where the great confusion begins.
His function is poorly defined; he has conflicting duties that
cover too wide an area; and the actual relationship between the
probation officer and the probationer is a mysterious matter.

The success of probation depends on the supervision
that the delinquent gets while he is in the community. Few
people other than the probationer, his family, and his lawyer (if
he has one and if he keeps in touch with the lawyer after the trial)
have an opportunity to glimpse the workings of this large sub-
profession of the criminal court bureaucracy. The meeting between the probation officer and his probationer is and should
be private, like the conference of lawyer and client. No one
knows what happens at these interviews or on what terms they
are conducted. The attitudes of the probation officers who came
in contact with the Office for Juveniles varied from one individual to the next, all the way from the harshly punitive to the
concerned and helpful. We lawyers, in dealing with children on
probation, often mentioned their probation officer, to see if we
might get some help and guidance from this adult, who should
know the child well. Some of our clients were hostile toward the
officer; most were disinterested and vague—"He just talks to
ya" or "Mine don't give me no trouble."

One thing is certain: most probation officers see their
probationers infrequently and briefly. In the largest population
centers, a child placed on probation is generally seen on an
average of once a month. In some big cities the probation
officer sees the child only every three months or even less frequently (*Juvenile Delinquency and Youth Crime*, p. 83). In many
juvenile courts the probation officer has such a large case load
that his contacts with the child are so hurried and infrequent as
to be meaningless. Such brief, official contacts are not likely to

promote a relationship of trust or confidence. Even if a child is in trouble or recognizes that he needs help, the probation officer is probably the last person he will turn to: One word from the probation officer to the judge will usually suffice to have the child returned to court and committed to an institution.

There is nothing punitive in the juvenile court philosophy even when it results in jailing a child. The juvenile probation officer is also a part of this helping philosophy. He is supposed to be the child's friend, his support and confidant in time of trouble. But the probation officer is also an employee of the court answerable to it for the conduct of the probationer. The ambivalence of this position is immediately apparent to any child, even an illiterate slum dweller. Frequently, I have been asked to speak to school children about "the law." At these sessions the children invariably ask about the probation officer. Usually the first question is, If you tell your probation officer you have done something wrong, will he turn you in? The answer, of course, is that he must do so; this is his job. The boys and girls are dismayed. I have often heard this kind of reaction: "Some friend he is!"

There is little law governing this very common and important relationship between probationer and officer. The *Gault* decision, while recommending increased use of probation, does not mention the rights, limitations, and duties involved. The probation officer frequently questions the child about his activities. It is his duty to do so. When a policeman questions a suspect, he is required first to warn him of his rights. The Supreme Court, in the 1966 *Miranda* case, held that a policeman must tell the suspect that he has a right to remain silent, that if he starts to talk he may stop at any time, that he has a right to a lawyer and to have the lawyer present, that if he cannot afford counsel it will be provided for him, and that anything he says may be used against him. If a person does not receive these warnings and makes a statement or confession to the police, that statement or confession may not be used in court against him.

But what of the interrogation by a probation officer and the use he may make of the information he obtains from talking to the child? Revealing misconduct to a probation officer is closely analogous to the confession given to a policeman. In both cases the statement will be used against the individual. Even a child recognizes that a policeman is a law-enforcement official whose duty is to arrest people and ferret out criminal conduct. A statement made to a policeman is introduced into evidence in open court. A probation officer is often mistakenly assumed to be just a social worker, not a law enforcement official. The statement made to him may get to the judge by way of a written report, which the child never sees and often is not even aware of. In some instances, the conversations between probation officer and probationer come close to entrapment.

This problem arises because the probation officer has incompatible functions. An agent of the courts, essentially engaged in law enforcement, cannot also be a friend and confidant of a convicted person, whether he be an adult or a child. Thus noble plans for young assistant district attorneys to "take a brother" from among the juvenile gang members are doomed to failure. (This well-financed and well-publicized plan for coping with juvenile crime was promoted by Philadelphia District Attorney Arlen Specter.) A biological brother may or may not turn his sibling over to the police. A probation officer or a district attorney must do so.

The official prescribed functions of a juvenile court probation officer combine many unrelated duties. He is the investigator for the court before trial who prepares a report on the facts of the case. He is also a social worker who prepares a report on the background of the child and his family. All this is done *before* the child is brought to trial. Trial by inquisition was presumably abolished by the Common Law during the Middle Ages. But it lingers on in juvenile court, where the employees of the court investigate the alleged crime and report the evidence to the judge before the trial. The social background of the child, which theoretically is useful in sentencing or making an individualized disposition of the child, is available before the trial and may either consciously or unconsciously influence the judge's finding of guilt or innocence. A jury is never permitted to know the prior record of a defendant. If accidentally it is revealed during trial that an adult defendant has a record, this is grounds for an immediate mistrial. Attorneys for children frequently protest that the juvenile court judge should not read these reports before he hears the evidence presented in open court.

I have on occasion asked that the record show that the judge is reading the child's file during the trial. Of course, this does not endear an attorney to the court. It does, however, protect the rights of the child to a reversal on appeal in the event that he is committed to a correctional institution. There is not much a lawyer can do if the judge reads the report before he comes into the courtroom.

One day I protested for the record that the judge was opening the child's file. He facetiously asked, "Counsel, may I just take a peek?"

And I truthfully replied, "Not while I'm watching you, your honor."

Besides preparing reports, the probation officer testifies in open court. Sometimes he will say things that are favorable to the child. Sometimes he will request that the child be given another chance, more time to improve his behavior and the like. Other times he is obliged to report unfavorable impressions about the child's behavior. He may truthfully testify that the neighbors have made complaints, the parents have told him the boy is staying out late, and so on. Much of this testimony is of necessity hearsay. It is based on what other people have told him about the boy. Such evidence should be inadmissible on a hearing to revoke probation or on the trial of a charge of delinquency. The probation officer's report should be used only after a determination of the facts as an aid to deciding what disposition should be made of a child who has been found to be guilty after a due process hearing.

The most important function of the probation officer is to supervise and help the child *after* the trial. The intake and investigative functions of the probation offices, however, account for more of the staff time than supervision after adjudication. The suggestions of the scholars largely neglect this "treating" function of the probation department. Instead it is recommended widely that intake and probation be used in lieu of court proceedings.

Probation is seen by the judge, the child, and his lawyer as an alternative to commitment. Instead of being sent to a correctional institution, a guilty child is given his freedom subject to the supervision and surveillance of his probation officer. It is here that a wise, sympathetic and strong father figure is most needed. Ideally the probation officer should be able to help a teen-age boy avoid further illegal acts and find a motivation and wholesome meaning to his life. This is not an easy task; it would require exceptional talents. It also requires sufficient time. A monthly half-hour interview or the mailing of a postcard will not do.

The qualifications of a juvenile probation officer have been aptly described as follows: "He must understand the motivations of human behavior, the influence of physical, mental and emotional health on conduct and family relationships. He must be informed as to community problems and their effect on individual attitudes and behavior" (John P. Kenney and Dan G. Pursuit, *Police Work with Juveniles* [Springfield, Illinois: Charles C. Thomas, 1959] p. 276).

It is hard to evaluate the work of a probation officer. The best person may fail with a particularly unregenerate child. Some youngsters learn a lesson simply from the experience of arrest and the fear of jail. They do not need the guidance or restraint of a probation officer. A probation officer may sound intelligent and sympathetic when speaking with a lawyer and still not be able to reach teen-agers. I have discussed cases with many probation officers. Some were genuinely concerned and helpful. Others were ignorant, vindictive, and punitive.

While written reports certainly do not tell the whole story, they do reveal something about the author of the report. Few lawyers have the opportunity to read these reports. They are confidential and for the eyes of the court only. I have received permission from the court to read many reports written by probation officers about my young clients. There is rarely any mention of positive action taken by the probation officer. One rarely if ever reads that a child went to a medical clinic, was enrolled in a special remedial school class, or obtained a job. The report simply records impressions and hearsay. The one reprinted below is not typical, because there is no typical report. But it is not unusual.

Richard K. was sixteen at the time he was on probation. (All of the information with respect to Richard was obtained from the official court records. I represented Richard. Because he was not committed to an institution, no transcript was made of the trial. He was continued on probation.) His parents were living together. His father was employed but his salary was so small that the family qualified for free legal services. At the age of fourteen, Richard had been found guilty of malicious mischief and disorderly conduct and was placed on probation. At the age of fifteen, he was twice found guilty of larceny of automobile and continued on probation. At sixteen, he was found guilty of attempted burglary. The boy had a verbal IQ of 97, performance 122, and full-scale IQ of 110. He was undoubtedly bright, but he read at a third-grade level. We attorneys thought that this was one of the factors contributing to his misbehavior.

Here is the verbatim entire report of the probation officer dated Janauary 25, 1966.

Richard is an intelligent lad, according to observation and experience of the Probation Officer. He is worldly wise for an individual of tender years. Playing in a Combo at dances and places of amusement will give one "worldly" education and not theory. The youngster is smart, has answers to cover up his acts of mischief. His motives are involved with criminal tendencies, and tainted with evil. A condition once embedded continues to exist. This individual cannot make a "mockery" of our Courts of law. By his effrontery before the Bar of this Court, his acts will not be condoned. The machinery of the law must be put in motion. Richard should be placed in an institution to correct him. Such an institution for an evader of the law and one who has "alibis" and looking for sympathy. As it was once said, "out of evil comes good, and out of good comes evil." By his acts of crime, institutionalization is the remedy—probation has failed which is the good side of the fence of our judicial mechanism. He has good intelligence, "waste not the human brain, put it to the use of wisdom needed in a troublesome world."

One must agree with the discouraged probation officer. Probation had indeed failed for Richard. But had either probation or Richard been given a chance? Richard dropped out of school. I do not know what has become of him.

Not all the reports were on this level. But this one was not unique. From time to time, the judges discussed the quality of the probation staff. Everyone recognized the critical importance of the probation staff in the work of the juvenile court. The Uniform Juvenile Court Act (Section 5) mandates the employment of probation officers and recommends that they be on civil service. The comment on this section is illuminating:

A competent probation staff is essential to achieving the objectives of the juvenile court system. The staff must be adequately trained, working loads must be limited, and conditions must be provided that permit the giving of the required time and attention called for by each individual case.

A probation service may be established on either a local or a statewide basis. Competent authorities disagree on the relative merits of the two alternatives. The National Council of Juvenile Court Judges favors a local system stressing the importance of having these services provided by court personnel responsible to and under the direction of the juvenile court judge since he is responsible for the successful conduct of the juvenile program. Proponents of the state- wide system stress the frequent inadequacy of local resources to provide the needed minimum service required and contend that better proba- tion service is provided by a state system, and that the prospect of the judge successfully achieving the objectives of the court's program is therefore enhanced.

Although probation officers are court employees, the judges often do not actually control hiring and firing. Court officers are not civil service or merit employees in many juris- dictions. In some states, probation is under the jurisdiction of the Department of Welfare. There is a continual struggle be- tween the judges and the department for control of probation. It represents many jobs and much patronage. It is a luscious political plum. Under either system there should be some re- view of work and some procedurally fair way of evaluating, hiring, and firing these officers who are crucial to any real effort at rehabilitation.

If probation is to be widely used as an alternative to institutionalization, there must be many changes. The duties of probation officers should be rationalized and redefined. The person who supervises the child after the trial should not be the same person who assisted in his prosecution. The use of proba- tion reports to prove delinquency certainly should be abol- ished. The probation officer should not be an adjunct policeman or detective.

If the probation officer is truly to be the key to rehabilita- tion, then he must not be put in an ambivalent position with respect to his young charges. If he is to help them, he cannot prosecute them. If he is to help them, he must have the resources with which to provide meaningful service. His case load must be small enough that he can see each child at least once in two weeks and oftener if he feels that it is desirable. He must have access to community agencies to help the child find tutoring, recreation, medical care, employment, or whatever else he needs in order to enable him to cope with his actual life situation. Just talking to a teen-ager for half an hour will not help him if he is sick or illiterate or bored and idle. A probation officer must be able to identify the boy's needs and then have the resources and authority to do something more than give him a sermon or a pep talk. If Richard had been given remedial reading lessons and perhaps formal musical training, his entire life might have been changed. This is the challenge and opportunity that awaits the probation officer.

Solid standards of education, training, and experience are essential. To obtain qualified people, it is necessary to pay competitive salaries and to give these people the status and respect the importance of their work deserves. As is the case with so many other persons who impinge upon the lives of ghetto children, there is a need both to upgrade the qualifications of the job and to employ qualified people who can "relate" to the children and their problems. The problem of the probation officer is not unlike that of the slum schoolteacher. Both the teacher and the probation officer must be trained, educated professional people. Of necessity, most of them will be middle-class. Many will be white. They must have adequate salaries and job security. They must also be understanding, not censorious; helpful, not punitive. Special skills are required; so are adequate time and resources.

Because most of the children in urban slums are black, it is a popular fallacy that a black person—any black person—will have better rapport and understanding than any white person. Some of the most overt and brutal hatred of poor black children is exhibited by middle-class Negroes. On the other hand, it is undoubtedly true that a middle-European refugee, despite his academic attainments, will probably have difficulty understanding the attitudes of children reared in permissive America, so different from his rigidly obedient childhood. He will have even more difficulty with black children whose patois is difficult to follow and who can barely understand his uncolloquial English. Between these extremes it should be possible to find people, both black and white, with formal education and some natural ability to surmount the formidable barriers of generation, class, education, and culture. If it can be done in the Peace Corps and Vista, perhaps a more imaginative form of recruitment and training could produce more effective probation officers. Failing that, the only alternative at present is mass institutionalization of a large segment of American youth.

Chapter Nine

BATTLEDORE AND SHUTTLECOCK

n. a game wherein a shuttlecock is driven or thrown back and forth

Funk and Wagnalls New Standard Dictionary of the English Language

The "subway rape case" was as famous in Philadelphia as the trial of Lizzie Borden was in Fall River. The press luridly described the "rape" of a little black girl in the subway by eight Negro youths. The police department immediately began patrolling the subways with dogs to prevent another "bestial" attack. The trial judge was lauded for the stern, speedy justice meted out to the dangerous fifteen-year-old felons. The public was confirmed in its belief that "those" people were really sub-human.

I was astonished when a pleasant-looking woman came into the office two years later and identified herself as the mother of two of the defendants in the subway rape case. Mrs. Y. said that her boys, Kenneth and Stephen, were not guilty. In the years since the trial, she had forgotten all the details. She did not know the names of the witnesses. All she knew was that her sons were innocent and they were in jail. She asked for our help.

In our long fight for these boys' release—appeals, writs, efforts to obtain a new trial—the Office for Juveniles got caught in the time-honored game of battledore and shuttlecock. This is apparently the favorite sport of judges, who bat a case from one court to another endlessly, never deciding the issues.

First, we decided that in order to unravel this mystery we would need the transcript of the trial. With some difficulty it was obtained. The entire transcript of the trial of eight boys, including the names of the prosecutor and the court representative, the names and addresses of the boys, the names and numbers of the arresting police officers, was all of forty-nine pages. The trial could not have taken more than twenty minutes.

The transcript disclosed that the boys were charged with "forcible rape, aggravated assault and battery, sodomy, disorderly conduct, robbery and larceny." The incident was alleged to have occurred on the evening of March 6, 1965.

On the night of March 7 the boys were removed from their homes by a uniformed police officer. He did not have a warrant for the arrest of any boy, although there was ample time to obtain warrants. The boys were not advised of their constitutional rights prior to interrogation, and they were questioned extensively. A police officer testified that the boys "admitted" the offenses with which they were charged. There were no signed statements, no formal confessions. The boys said they had been beaten with blackjacks and a rubber hose while being interrogated. In open court the two brothers exhibited severe bruises that, they said, were the result of beatings by policemen in the station house. The court was not interested in this testimony. No one investigated this alleged police misconduct.

The trial was held the next afternoon. Judge Juanita Kidd Stout presided. There was no reason for such a rush to judgment. All the boys were in jail.

Of the eight boys, only these two brothers had an attorney at the trial. He was retained at noon on the day of the trial, which began shortly after one o'clock. He was not given an opportunity to cross-examine the prosecution witnesses, to present witnesses on behalf of his clients, to make an argument, or to perform any of the functions essential to adequate legal representation.

At the opening of the trial, the arresting police officer asked the judge to advise the boys of their right to counsel. But Judge Stout stated that the boys had no right to counsel when they were being tried as juveniles. She further declared that this was a case "which requires swift justice." It was swift. By evening all the boys were a hundred miles away in jail.

The complaining witness, a girl, stated that on Saturday evening, March 6, 1965, she was in the subway station when several boys ran down the steps. One said "something dirty," another took money out of her pocketbook. Several boys held her and one boy exposed himself. The judge pointed to one of the defendants and asked the girl, "You remember seeing him there?"

The witness replied, "I think so."

On this positive identification, the judge ruled, "They were there. They are equally guilty." All eight boys were sent to jail. But there was no rape.

Kenneth testified that when he came down to the subway a sailor was running up the steps. Gregory H., another juvenile defendant, testified that someone had grabbed the girl's pocketbook, that it had nineteen cents in it, and that he returned it to her. This was not denied.

All of the boys were adjudged delinquent. Three of them were only fifteen years old at the time. Nonetheless, Judge Stout ordered them committed to the State Correctional Institution at Camp Hill, a jail for male offenders from the ages of sixteen to twenty-five. Commitment of a child under the age of sixteen to Camp Hill is illegal.

For weeks prior to this trial there had been a steady barrage of stories about juvenile crime in the press, on radio and TV, and at public meetings. Judge Stout had repeatedly talked about the need for swift, stern justice. On March 8 and 9 all of the papers carried long, hysterical accounts of the "subway rape case." The names and addresses of the eight defendants were published, also their prior juvenile "records." One of the boys had had his first "contact" with the juvenile court at age seven. These boys had been repeatedly arrested. Even under the loose procedures of the juvenile court they had not been convicted until this case. One can only wonder at the probable cause for the arrests and the nature of the evidence.

None of the boys or their parents was ever informed of the right to a rehearing or appeal. Because the trial was held within seventeen hours of the arrests, there had been no opportunity for the defendants to make an investigation of the facts. The six boys who had been tried without counsel had not known that they had a right to move for the suppression of the so-called confessions. The lawyer for the other two boys was not permitted to say or do anything.

After the trial, one parent retained a lawyer who petitioned the juvenile court for a rehearing. His client was not released. The mother of Kenneth and Stephen had been to the juvenile court many times during this two-year period. She pleaded with the various clerks and other employees to whom she spoke. None of them ever let her speak to a judge. None of them told her about free legal help. None of them mentioned an appeal.

When she heard of the Office for Juveniles, she immediately came to see us with an obstinate hope that something could be done. We struggled with the problem. What means of relief did the law afford in theory and in practice? The time for rehearing had expired. The time for appeal had expired. There was at that time no post conviction hearing statute. (Such statutes have recently been enacted in most states, but it is not clear whether they apply to juvenile court commitments.) A petition for rehearing would have to be addressed to the discretion of the court. Any petition filed in juvenile court would go to Judge Stout. No other judge would touch it. To file such a petition would be an exercise in futility. Even if a judge of the Court of Common Pleas did issue a writ of habeas corpus—which was extremely doubtful—the juvenile court could simply clap the boys back in jail on a bench warrant. And the State Supreme Court would not interfere.

In the case of King David M., who was held in jail for

several days for a shooting at South Philadelphia High School which occurred when King was admittedly miles away at his place of employment, we obtained his release on a writ of habeas corpus granted by Judge Herbert Levin. When Judge Charles Wright of the Juvenile Court learned of this order, he issued a bench warrant and had the boy put back in jail. The State Supreme Court refused to hear the case.

The only possible remedy for Stephen and Kenneth lay in federal court. It is not easy for a prisoner in a state institution to get a hearing in federal court. In recent years, so many state prisoners have sought relief in the federal courts that Congress passed an amendment to the judicial code restricting the right of federal judges to hear an application for a writ of habeas corpus from such prisoners. Before a federal judge can consider the merits of a habeas corpus petition, he must be convinced that the prisoner has "exhausted" his state court remedies. Scores of cases have wound their weary way on appeal from a federal district court, to the court of appeals, and finally to the United States Supreme Court to interpret and fix the meaning of the word "exhaust." Had the boys exhausted their state court remedies if, in fact, there were no remedies? In this case both logic and experience seemed to give an affirmative answer. I knew there was no meaningful remedy in the state court system.

Accordingly, on December 19, 1966, a petition for writ of habeas corpus was filed in the United States District Court on behalf of Kenneth. The petition was filed *in forma pauperis,* which means that the client takes a pauper's oath that he cannot afford to pay the court costs.

The federal court has an extremely elaborate and complicated form of seven mimeographed pages that the indigent prisoner must fill out in order to get his case before the court. It took me hours to comply with its ramifications and requirements.

How could seventeen-year-old Kenneth answer such

questions as question 14: "State concisely the ground on which you base your allegation that you are being held in custody unlawfully." Or question 17: "If any ground set forth in (11) has not previously been presented to (a) any state court, state which ground set forth in (11) was not so presented, and why not. . . ." Kenneth was in ninth grade when he was jailed. Two years later he was still at a ninth-grade level. He had not had one day of schooling while in jail.

I struggled with the form. Finally the petition was completed. It alleged that Kenneth's rights to due process of law had been violated in the circumstances of his arrest without warrant, the conduct of the trial, the failure to have adequate representation by counsel, the glaring publicity, the denial of any schooling while in jail even though he was of compulsory school age, and illegal peonage in that he was forced to work in a factory for wages of fifteen cents an hour.

Argument on the petition, limited to the question of exhaustion of state remedies, was had before Judge Francis L. Van Dusen. A lengthy brief was filed. A Philadelphia assistant district attorney argued that a remedy was available in the juvenile court. On January 25, 1967, Judge Van Dusen filed a memorandum opinion* in which he wrote that he had "requested the President Judge of the County Court to schedule a hearing for the relator." Meanwhile the petition for habeas corpus was held in abeyance.

We were then faced with unhappy alternatives: an appeal from Judge Van Dusen's order or a petition in juvenile court. Normally an order that does not finally dismiss the case or decide it on the merits is an interlocutory order and not appealable. There were circumstances here that might have justified an appeal. It would probably take three to six months to get the court of appeals to decide whether or not to hear the appeal. Meanwhile, Kenneth and the other boys would remain in jail.

---

*In the Matter of Young, U.S. District Court for the Eastern District of Pennsylvania, Memorandum Opinion Misc. #3435, January 25, 1967.

The alternative—to get a new hearing—was also undesirable. At a new hearing, the juvenile court would carefully avoid all the outrageously unconstitutional aspects of the original trial. These violations of the rights of the boys would then be forever buried and unreviewable. The only matters that would be considered on appeal or habeas corpus would be what occurred at the second trial.

Agencies interested solely in law reform might have chosen to appeal. I, too, was vitally interested in law reform. But I also represented two flesh-and-blood children who were in jail while these legal maneuvers were being performed. It was like a minuet, two steps forward and a bow to the federal judge, two steps back and a curtsy to the state judge. The lawyer danced while the judges called the tune. And the children stayed in jail.

With misgivings, the petition was filed in juvenile court. I filed on behalf of only one boy so that the issues lost in this case might still be available for the other boy. Judge Bonnelly promptly ordered a rehearing *de novo*. Such an order requires that the whole case be tried over again as a new case. The state must produce its witnesses, prove a crime, and prove the guilt of the defendant. The new trial was held on February 23, 1967, before Judge Clifford Scott Green of the juvenile court. Preliminarily the district attorney's office argued that the juvenile court had no jurisdiction to hear the matter. This was exactly the contrary of the argument that had been made in federal court. Judge Green was not impressed. He proceeded with the trial.

The complaining witness, the victim of the alleged rape, appeared. She testified that there was no rape. She could not account for her presence in the subway or her behavior that night. At the conclusion of the trial, Judge Green ruled that there was no evidence of rape or sodomy, that the commitment of a fifteen-year-old to Camp Hill was illegal because the statute sets sixteen as the minimum age for inmates in that prison. Kenneth was then adjudged delinquent on the basis of testimony that he was one of the boys who had "grabbed her" and held her arm or leg. The identification was dubious. At most this was assault and battery, a misdemeanor, the maximum penalty for which is two years in jail. Kenneth had already served twenty-three months on an illegal commitment. Judge Green changed all that. He legally committed Kenneth to a different jail to remain until the age of twenty-one.

What was the net result of all these petitions, extensive briefs, arguments, and a new trial? The federal court had deprived Kenneth of his federal remedy. The juvenile court had given him a new trial without constitutional infirmities. No one could say that he did not have a state remedy. Now all the blatant unconstitutionalities of the original trial were wiped out. After two years of illegal imprisonment, Kenneth was serving another four years legally. A decent interval after this second trial, Judge Bonnelly quietly released all the boys.

In the "subway rape case," the game of shuttlecock was played between the federal court and the juvenile court. This time the courts were not content simply to bounce the case back and forth with official court orders and decisions. These judicial players had a system of under-the-table signals. To whom can a lawyer complain on appeal when the courts confer privately?

Only twice in the experience of the Office for Juveniles, although we filed many petitions, were we able to obtain writs of habeas corpus. In both these cases, even though there was not a shred of evidence that our clients had committed the offense, they were put back in jail by the juvenile court in violation of the writs of habeas corpus.

Sometimes the game of shuttlecock can be skillfully played by one judge alone, like solitaire. In the case of Wilson H., Judge Clifford Scott Green played it all by himself. He didn't do it with mirrors, but with the canons of ethics. Wilson, a seventeen-year-old black boy, was arrested on October 11, 1966, at about nine o'clock in the evening. He was walking peacefully down the street. Perhaps he had had a drink. He

accidentally brushed against a police car. The policeman
promptly grabbed him and handcuffed him. Then in full view of
more than a half dozen people, three policemen pushed Wilson
up against the car and beat him. The boy was handcuffed while
he was beaten. He was taken to the police station. The witnesses
called a committeeman—that much maligned unpaid antipoverty worker who does favors for poor people in the hope of
getting their votes and in the process gives them an experience
of "participatory" democracy. The committeeman went down
to the police station and saw Wilson about one o'clock in the
morning. He testified that the boy was in a cell and still bleeding. Wilson had been knocked unconscious in the police wagon.

There was nothing unusual about this case except the
presence of the eyewitnesses. Wilson was charged with the
usual crimes of resisting arrest, assault and battery on a policeman, and disorderly conduct. Despite repeated requests for an
early hearing, I could not get the case listed for trial until June
21, more than eight months after the episode. By then Wilson's
wounds had healed. (He now has a permanent scar on his head.)
There was a full-scale trial that lasted more than three hours.
(No transcript was made of this trial, because it was a nullity.
The testimony is reconstructed from my notes.) One policeman
admitted using a blackjack on Wilson *after* he was handcuffed,
in order "to subdue him." That cop was at least fifty pounds
heavier than Wilson. The defense witnesses testified fully. Their
stories were consistent. They had a clear view of everything.
The judge's questioning revealed that the witnesses were not
friends or relatives of Wilson. At the conclusion of the testimony, Judge Green suddenly disqualified himself from deciding the case, to everyone's great astonishment. There was not
a particle of evidence that Wilson had committed an offense.
The case against the cops was airtight.

Judge Green told me that he *must* disqualify himself because there was a discrepancy between Wilson's statements
made on the witness stand under oath and the report of the

intake interviewer. The intake report was not a stenographic transcript but a summary of what had presumably been said. At the hearing before the intake interviewer, Wilson was not represented by counsel, he was not advised of his rights, he was not under oath. Because that hearing would determine whether he should be released pending trial, he naturally did not disagree with anything the interviewer said. Of course, he did not see what the interviewer wrote in the report.

The judge had no business reading inadmissible evidence prior to the trial. *After* the trial, he suddenly discovered that he had been prejudiced by the report. He told me he didn't believe a word of Wilson's uncontroverted testimony at the trial. I asked Judge Green if he thought Wilson had beaten himself. Judge Green gave me the choice of letting him, who admitted his prejudice, decide the case, or else having a new trial. Judge Green would probably have found Wilson delinquent and perhaps committed him to jail. In the meantime he was free pending trial. Obviously, I had to agree to try the case all over again. Would I be able to locate these witnesses and persuade them to come again and testify? If there was the slightest discrepancy between their testimony at the new trial and the testimony already given, this would be seized upon to impeach their credibility. At the second trial, we would face many more difficulties. The policemen would be briefed to excuse and explain their reasons for "subduing" Wilson. In the meantime, Wilson was a prime target for arrest by the policemen who had beaten him. The court dismissed everyone and promised to list the case for an early hearing. Six months later Wilson still had not had a trial on these charges or an opportunity to present his evidence against the police.

The judge, Wilson, and all the witnesses were black. The policemen were white. The witnesses muttered that the judge was trying to protect the cops. They were outraged. Wilson was neither angry nor surprised. He hadn't expected anything else. In fact, he was relieved to be able to go home instead of to jail.

This time the shuttlecock had been knocked way out of bounds. Because there had not been a trial, there was nothing to appeal. Wilson was free so that habeas corpus would not lie. No court would mandamus a judge to hold a hearing in a particular case when the defendant was free and when there is a huge court backlog. Wilson cannot sue the judge for refusing to try the case. Wilson will never get the speedy public trial that the Constitution guarantees him.

When I protested this peculiar proceeding, the judge pointed out that no one was hurt. It is true that no one suffered a harm that the law could redress. Wilson was at least out of jail. Many civic groups had been deeply concerned with this case. The highly respected North City Congress, a grass roots organization funded by charitable foundations, had sent observers to the trial, and a number of them spoke to me afterward. They were confirmed in their belief that there is no justice for the poor in the courts of the United States. What was hurt on June 21, 1967, was the administration of justice.

Chapter Ten

COMING OF AGE IN THE GHETTO

... I learned to speak the language, eat the food, and use and interpret the postures and gestures of the people.

MARGARET MEAD, *Coming of Age in Samoa*

It is estimated that there are 22,467 forcible rape cases a year in the United States.* The charge of rape is easy to make and difficult to disprove if the accused and accuser have been in a compromising situation. The life style of teen-age boys in the ghetto makes possible easy casual consensual relations and frequent false charges of rape. Many of our clients were accused of rape. Very, very few were guilty.

Paulinus G. was accused of rape. In most cases the complaining witness and the accused are of the same race. Mrs. Gladys G., Paulinus, Francisco, Sam, and Gary all were black. So were all the witnesses and the judge. All four boys were charged with delinquency—the rape of Mrs. Gladys G. It sounded like a vicious, brutal crime. I went to the detention center to interview these young clients with some misgivings. I spoke to each of the boys separately and took careful notes of their stories. They had been apart since their arrests and had had no opportunity to concoct an alibi or defense. Their stories were absolutely consistent. They were all to be tried at once. Because there was no conflict of interest, I decided to defend them all and free my colleagues for other cases. (Because the boys were eventually released, no transcripts were made of this case. This account is

*President's Commission on Law Enforcement and Administration of Justice, *Challenge of Crime in a Free Society*, 1967, p. 18.

reconstructed from my notes—as are the other case histories in this chapter.)

The prosecuting attorney in juvenile court changed frequently; it is an assignment that the lawyers dread. On the morning of this trial there was another new assistant district attorney. David K., fresh out of the University of Pennsylvania Law School, was about to prosecute his first case, and he was nervous. (This is a psuedonym.) I discussed the case with the assistant prosecutor, who related his thoughts and reactions to me. He had little time to prepare for this big moment. At nine o'clock he was handed a stack of more than thirty files and told to go to courtroom A and press for adjudications.

He opened the files and began hastily reading the yellow carbon tissue sheet of the police report known as "the 49." Because he had never seen one before, he read slowly, "Paulinus G. 3/21/52 N male Baptist." From the address it appeared that the boy lived in one of the worst slum areas. He was in his third year of high school at one of the virtually all-Negro high schools. Previous record: larceny of auto—discharged as to offense—placed on probation. David paused, a little puzzled. If Paulinus was put on probation, why was he acquitted? Then he reversed the question. If he was acquitted, why was he on probation? The courtroom was filling up with a strange assortment of people. He hurried down to the charge: rape, A & B (assault and battery), Agg. A & B (aggravated assault and battery), larceny, conspiracy, and RSG (receiving stolen goods). The names and addresses of three other boys were given. Paulinus hadn't confessed, or had he? David scanned the report: "Def. admitted having intercourse, denied rape."

David sat down at the district attorney's desk located conveniently inside the bar of the court. Being a polite young man, he was embarrassed that there was no chair or table for defense counsel. I had to remain standing while everyone else, except the defendants, could be seated. It takes strong arches to try cases in the juvenile court.

There was a stir, and some confusion. The mothers and witnesses were told to sit down and be quiet. The four boys were standing at the bar of the court. The crier arranged them in the order in which the cases were numbered—this is standard practice, so that the judge will know which boy belongs to which file. If they stepped out of order, the wrong one could be sent away. The three smaller boys were hard to tell apart; they were all small and dark. According to the file, Sam and Francisco were ten and Gary was eleven. Was it possible for boys this age to commit rape? Paulinus was five feet ten inches tall, slim, light-skinned, and good looking. He had a scar, perhaps from a knife or a razor, on his left cheek, which gave him a rakish, debonair look. Paulinus looked at me in surprise. Despite our long conversations, he never really expected me to come to court on his behalf.

The boys were charged with rape and also with assault and battery, aggravated assault and battery, larceny (of a gold wristwatch), receiving stolen goods, and conspiracy. For the record I pointed out that the delinquency petitions were defective (and thus contrary to the defendants' constitutional rights) in that they did not specify place, time, victim, items stolen or received, or any details of the alleged conspiracy. David supplied the information. The charge of conspiracy was dropped.

The first witness was the arresting police officer.

Before he began to testify I moved for sequestration of the witnesses. The judge remonstrated with me. "Is this really necessary? We are in juvenile court." But I persevered. These children were charged with very serious crimes. The credibility of the complaining witness was at issue. The children would be prejudiced if the witnesses were permitted to remain in the courtroom during the testimony. Obviously, if the complaining witness heard the testimony of the policemen, she would not contradict them. It was my hope to impeach her credibility by catching her in a couple of lies. The witnesses were ordered out of the courtroom.

The arresting officer read from his notebook. He stated that in response to a complaint he had gone to a certain address, walked up to the third floor apartment, and found the complaining witness, Mrs. Gladys G., nude on the bed. Paulinus was just exiting through the bedroom window when the officer and his partner seized Paulinus. The three little boys were sitting on the floor in the other room of the apartment playing cards. When the police entered, the little boys had yelled, "The fuzz are here!" A half-empty bottle of wine was found in the apartment.

The four boys had been taken to the police station. Mrs. G. told the police that Paulinus had raped her and stolen her watch. That he had dragged her upstairs from the street with the help of the three other boys. All four boys were held in custody. (It was thirteen days since the arrest.) Paulinus admitted having intercourse with Mrs. G. but said it was consensual. Sam, Francisco, and Gary first denied having relations with Mrs. G. but later said they had. The parents were not notified until after the boys had made their statements. Mrs. G. went home from the police station with her husband.

On cross-examination, the policeman admitted that none of the boys had been advised of the right to remain silent or the right to counsel. He also testified that he had gone to the apartment where he made the arrest as the result of a complaint made by a Mr. J., a Negro male about forty years old, who said that a woman was being raped at that address. Mr. J. was not called as a witness. No one seemed to know anything about him. The officer admitted that he had not heard any noise as he approached the apartment. It was very quiet. If anyone had yelled, could he have heard it? Yes, the officer said his hearing was good and he would have heard any screams. I asked him to describe the bedroom. He said that there was no furniture in it except a big mattress on the floor covered with a blanket. Mrs. G.'s clothes were in a pile on the floor. There were two paper cups with wine by the bed and some cigarette butts.

This was rather a cozy scene, wasn't it?, I asked. And the officer agreed. As for Paulinus, how was he dressed? The officer looked at him and said he was wearing the same green shirt. When questioned more closely, he remembered that Paulinus' shoes were unlaced and his belt was not buckled.

Mrs. G. was the next witness. She was about five feet two inches tall, very slender, with silky hair. She didn't wear lipstick. But she had on enormous sunglasses. She looked so fragile that David, the assistant district attorney, asked that a chair be brought for her.

Mrs. Gladys G. spoke in a soft voice, almost a whisper. The boy in the green shirt had dragged her by force to an apartment—she didn't know where—had taken her to the bedroom and raped her. Yes, she had resisted. But he was too strong for her. She choked at the awful memory, and a court employee brought her a glass of water. She was a pathetic little figure. Everyone in the courtroom glared at Paulinus.

Cross-examination began gently. In answer to friendly questions, Mrs. G. stated that she was married and the mother of three children. The oldest was eight years old. She didn't know where the incident occurred. She had never been on that street before. She was about a block away when the boys first approached her. The four of them dragged her along and pulled her up the stairs. But she resisted. How? Why? she screamed. She screamed the whole time. On the street, going up the stairs, and in the apartment. Didn't anyone hear her? There wasn't anyone on the street. But, of course, the police heard her. They came in the room and rescued her. The time was fixed at 3:30 P.M. Only Paulinus had raped her. Not the little ones. Mrs. G. was asked where she was going when she saw the boys. She was shopping. Further questioning brought the admission that she hadn't bought anything yet. She didn't have any packages. And where had she been the night before? Was she at home with her children? Mrs. G. hesitated.

David jumped up and objected. The question was irrelevant and beyond the scope of direct examination.

At the next question, Mrs. G.'s little-girl whisper vanished. She was asked if she had seen Mr. J. (the man who had alerted the police) that afternoon. Her denial was vehement. David didn't have a chance to object. But she admitted she had seen him on other occasions. I asked the court to request the witness to remove her sunglasses so that the defendant, counsel, and the court could see the witness. Mrs. G. said that she preferred not to. She had an eye ailment. I asked if perhaps it was a black eye. David objected and was sustained. I then observed that the witness was wearing a gold wristwatch. Was that the one she had worn on the day of the incident? Mrs. G. admitted that it was. So, I suggested, it hadn't been stolen, perhaps just misplaced. She agreed. The charges of larceny and receiving stolen goods were dropped by agreement of counsel.

I called two witnesses for the defense. A woman who had an apartment in the building where the incident occurred testified that she had been home all that afternoon. She remembered it clearly because she had been to a funeral earlier in the day and she felt so bad she didn't even turn on the TV. She hadn't heard any screams or any noise until the cops came. She was asked if she had seen Mrs. G. before. And she said that Mrs. G. had come into the building on several occasions, each time with a different man. She said there was a vacant apartment on the third floor. It was supposed to be locked but apparently somebody had the key.

The second witness was Paulinus' aunt. She testified that Mrs. G. had left her husband and children on many occasions, that her reputation in the neighborhood was that of a cheap, no-good whore.

I then moved for the discharge (acquittal) of all four boys. There was absolutely no evidence against the three little ones. And Mrs. G.'s testimony was not worthy of credence.

The judge said that first he wanted to ask the boys some questions. I objected that they did not have to testify, they had a right to remain silent. There was no evidence that the three little boys had committed any offense. As for Paulinus, at most it was fornication or adultery, depending on the uncertain marital status of Mrs. G. And considering the ages of Mrs. G. and Paulinus, he was doubtless the victim of a designing adult. I suggested that Mrs. G. be prosecuted for contributing to the delinquency of a minor. This was quickly brushed aside.

The judge insisted on questioning Paulinus. To permit him to testify would surely result in his admission of fornication, violation of liquor laws, and possibly trespass and other minor offenses. The fact that these charges were not specified in the petition is irrelevant in juvenile court, where the only offense is delinquency. On the other hand, to instruct Paulinus not to testify would result in his being held in contempt for refusal to answer the judge. Usually the word "contempt" is not used. A child is just held in custody until he "cooperates." A child who refuses to talk to the court psychiatrist or his probation officer may be locked up until he is willing to talk. And "talk" means to tell about the offense of which he is accused. Whatever the boy says will go into a report that is given to the judge. And this will be used to impeach or contradict his testimony given in open court.

There was no practical way in which I could assert Paulinus' constitutional privilege against self-incrimination. I had to let him testify. Paulinus' story was simply told. He had gone to the apartment after school. He often went there. It was a sort of clubhouse the boys went to when they had nothing to do. High school is over at two thirty. It was a cold day. The apartment was warm. There was almost always someone there to talk to. When Paulinus arrived, the other boys were there playing cards. They had some cigarettes, which they shared. A man and a woman came to the apartment. When they saw the boys, they went away. The woman was "her." She came back in a few minutes. She brought the wine and gave some to Paulinus. Then he asked her to go to bed with him and she did. Then the cops came.

David began his cross-examination when the judge had finished questioning Paulinus.

Did Paulinus mean that he asked a woman to go to bed with him after seeing her two minutes?

Paulinus said it wasn't two minutes. It was at least five. Visibly shocked, David asked whether Paulinus asked a strange woman to go to bed with him after five minutes. Paulinus said Yes. That was what he usually did.

David pursued him. Was Paulinus testifying that Mrs. G. agreed to his request without any force? Did he give her money, or what?

This time Paulinus was shocked. "Me? Give her money?," he repeated, his voice rising in amazement. Where would he get money? Why should he pay her? Besides, she told him her name was Rosemary and she loved him.

David could not stop. And what if she had said No?, he asked. Paulinus said that would be all right with him. There would be other girls. A few said No. Most said Yes. Paulinus admitted matter of factly that this was the purpose of the apartment. He didn't know who owned it. But he used it often and so did other people. Defense counsel's objections that these questions were immaterial and irrelevant were swept aside by the judge.

After considerable discussion all the boys were released in the custody of their mothers.

There was a tense moment when the school records of all four boys were reported by the school representative. It seemed that Gary had been absent a good many times. I called his mother to the stand. In response to very leading questions she promised to see that Gary would get to school every day. Paulinus' record was not too bad. As the school representative remarked, he would soon be seventeen and drop out of school. Apparently the school was waiting for that happy day.

The little boys were discharged (acquitted). Paulinus was "determined." This is a concept peculiar to juvenile court. It is halfway between innocent and guilty, like being a little pregnant. Because the boy who is "determined" goes home, it is a dangerous thing to challenge this finding. An irritated judge can easily change it to adjudicated (guilty) and send the boy off to a correctional institution (jail).

If the boy should get arrested after he reaches eighteen, this record of "determined" will go along with him and weigh against him on an application for bail, a presentence investigation, and fixing of the penalty. It will go to the Army and to prospective employers. I was concerned about the far-reaching effects this single ambiguous word might have on Paulinus' future. In some cases, after the judge's temper had cooled, I would file a petition and get an order "expunging" the record. Even then the record is not wiped clean, it is simply marked "expunged" and continues to follow the boy.

None of these considerations bothered Paulinus. He was glad to get out of jail and go home with his mother. She was still fuming about that "lyin' bitch." Paulinus' behavior occasioned absolutely no comment. The witness who lived in the building where the incident occurred told Paulinus to knock on her door whenever he visited the apartment and she'd give him something to eat. It was assumed that the empty apartment would continue to serve its many sheltering purposes.

The four mothers received their sons back with love and joy. There was no great indignation over the fact that the boys had been jailed for two weeks on palpably fradulent charges. There was just relief that they had got out so soon. No one worried about the school that was missed, the problems of making up assignments, or keeping up with the class. In the ghetto, children miss an enormous amount of school. They are often sick; they oversleep; a rival gang is on the warpath. There are many reasons why it may be wise to stay home.

The boys cheerfully gathered up their possessions and went out to the little knot of voluble mothers, witnesses, and neighbors. It was a time to be happy. They moved en masse to say good-bye to me, to repeat again and again their thanks, to offer small sums of money, and a request to take me to the corner "greasy spoon'" for a coffee or a soda. There was always something embarrassingly pathetic and wrong that people should be so grateful for what was, in truth, a legal right. I never encountered a single parent or child who did not thank me and my colleagues fulsomely, even if the child was sent to jail.

I tried to explain to Paulinus and his mother my concern about the decision "determined." His mother patted my shoulder. "Don't worry, honey. You done everything you could. He's free now."

Hector J. and Lawrence L. also spent most of their days on the street. Life was generally pretty dull, and they kept looking for something to happen. One late afternoon as they were wandering down a slum street they heard a commotion in an alley. Naturally they rushed over to see the excitement. They came very close and then stood and watched. This was what they always did. Sometimes they would see a knife fight; sometimes a mugging or armed robbery. This time they watched a rape. The boys did not know either of the adults. In the midst of this activity, a police car arrived. An unidentified person in a second-floor window had phoned the police. The police officers took the two adults and the two children to the police station. The man was arrested for rape and released on bail.

The boys were charged with delinquency and held in custody. Lawrence's father had a good job. He immediately retained private counsel who got Lawrence released pending trial. Hector's mother was on assistance. She came to the Office for Juveniles. We promptly obtained an order releasing Hector. Many weeks later the boys' case came up for trial in juvenile court. The adult defendant naturally refused to testify in juvenile court in advance of his trial. The woman victim of the rape testified that the boys had not touched her. She said there were two boys watching but she could not identify them. The police-men did identify the boys. There was no doubt that Lawrence and Hector were at the scene. They did not avert their gaze. It was equally clear that the boys did not *do* anything.

The judge was highly indignant and deeply concerned that these boys exhibited such prurient, immoral conduct. He called for the school records of both boys. Lawrence, having private counsel, was taken first. He had more than seventy unex-cused absences. He also had a long record of prior arrests for larceny, disorderly conduct, and other minor offenses. Law-rence's counsel made a persuasive argument. The gist of his plea was that Lawrence's parents were moving to the suburbs. They would take him away from the ghetto, its problems, and crimes. The court was moved and sent Lawrence back to his parents with good wishes and congratulations on this momen-tous step out of the ghetto and on the road to morality and good citizenship.

The judge then turned his attention to Hector. His school report showed almost as many absences as Lawrence's. Hector, too, had several prior arrests. The judge immediately decided that a correctional school (prison) was just what Hector needed. Legal argument—that Hector had not committed a crime—fell on deaf ears. The boy is in need of care and guid-ance, which gives the juvenile court jurisdiction under the stat-ute. The fact that he had not been charged with being in need of care and guidance, but with the crime of rape, was consid-ered an irrelevant trifle. I argued that Hector's mother provided a good home for him—clean, loving, and moral. Of course, it was in the ghetto. She could not afford to move away. Such a home, in the view of the court, did not provide the care and guidance that Lawrence's family by virtue of their move to the suburbs could give to him. Hector was ordered committed.

I immediately filed a petition for rehearing alleging a denial of the equal protection clause of the Constitution. Here were two boys whose conduct with respect to the "crime" had been identical. Their prior records were closely similar except that Lawrence's prior record was worse. The differentiation of treatment, I alleged, was an invidious discrimination based solely on the wealth of the parents. Hector was soon released. The judge decided that a taste of prison was sufficiently beneficial and he didn't need a whole diet of incarceration.

Apathy, indifference, and lack of drive characterized many boys of the ghetto. But these stereotypes were far from unversal. Many girls and some boys showed ambition and determination. Their desires were for the good material things and pleasures of the world. As in every economic group, only a few were moved by great passions. Warren G. was one of these. I thought of him as I read a Sunday supplement story "The Greeks and Their Golden Girls." It described the opulent gifts that tough up-from-poverty Greek millionaires lavish on their ladies. The Greeks buy ruby necklaces, diamond tiaras, art collections, yachts, villas, chateaux. Nothing is too extravagant, luxurious, or ridiculous for such a man to buy his girl friend or new wife. Warren bought his girl a dress for seventy dollars.

The middle-class, middle-income college boy buys his fiancée a minuscule diamond or has his mama's engagement ring reset. Good taste as well as the habit of thrift and the sour-grapes shunning of ostentation dictates his choice of the small gift and her joyous acceptance of it. The boys and girls of the ghetto have no habits of thrift; they do not save for a house in the suburbs that they will never have. Nothing is too big, too luxurious, or too expensive for a boy from a cold-water flat with rats and roaches to give to his girl.

Warren gave Delores whatever luxury her heart desired. And Delores was happy to receive these tokens of his affection. It was a cruel fate that cast Warren in jail. He had been there more than a week when his mother came to the office to see me. Warren is the oldest of her large brood. They all live on public assistance. This was the first time Warren had ever been "in trouble"—the polite ghetto euphemism for jail and arrest. Warren's mother told me he was a good boy. She didn't know what the charges against him were.

Warren's seventeenth birthday was March 24. On that day he legally quit school, although he could have graduated in less than three months. A high school diploma did not seem nearly so important to him as pleasing Delores.

Delores was also seventeen, but she was going to finish school. She wanted a new dress to wear to the high school graduation dance. She saw a filmy white chiffon with plunging neckline and insets of lace for seventy dollars. Then there were white satin shoes and a string of fake pearls and long earrings needed to complete the ensemble, to paint the perfect picture of the sweet girl graduate. Delores had walked Warren past the store window many times. On March 25 Warren left school and hurried over to Ben's auto body repair shop. Warren is a smart boy and Ben paid him ninety dollars a week. Warren also got tips for delivering cars to free-spending, well-dressed members of the black working class.

Warren bought the gown, the slippers, the pearls, and even a white satin pocketbook for Delores. But there is a snake in every Eden. And so it was on Columbia Avenue in North Philadelphia's jungle. Oscar appeared, in a red second-hand sports car, with processed hair, and a gray flannel suit. Oscar was a graduate of Columbia Avenue who attended Cheyney, a 90 percent Negro, recently accredited college, owned by the Commonwealth of Pennsylvania. Warren, with his nappy hair and grease-rimmed fingernails, whose idea of a big date was to take a girl to the movies, didn't have a chance. Delores' mother had always taught her that it was just as easy to love a rich boy as a "nigger on DPA." Delores belatedly bethought herself of her mama's teachings. Oscar was obviously the boy who should take her to the graduation dance. In two days, Delores had made her arrangements with Oscar. The only problem was how to get rid of Warren.

For this delicate matter, Delores consulted her mama.
Mama knew all about Oscar's father who was a successful numbers writer. Like every mother, she wanted the best for her
daughter and the best was personified in that nice college boy.
Mama advised Delores not to have a scene with Warren, who
was known to have a bad temper and might, if sufficiently pro-
voked, give Delores a black eye, which would be difficult to hide
from Oscar. The plan was simple. Delores was to admit Warren
to the house as usual. But Mama would come upstairs and chase
him away with a show of outraged virtue.

The scene unfolded that night according to the script.
But the unanticipated occurred. Warren refused to get out of
Delores' bed and leave when Mama appeared. Unpleasant
words were exchanged. Fearing that Oscar might be arriving
soon, Mama ended the little drama by calling the police.

When I saw Warren he had been in jail almost two weeks.
He was in the basement cellblock, sitting on a bench in withdrawn misery as his cell mates joked, pissed, and laughed while
waiting for their trials. His ugly, intelligent face was contorted
with pain. He knew that he was charged with rape. Slowly, with
evident effort, he told me about Delores. He said she was his
girl. She was beautiful and he loved her. He had bought her not
only her graduation gown and all the trimmings but many other
things. He was sure that she loved him too, and was just under
the domination of her spiteful mother.

The day of the trial, I asked the court crier to list this one
late in the day. Then I went through the court waiting room
looking for Delores. With little effort I found her amid the
scores of weary mothers, bored little brothers and sisters, and
disdainful teen-agers. There were at least one hundred people
sitting in the dim, ill-ventilated room—just waiting. Most of the
people were black. There were few girls. Delores was far from
beautiful but she was very well dressed. She was plump and
sweet looking. Mama was big and domineering. I explained that
I was Warren's lawyer and that I would like to talk to them if they

were willing to talk to me. We went into the corridor, the only place that a lawyer can hold a conference.

Mama assured me she had nothing to say to me. And then she proceeded to tell me that she didn't want Warren for her daughter, that Delores was brought up to be a lady, and that she was going with a college boy. I asked Delores if she had gone out with Warren before. She said she had. But it was all over and she never wanted to see him again.

Before the trial, I repeated this conversation to Warren. His eyes filled with tears and he turned away from me. I felt as if I had stabbed him. But there was more to tell Warren. He had an IQ of over 120. His school grades were good. I piqued his wounded pride and told him how superior he was, that he must go back to school and on to college. There were smarter and prettier girls than Delores. They would appreciate an educated man. Our only problem was to get him out of jail and back to school. He promised to cooperate.

This was another case for sequestration of witnesses. It was essential that Delores testify without Mama's intimidating presence. In most cases both boys and girls will tell the truth if they are not afraid of a parent, or a bigger and stronger boy who is in the courtroom and may take his revenge later. The young assistant district attorney made no objection to the request for sequestration. A very irate Mama was ordered out of the courtroom.

Delores testified in a whisper. Warren had forced her. No, she didn't want to. She wasn't that kind of a girl. The district attorney spoke kindly to her and so did the judge. She was really a nice girl. I avoided the "rape" and began to question her about Warren. How long had she known him? Did he take her to the movies? Did he visit her at her home? He'd been there before? Many times? Yes, she acknowledged everything candidly. And then we got to the question of the graduation dance. Reluctantly she admitted that Warren had bought the dress, the slippers, the pocketbook, the gloves, the earrings. And the underwear? Yes, the underwear, too. She and Warren had gone shopping together and he had paid for everything.

When Mama was called back into the courtroom, the judge asked her whether she knew who had bought her daughter's clothes. Mama's righteous indignation evaporated as she hemmed and hawed. One could almost see her shrink as her self-righteous dignity oozed away.

The judge called Warren's mother to the bar of the court. Did she know that Warren had spent all this money on Delores? Yes, she knew. But it was what he wanted to do. It did not seem odd to her that a boy would spend seventy dollars for a girl's dress when he didn't own a decent pair of shoes and his family was on relief.

Warren was discharged. Delores looked pleadingly at him as she followed Mama out of the courtroom. But Warren resolutely gazed out of the window. His mother held his hand gently as she and Warren went out of the courtroom. The money was forgotten. Warren was free and she was happy. They went back to their flat in the ghetto.

Four girls were in the waiting room one day when I returned from court. It was unusual to see more than one girl on a single day. National statistics on crime and delinquency indicate that only 13 percent of all juveniles arrested are girls. Our figures were closely similar. The Office for Juveniles kept files in chronological order. An examination of 125 consecutive files from May 16, 1967, to May 31, 1967, disclosed that 107 clients were males and 18 females. Of these, only one girl was charged with an offense that might be considered criminal. That was shoplifting. All the others were charged with runaway, incorrigibility, and truancy. Of more than three thousand children who passed through our office, only one girl client, Madeline W., was charged with a crime of violence—assault and battery.

Madeline was emotionally disturbed. She needed therapy, but instead she was in jail. She wrote us heart-breaking letters telling that her family didn't like her, the jail matrons hated her, her school teachers had no time for her. In each letter was this cry: "No one will lissen."

There can be no doubt that girls rarely commit crimes of violence. They do not kill, mug, shoot, stab, steal for profit, or even take automobiles. Yet they suffer disproportionately.

The legal problems of girls are sex and shoplifting. But shoplifting, by the girls of the ghetto, is just another aspect of their sexual problems. Boys steal radios, television sets, watches, all kinds of readily salable goods. There are numerous Fagins who not only act as fences for the boys but put them in the business of burglary. Not one girl was accused of stealing from a dwelling or a school. Not one girl was accused of purse snatching. The things girls were accused of stealing were always cheap clothes or jewelry for their own adornment. All of these girls try desperately to be clean, neat, and attractive. Somehow they succeed. A girl in an ill-heated slum will wash her body, her hair, and her clothes. Her mother, her brothers, and her little sisters may be filthy and unkempt. By puberty, the girls of the ghetto have learned how to be attractive. If they cannot buy a lipstick or a pair of stockings, they may yield to temptation and filch them.

Middle-class girls have the same two categories of problems—sex and shoplifting. But they are handled very differently by the law. Before opening the Office for Juveniles, I had represented a number of middle-class girls accused of shoplifting. In fact, all of them were guilty. They were caught red-handed taking quite expensive items from department stores. None of these girls was in want; all of them had not only necessities but luxuries. Zelda F. was a habitual shoplifter. But she claimed it was the fault of the stores. They shouldn't leave the goods lying around on counters. Candace M. was more adept, and she stole much more expensive things. Candace attended a fashionable private girls' school. Her ploy was to go to an expensive specialty shop wearing her Somali leopard coat over a slip. She would try on a two-hundred-and-fifty-dollar or three-hundred-dollar dress, put her coat on over it, and saunter nonchalantly out of the store. Candace got away with this at least six or seven times before she was caught. Her father paid for the dress. He paid my fee. And I persuaded the store to withdraw the charges. Candace and Zelda are now honor students in college. Judy K. is a rebel. She wears her hair long and stringy, her skirts very short. She is not interested in adorning herself but in fighting the corrupt bourgeois system. She "liberates" goods from the ten-cent store and the supermarket as a form of protest against the state. Her bourgeois father also paid up when she got caught. And the charges against her were dropped.

These cases were adjusted so easily and quickly that I felt constrained to give the girls a lecture about the evils and dangers of this little game of larceny they were playing. Were their lives so dull and drab and meaningless that they had to resort to thievery for kicks? I could not tell them, Crime does not pay. They knew that there were no penalties for them. I begged the parents to make their daughters earn the money for my fees and to reimburse the stores. But the parents and the girls just wanted to forget about the law and its intrusion into their lives as quickly as possible. The fathers wrote the checks and the girls went home.

Uvelia J. was not at all sure that she would go home after a hearing on a charge of shoplifting. Nor was I. When a poor black girl is charged with shoplifting, all the normal rules of law are reversed. The prosecution does not have to prove guilt beyond a reasonable doubt. The accused must establish her innocence beyond the least shadow of a doubt. Uvelia was employed. She made sixty dollars a week and helped support her mother and sister. Uvelia did not feel poor or underprivileged. She offered to pay for an attorney. She expected that she could get a lawyer for five dollars. Uvelia had left high school at the age of sixteen, got her working papers and a job. She read fluently; she was neat, pretty, and proud. It is no slight achievement to be self-supporting when 40 percent of one's male contemporaries are unemployed, and most of one's girl friends are pregnant, or taking care of their babies, and living on public assistance.

"Why would I steal a skirt? I had the money in my pocketbook to pay for what I want," she said bitterly. And she showed me the uncashed salary check. The notes of the intake interviewer showed that the store floorwalker had seen her through a mirror, that she had gone into a dressing room with some garments from a rack, emerged a few minutes later carrying a paper bag. He stopped her just as she was leaving the store and called the police. In the bag was a skirt. Such testimony would make out an open-and-shut case, unless we had strong evidence of innocence.

Uvelia said she had brought the skirt from home. She had taken it to work with her in a paper bag. It was one she had had for a couple of weeks. She was looking for a sweater to go with it. I called the store where she said she had purchased it, described the skirt, and asked them if they had any records. Of course, Uvelia didn't have a charge account. They had no record of her. But they did have records of the sale of that skirt in her size on the day she claimed to have purchased it. After considerable persuasion and pleading, the store manager promised to send someone to court to identify the skirt and to testify that it was their merchandise. Uvelia's employer could not come to court, but sent a written affidavit of good moral character. We could not subpoena these witnesses because the office did not have $7.60 per witness for witness fees and carfare, which must be tendered when the subpoena is served. The subpoena itself costs fifty cents. Before the trial I notified the prosecutor that I would demand that the complaining witness, the floorwalker, be present and that the skirt and the bag be produced.

The floorwalker was in court. He was the state's only witness. He testified that it was his job to watch the customers. The store lost thousands of dollars in purloined goods each year. My objection to this testimony was overruled.

The floorwalker said he had been looking through a mirror and he saw Uvelia go into the dressing room without a package and emerge shortly with a bag. He hurried down and nabbed her just as she was leaving without paying for anything.

On cross-examination, he was asked to locate himself, the mirror, and the dressing room. I had been to the store to look over the layout before the trial and I knew he could not see the dressing room from where he would have to stand in order to see the mirror. With some prodding he admitted that he hadn't seen Uvelia go in or out of the dressing room. He just saw a girl leaving the store with a paper bag.

"And you assumed that a young colored girl carrying a bag would be shoplifting?" I asked.

He agreed that this was his assumption.

I asked him to produce the bag and identify it, which he did. He didn't know the price of the skirt. No, he didn't see any tags on it. But she could have removed them.

Our first witness was a woman employee from the other store. She identified the skirt as being their merchandise. She said that a skirt of that size and description had been sold two weeks before. Of course, she didn't know to whom it was sold. She was asked to examine the skirt carefully. She gave her opinion that it had been worn a number of times.

Uvelia testified in a quiet manner. She produced her salary check. She told about looking for a matching sweater. She had taken the skirt to work with her in a paper bag. She also had one tan glove with a rip in the finger. She intended to buy a spool of matching threat to mend the glove. The bag was examined and the torn glove was found in the bottom. The judge discharged Uvelia.

The abashed floorwalker went over to her and said, "No hard feelings. There's nothing personal, y'know."

Most of the girls the office encountered were victims of adult abuse or neglect. There were many girls pregnant as a result of forcible rape by fathers, uncles, paramours, and neigh-

bors. Without exception the girls read fluently; they liked
school. Except for Mary Ann S., who was distraught and dishev-
eled, and Madeline W., who was emotionally disturbed, the girls
were stylish and attractive. Many were hopeful and ambitious.
Each of them with only a little help could move so easily into the
mainstream of middle-class life.

In the Office for Juveniles we learned that living in the
ghetto was itself a strong factor in every phase of a child's
contact with "the law." The policeman's decision to arrest a
slum child was not just subconsciously dictated by a feeling that
this was the way to handle "them." It was scientifically built into
the system. A point scale of factors of delinquency developed
by Dr. Marvin Wolfgang as a sociological measurement device
was used by the police department as a standard for determining which young people to release at the station level and which
ones to turn over to intake. We also discovered that poverty and
the ghetto were a determining factor in disposition—that is, in
the judge's decision to send a child home or commit him to an
institution.

When a child comes from a broken home—no father and
a mother struggling to maintain herself and her children on a
bare subsistence allotment from the state—and the child gets
into trouble and plays hooky from school, it is easy to conclude
that he will be better off in an institution. But a moment's reflection suggests that this is not true. It is also grossly unfair. The
rich child of a broken family often gets into scrapes and plays
hooky. Yet most of these children of divorce grow up to be
respectable and law-abiding adults. Many of our distinguished
citizens grew up in dire poverty in an era when there was no
welfare and the truant officer rarely brought delinquency proceedings against the slum children of immigrants. It is perfectly
evident that our juvenile institutions like our adult jails are the
spawning grounds of serious crime.

There is an old maxim in the law, Equality is equity. In
a court of law, children should be judged and punished for their
own conduct, not the status of the family. Often one boy goes

to prison while his equally guilty or equally innocent friend of a better economic background goes free. I have spoken to many of these children and witnessed their burning sense of injustice.

These differences in treatment, which were so apparent to us, were proved with statistical nicety in a study of juvenile arrests and dispositions in Contra Costa County, California. The researchers from the University of California compared two sections of the county—one wealthy and the other relatively poor. The children from the wealthy area were arrested less frequently. Those who were arrested were almost always released at the police station level. Those who were brought to court for serious offenses were rarely sent to institutions. By contrast, the poorer children were arrested more often, a larger percentage were taken to court, and a considerably larger proportion were sent to correctional institutions. The disparities increase when one compares the wealthy white suburbs and the black slums.

The daughter of a wealthy manufacturing family was recently adjudicated delinquent for smoking marijuana. She, of course, was placed on probation and sent home to her family and back to school. Similarly, the sons of prominent politicians and other public fiigures have been held delinquent for smoking pot. They have not been jailed. Significantly, there is considerable pressure now to reduce the penalties for marijuana possession so that college students will not be jailed for several years. There is no comparable effort to mitigate the severity of penalties for the offenses which are commonly committed by poor children.

With the exception of New York City, where hard drugs are readily available, the slum child is far less addicted to drugs than the white middle-class suburban high school student. We did not have a single case of drug use among the more than three thousand children accused of delinquency who came to the Office for Juveniles. But many of our clients were sent to correctional institutions for glue-sniffing, which is the slum child's cheap substitute for marijuana. The ghetto child does not drink much whiskey. It is too expensive. He gets drunk and sick on cheap wine. For glue-sniffing and wine drinking and poverty he is often sent to a juvenile jail.

A recent article in *The Philadelphia Inquirer* (March 15, 1970) bears this out. The article reports that in 1968, 231 juveniles appeared in court on narcotics charges, and in 1969, 403 juveniles. For the first seventy-one days of 1970, there were already 160 cases. Two-thirds of these 160 juveniles were white. Most of the drug cases don't even get to court.

The difference in treatment of the slum child and the middle-class child for premarital sex is also striking. Numerous surveys show that the majority of college girls have premarital sex relations. So do many suburban high school girls. Obviously many middle-class boys also have premarital sex relations. Rarely are these young people brought to court and charged with juvenile delinquency. The prosecutors and the courts sensibly refuse to become involved with the private lives of these young people despite the obvious violations of the criminal law, just as they refuse to become involved with the much publicized babies born out of wedlock to movie stars and members of the jet set.

The middle-class mores of an earlier day are codified in the law. Fornication, bastardy, and adultery are crimes. But the poor, like the rich, do not subscribe to these norms. Extramarital sex in the slums—where divorce is impossibly expensive—is not deviant behavior for adults or youth. It is the norm. Kinsey has shown that sexual strength and desire are at their highest in late adolescence. There is little social pressure on the young people of the slums for celibacy. Their lives are meager, idle, and lacking in the pleasures and activities that fill the hours of the middle-class teen-ager. The slum youth has no reason to be frugal or abstinent. He has little motivation for study. *Carpe diem* is, of necessity, his philosophy. This seizing of present pleasures, both monetary and sexual, is the only sensible way of life for those who have little expectation that tomorrow will be any better than today. They know it may be worse.

Chapter Eleven

PARENTAL STATE: INFANTILIZED PARENTS

[The purpose of the Juvenile Court] is not penal but protective
—aimed to check juvenile delinquency and to throw around a
child, just starting, perhaps, on an evil course and deprived of
proper parental care, the strong arm of the State acting as
parens patriae.

In re Holmes, decision of JUSTICE HORACE STERN of
Pennsylvania

"Floyd don't have no respect for me," Mrs. T. whined. "I
want the court to learn him to have respect."

Mrs. T. was one of the fairly small number of parents who
wanted the juvenile court to take their children off their hands.
The well-to-do parent who finds his child a problem and an
emotional burden can pack him off to boarding school in winter
and to camp in summer.* The indigent parent turns to the
juvenile court. All too often it obliges him, without giving a
thought to the rights of the child.

Mrs. T. was large and neatly dressed, with fresh nail
polish and earrings. The secretary had already ascertained that
Mrs. T. met the office's standards of indigency. I wondered, as
I often did, how these mothers managed to look so smart and
attractive on an income supposedly 20 percent below subsist-

---

*Parents occasionally consult a lawyer not only to find ways to prevent a child
from inheriting money, but to try to rid themselves of their responsibilities.
Middle-class parents of handicapped children frequently use political influence
to have such children placed in state residential institutions even when they
know that these places simply warehouse the children and provide no real care.
Educated middle-class adults who have adopted a child in good faith and then
discovered that the relationship is burdensome have consulted me in an effort
to rescind the adoption and get rid of the child.

ence level. The system requires lying for survival. Despite my own ethical standards, I gradually became accustomed to this sordid business. Either one pretended ignorance and accepted the lie, or one became a detective seeking out the discrepancies in the story, entrapping the ignorant and illiterate into betraying their crude strategems.

"Where is Floyd?" was my first question to Mrs. T. If the boy's location could be pinpointed, it was easier to find out what the charges were.

It happened that seventeen-year-old Floyd was roaming the streets with his friends, that "no good lot" who would get him into trouble, in the opinion of Mrs. T. About five minutes' interrogation finally convinced me that Floyd had not been arrested and was not wanted by the police. There were two other possible reasons that a slum boy would need a lawyer: trouble with school or with a girl. Mrs. T. refuted both propositions. Floyd "done good" in school. He passed all his subjects. She was never bothered by the "home and school representative," the contemporary nomenclature for the truant officer. As for girls, evidently Floyd distributed his favors widely. No girl or her mother had been around to see Mrs. T. Truly Floyd was an exemplary young man. He had no police record. Because in his neighborhood 70 percent of the boys had at least one contact with the police before reaching the age of eighteen, it appeared that Floyd was not only exemplary but adept. More questioning brought the reluctant admission that Floyd had not noticeably violated the curfew laws.

Mrs. T. returned to her original complaint. Floyd didn't respect her. Of course, I sympathized. As an adult and a parent, I could understand her problem, which is of course quite widespread. This, however, is not a legal question. Why did Mrs. T. consult a lawyer?

Mrs. T. said she had been told that she could file a petition against Floyd and the juvenile court would send him to a school where "they'd learn him to have respect."

"Mrs. T.," I carefully explained, "the juvenile court is not a parent. If you haven't been able to teach him respect in seventeen years, what do you expect the court to do in five minutes?"

"They c'n send him away. Mrs. Handy's Darryl was sent away and it kept him out of more trouble."

A light began to dawn.

"What do you live on, Mrs. T.?" I asked her.

"What d'ya mean?"

"Where do you get your money? Do you have a job?"

Mrs. T. was offended at the question. "DPA," she replied. A tacit "of course" was implied. Obviously, she thought that I was more dense than most white people.

"Where is Floyd's father?"

"Gone."

"Are you ill, Mrs. T.? Why can't you work?"

"I don't want my boy to get in no trouble. I wants him sent away." The question about her unemployment was blandly ignored.

I tried once more. "There are only two things the judge can do. He can give Floyd back to you or he can put him in jail —and I mean jail. What do you want?"

"He's got no respect. I wants him put away." She was vehement.

"Is that what you really want, that your son should be in jail with murderers and thieves, that he should not be able to walk the streets in freedom, that he shouldn't go to school, that he should spend his youth behind bars? Do you want him caged like an animal? Is that what you want or what your boyfriend wants?"

Mrs. T. flushed beneath her dark brown skin.

"Even parents have to earn respect, Mrs. T.," I said.

Mrs. T. rose in anger. All two hundred pounds quivered with indignation. "I'll tell my caseworker. I come to the wrong place. She'll tell me how to file that petition."

"You *have* come to the wrong place," I told her. "And if

you get Floyd locked up, I promise you, I'll get him out." My voice dropped to a whisper. We two mothers looked at each other in silent combat. Fury filled the room. I looked down at last, ashamed.

Mrs. T. walked heavily out of the office and down the stairs. As I listened to the clump, clump, clump of her heels on the uncarpeted steps, I wondered how I, a presumably civilized person, could treat another human being as badly as I had treated Mrs. T. We sent a letter to her and to the public assistance caseworker explaining the purpose of the office, the law, and the presumption of innocence.

As I struggled with the shame of my reaction to Mrs. T., I began to realize why I had been so angry. After many months and hundreds of cases of abused children, the entire office had imperceptibly come to view the world from the client's point of disadvantage. "They" were the enemy. "They" were composed of judges, caseworkers, school administrators, and policemen —the forces of society that deprived children of their freedom.

This was the first time I recognized the complicity of the poor themselves in perpetuating and feeding the machine. Mrs. T. was not evil. She was not even unusually selfish. What had happened was that she, like the bureaucracy, had adopted the conventional wisdom: The juvenile court is a parent who will throw a protective arm around a child and guide him safely through the dangers of adolescence. Many lawyers, professors, and psychiatrists, who have observed the operations of juvenile courts, still cling to the notion that the juvenile judge can and does minister to the needs of a child.* Surely a ghetto mother

---

*Judge J. Sydney Hoffman, of the Superior Court of Pennsylvania, who sat for many years as a juvenile court judge in Philadelphia, disposing of as many as eighty cases a day, testified on July 24, 1968, before the Pennsylvania Joint State Government Commission Task Force on the United States Supreme Court decision concerning juveniles, as follows: ". . . The kindness of a juvenile court, the ability to put his arm around a child and do something for him, and perhaps the relaxation at the proper time of the rules of evidence, all these things are absolutely required and absolutely necessary. Don't handcuff the judges. . . ."

distraught by the brutal life of the neighborhood should not be too harshly criticized for adopting this convenient view.

The juvenile court stands *in loco parentis,* the law says. But when the state assumes the role of a parent, the parent is relegated to the status of a child. The parent no longer has authority or control over his offspring and is relieved of responsibility for him. But the court is not a parent. It does not provide a home for the child. The judge is not a father. He cannot give counsel, guidance, or care to a child he sees for five minutes. The judge can only process the children as the conveyor-belt system carries them into the courtroom and out to the streets or institutions.

Denise M. was shunted into an institution on the conveyor belt. She is a fourteen-year-old black girl who had stayed away from home for several nights. Denise was sleeping at her girl friend's house because one of the roomers in her own home had tried to molest her. She was afraid to go home. She couldn't call her mother, because they have no telephone. Her mother notified the police. Picked up outside of her school, Denise was taken to the Youth Study Center and held for several nights. Her mother was notified, but the authorities would not release this "delinquent." Denise's mother, having heard about the Office for Juveniles, came to us. We were able to get Denise freed, and a grateful mother took her frightened little girl home. The court refused to consider filing charges against the roomer, although it has jurisdiction over adults contributing to the delinquency of a minor. But Denise had been charged with runaway, truancy, and incorrigibility.

Patricia O., a seventeen-year-old white girl, was also charged with incorrigibility. Her mother is an alcoholic. When drunk, she has a vile temper. Patricia had promised to go to a church social affair. Her mother insisted that she stay home and care for her ill father, even though he preferred that Patricia go out and the mother stay home. The mother finally called the police. As in most cases involving family disputes, the adults remained at liberty and the child was held in detention. Patricia was released the next day when the office got in touch with the judge. I had a stern talk with Patricia's mother, and she was truly contrite. She withdrew the charges, with the prosecutor's agreement. Mother and daughter, who had not spoken to each other the entire time they sat in the outer office waiting to see me, smiled shakily. They promised one another to be a little kinder and more considerate. We sent out for coffee, and mother and daughter went home on friendlier terms.

Arlene J.'s mother was more difficult. In most cases, once a mother understood that she had put her daughter in jail with thieves and prostitutes, she was willing to withdraw the charges and take the girl home again. Arlene's mother was good and self-righteous, a huge black pillar of virtue. She wanted Arlene, a slim little reed of a girl with dancing feet and a provocative figure, to "behave like a lady." By this she meant instant obedience, no parties, no fun on weekends. Life in Arlene's home was like a nunnery. Arlene's father had left some years before.

I cross-examined the mother gently. She agreed that Arlene hadn't committed any crimes. But she feared the girl might get in trouble. She wasn't going to bring up her daughter to lead a loose life. Arlene didn't come home after school. She went on and on with her complaints.

Finally the exasperated judge burst out, "Madam, if I were your daughter, I wouldn't go home either."

After that, the mother agreed to take Arlene home and Arlene gladly went with her.

These girls did not belong in court. Neither do a fourteen-year-old unwed mother or the fifteen-year-old father. The boy cannot support himself, much less the child. It is futile to enter a support order. The boy is, under the law, required to attend school. Even if he quit, he probably could not get a job. The new baby gets its public assistance allotment. Should the arrangement be sanctified by a marriage certificate? In one case where the children asked to be married, I encountered a problem. The boy, as a minor, needed the consent of a parent or guardian. His mother was dead. She had not been married to his father, who had never formally acknowledged him and was reluctant to do so. A grandmother was finally located. A similar problem arose with consent to the adoption of an illegitimate infant. The mother was a minor. Her mother was dead. The search for an adult in loco parentis turned up five generations of illegitimacy.

But these cases often work out acceptably. The grandmother usually welcomes the baby warmly. Often the girl moves in with the boy's mother, who helps her care for Junior. The young parents return to junior-high school. If there is hostility between mother and daughter, there is usually a relative or even a friend who will let the girl live in her home. These arrangements could often be made more easily without the intervention of the court. But the school, the police, and the families have been conditioned to believe that every problem involving a child should go to the juvenile court.

There is a widespread belief among the poor that they have no right to decide where or with whom their children shall live. Sixteen-year-old Fareed T. wanted to live with his married sister and her husband. His mother was ill and couldn't cook or care for him. The family asked me to get an order from the juvenile court permitting Fareed to live with his sister. They were astonished to learn that permission was not necessary.

The most heartbreaking, hopeless cases involving poor children are those in which a boy or girl, innocent of any crime, is in jail because there is no other place he can go. Many a girl tells the judge that she would rather be in jail than return to her home. And so she goes to jail for weeks or months. The court seldom inquires into the fears and problems of these children —threats of molestation, fear of beatings and danger on the street, deep hostility between parent and child. The welfare department is simply requested to find a nonexistent foster home. Few courts have a guidance counselor or family therapist to attempt the difficult job of reconciliation. The voluntary agencies are not called upon to help these people.

On January 16, 1968, three girls who had been arrested the preceding night and held in the detention center were brought before Judge Vito F. Canuso. Susan W. and Deborah H. are white; Elissa M. is Negro. The judge was given a report on each girl. Except for names and dates, all the reports were the same. All three mothers requested that their daughters be held in jail. This is the report on Deborah:

> *Deborah H. was arrested 1-15-68, about 2:45 A.M.*
>
> *On Saturday, December 16, 1967, at about 7:05 P.M., Mrs. H. reported her daughter, Deborah, as missing from home.*
>
> *A Mrs. G., on January 15, 1968, notified the police that Deborah H. was sleeping in the rear bedroom of her residence and that she knew the girl was a runaway from home. Deborah came to her house to see her daughter, Barbara, on January 13, 1968. Sunday she learned that the girl was a runaway so she waited until she had gone to sleep and then called the police.*
>
> *Mrs. H. reports that this is the fifth or sixth time that Deborah has run away from home. She drives her to school, but as soon as she drives away Deborah takes off. She needs help and requests that the girl be held.*
>
> *Court In is being recommended.*

Every day in every city, the court sees girls like Deborah. Most of them are clean, neat, and pretty. Most are literate. What can a judge do to or for these girls? His only alternatives are to return the girl to what is evidently an impossible home situation or to hold her in jail. There are no nonpunitive shelters for girls or boys of this age.

Even more terrible than the home that the child flees is the parent who refuses to take back a child who wants to return. The saddest child in this situation was Bonnie Lee R. I saw her in the second-floor jail of the Women's Misdemeanants' Court.

It was a stifling hot day. The director's office was air-conditioned, and there were flowers on her desk. "Bonnie Lee is stubborn," she told me. "Perhaps you can talk some sense into her. I'll ring and have her brought down."

I thanked the director, but said I preferred to see Bonnie Lee in her own room.

"As you wish. But it's no place for you."

After going upstairs, I decided it was no place for anyone —certainly not for a sixteen-year-old girl. The stairways are locked with iron gates. Each inmate has a tiny cubicle opening off a long corridor. The place is clean, but it reeks of disinfectant. Bonnie Lee was sitting on her cot crying. She had no book, no radio, not even a paper and pencil. Her clean cotton dress was stretched tightly across her stomach. She was about five and one-half months pregnant.

Bonnie Lee was a pretty freckle-faced girl. When she smiled she looked like an ad for breakfast food—a wholesome, all-American girl. She had been an honor student in high school.

Her mother (divorced and remarried) had been to the Office for Juveniles. So had the grandmother. Each of them adamantly refused to let Bonnie Lee live with her unless the girl would agree to give up the baby for adoption. A social agency had already agreed to place the unborn baby. There is a shortage of white babies for adoption. "Bonnie Lee should go back to school. The baby will be better off with a nice young couple to love it," said her mother, echoed by her grandmother. They were convinced they were right. So were the family service and the children's society (both voluntary charitable organizations), which they had consulted. And social workers from those agencies were busy trying to convince Bonnie Lee to give up her unborn baby. No one even considered that she had a legal or human right to her own child. Bonnie Lee loved the baby's father and intended to marry him. No one considered whether the father had any rights. All their energies were bent upon keeping those two apart. Bonnie Lee's father was in California. Neither he nor her mother would pay for Bonnie Lee's confinement or even a maternity dress. The court did not enter an order against the mother to compel her to pay for the support of her daughter. The mother was not indigent; it was her legal duty to support her minor child. In default of any other place, Bonnie Lee was in jail.

After several court hearings in which the bewildered judge implored the agencies and the relatives to find a temporary home for Bonnie Lee, he finally permitted her to live with a responsible family recommended by the Office for Juveniles. This family offered her a home in return for baby-sitting services. The social workers objected and so did her mother. One social worker insisted on convoying Bonnie Lee to the home in the suburbs (a fifteen-minute train ride), lest she get in trouble en route. Eventually Bonnie Lee's father sent her the bus fare to California. She had her baby there, and a few months later she married the father. Certainly no mother could love her baby more than Bonnie Lee loves the child.

Countless other children are in jail on charges of incorrigibility. In these cases the parent makes the complaint. Often he is told by the school or the public assistance social worker that the court will "help" the child. Sometimes the parent is simply angry or exasperated over a relatively trivial matter. But the child goes to jail (detention).

No adult could be imprisoned on such vague charges. He must be accused of an offense against the penal code. In addition to the all-inclusive term "delinquency," there are special "crimes" for children, violation of statutes or ordinances that are applicable only to minors. Curfew is one of these laws. A child who stays out past the magic hour can be arrested. He then becomes a delinquent with a "record." This delinquency record seldom specifies the charges. A prospective employer or school assumes that a delinquency charge is the equivalent of a real crime.

When we realized that so many children in detention were not even charged with a penal offense, we decided to make every effort to get them released immediately.

The Office for Juveniles obtained a list of the Youth Study Center population for November, 1966, and promptly launched a home-for-Christmas program. Parents of children who had been in the center more than one hundred days on charges of runaway and incorrigibility were contacted. We explained to each parent that his child was not getting help in the center. Did the parent know that he or she had signed a petition charging the child with delinquency? Did he know that the child can be held in an institution until the age of twenty-one on the basis of such a petition? Few parents understood what they had done; if it had been fully explained to them at the time, very few would have signed delinquency petitions. All of these parents were indigent. Most of them were black. Again, it was poor black children, innocent of any real crime, who were in jail. Eighteen parents gladly signed petitions to withdraw the petitions previously filed. There were no objections on the part of the prosecuting attorney, and the judge ordered these children released in the custody of their parents. In the succeeding eighteen months, not one of these children came into contact with the law.

Although the detention center was overcrowded, the court decided it did not want any more children released. The director of the center was instructed by the court not to permit the Office for Juveniles to see any more monthly population reports.

A number of white mothers on the fringe of poverty launch active campaigns to get their children sent to correctional institutions. These children are usually committed to predominantly white, private, church-controlled institutions. The cost to the taxpayers ranges from about four thousand dollars to more than ten thousand dollars per child per year. Probably none of these private juvenile jails could stay in operation without a steady stream of court-supplied inmates and public money. It is well-known that they have a selective admissions policy: the child must have a reasonably normal IQ, no serious emotional problems, no serious crime. They also have an unwritten but carefully observed *numerus clausus* (racial quota). I know of no judge, black or white, who has challenged this system. Nor have any of the organizations to abolish racial discrimination or to promote separation of church and state.

Undoubtedly some of the children committed to these institutions do graduate from high school and benefit from the strict discipline and rigid routine. But such commitments raise both legal and moral questions. Should this burden be placed on the taxpayer? Should some white delinquents be preferred over black delinquents by being placed in these institutions rather than in the regular state institutions? And should the juvenile court be used to provide involuntary boarding schools for poor boys at the price of stigmatizing an innocent child a delinquent?

Many children who are not dangerous criminals are in jail because the juvenile court gives the parent the option of abandoning his child to the correctional system. Often two boys are arrested together on the same charges—violating curfew, drinking wine, riding together in a stolen car. Clearly these are bailable offenses, and the child should be released—to go home and attend school—pending trial. But every day in all parts of America intake interviewers and juvenile court judges ask the parent if he wants his child at home. The two boys arrested together are equally guilty; but one boy's parent may obtain his release, while the other boy will remain in jail because his indifferent mother or father says, "You keep him, Judge. I can't do nothin' with him."

I often discussed this problem with the judges. Why do they let parents slough off their responsibilities by leaving their children in jail? Why should the state have to support the child? Don't the judges see the injustice of letting the relatives, rather than the court, control the key to the jails?

The invariable reply was that the child was better off "in custody" (the term "jail" was avoided here) than with parents who didn't want him.

Ever since the Moynihan Report, it is fashionable to deplore the disintegration of the Negro family. Perhaps one source of the problem is rooted in four hundred years of slavery. Another may be the migration from rural to urban America since the Depression. But an immediate and continuing cause of the problem may very well be the detachment of the Negro boy from his family by the juvenile court.

A ghetto boy who impregnates his girl friend is charged with delinquency. Often he is given the option of a correctional school (jail) or enlistment in the Army; the patriotic judge will expunge the boy's record if he is accepted in the armed forces. If the boy fails the literacy test and is rejected by the Army, he is sent to a correctional institution (which he will leave just as illiterate as when he entered). In either case—Army or jail—the boy is separated from the girl and his baby for several years. Any chance of creating a family or establishing emotional ties is destroyed. The middle-class boy who becomes a father returns to school or college. He has no record, expunged or otherwise. He is still a part of the family and the community, and he is not forcibly separated from his child and the child's mother.

In most cases of juvenile delinquency, the relationship between the teen-ager and his parents is probably not ideal to begin with. But when the court orders the child to be held in jail at the wish of the parents, the relationship is destroyed. Any possibility of reconciliation in the course of daily living is gone. And these are not letter-writing families. The child is left in prison longing for affection.

Wilbert W. writes to me from jail: "Dearest Mrs. L. G. Forer, I will all way rember you." The letters are crudely formed. The note looks as though it was written by a first grader

—but Wilbert is seventeen. He is not a hardened criminal; he needs the affection of even an inadequate mother. His mother misses him, but it is difficult for her to get paper, pencil, a stamp, and put into written words her longing for her son. In time they will become strangers.

The poor Negro family is being destroyed by unnecessary commitments of young black boys and girls. The sense of family is eroded as the court inculcates in the ghetto mother and father a feeling of dependency and lack of authority to control the destinies of their own children. In the juvenile justice system the caseworker and the court are stern parental figures to be deceived and outwitted, not only by the child but also by his natural mother and father, who believe they can keep their children only by the grace of the court. The court has become the all-powerful social parent to fall back on when people find it difficult or burdensome to carry on the responsibilities of biological parenthood.

Chapter Twelve

HE THAT HATH NOT

For he that hath, to him shall be given; and he that hath
not, from him shall be taken even that which he hath.

MARK 4:25

Alfonso L. wants to go to school. Many of the kids in his
neighborhood are adept at dodging the truant officer. They
hang around bars and college campuses shining shoes, stealing
dimes from newstands, and playing stickball. Not Alfonso. He
walks to school almost every day and goes into the third-grade
classroom. The teacher will not let him stay.

Alfonso's problem might never have come to anyone's
attention if he had not been arrested. The police notified Aunt
Maggie to come to the detention center where Alfonso was
being held. Aunt Maggie borrowed the carfare from a neighbor
and went to the center. She had never been there before, and
she didn't know what to do. A kindly volunteer sent her to the
Office for Juveniles.

Aunt Maggie didn't know why Alfonso was in the center
or what he had done. She only knew he had not been home for
four days and nights. She was worried sick about him. This was
what she told me. I investigated and learned that Alfonso was
charged with larceny. Larceny of what? A Tootsie Roll. Alfonso's release was promptly obtained by making a phone call to
a judge.

The alleged larceny had occurred at ten thirty in the
morning, according to the police report. I questioned Alfonso
about the incident. (The testimony in this case was not tran-

scribed. The conversations and statements are reconstructed from my notes. The quotations from reports on Alfonso are transcriptions from the court records and from the school records.)

"Alfonso, you were in the drugstore at ten thirty on Tuesday morning. Is that right?" He nodded. "Why weren't you in school?"

"They won't let me go to school," he answered.

"Who won't let you go?"

"The teacher."

A likely story, was my initial response. But so many crazy things happened to these kids, one could never be sure. I called the school and found out that Alfonso was indeed correct. He was not permitted to go to school. Two years before he had been dropped from the school system.

The law of Pennsylvania, like the laws of most states, requires all children within certain age limits to attend school. Failure to go to school is an offense punishable by being incarcerated in a correctional institution. The parent or guardian who fails to see that his child does attend school may also be punished by fine and imprisonment. In addition, the law gives the child the right to attend school in the district in which he resides. He is also entitled to a hearing before he may be permanently expelled.

There are similar laws in every state. Children must go to school. Expulsion is a drastic step.* It deprives the child of the right to free schooling. The middle-class child who is expelled from public school is usually sent away to a boarding school or military school. The poor child simply does not have any more schooling. The children of poor and ignorant parents do not know that they are entitled to a hearing.

*In 1961 and 1967 the federal courts in two cases established the principle that a hearing must precede punitive action by a school that has important consequences for the student such as expulsion. Legal seminars on school law discuss the procedural aspects of the expulsion hearing. But they do not consider the rights of the "excluded" child.

Obviously, the first thing to do was to get Alfonso a hearing. I discussed this with counsel for the school district. Then I learned that Alfonso was not expelled; he was "excluded" from school. There is nothing in the code about a hearing for a child who is excluded. The code does provide that a child who is emotionally disturbed is relieved of the obligation to attend school. But is the school relieved of the obligation of accepting him if he wants to attend school? This was a different issue.

The school district expressed concern about Alfonso. They knew all about him. There were files and files of reports on Alfonso. I was permitted to read them.

Alfonso is a small and shy twelve-year-old. Like most ghetto children, he does not talk much. I gave him a pencil and a piece of paper. He wrote his name in large unsteady capital letters. He can add two numbers. Subtraction is more difficult.

From the files I learned his IQ is 83. Reading level: 0.6 (normal first-grade level would be "1"). Alfonso lives with his great-aunt Maggie, who is seventy-two years old and has cataracts. He has always lived with Maggie. Alfonso has never seen his mother, who disappeared shortly after he was born. His father shows up occasionally. Alfonso is afraid of him. When drunk, Mr. L. is terrifying.

Once a long time ago Alfonso hit a little girl who was mocking him. The teacher ordered him out of the classroom. A policeman was called and Alfonso was taken home. It's all in the record.

Unhappily Alfonso wanders the streets alone wondering why the school doors are closed to him. Sometimes the other children laugh when they see Alfonso coming on his vain and hopeless journeys. This infuriates Alfonso.

Sometimes Alfonso has nightmares just remembering his father. His other memories are not pleasant either. The jeering children in the classroom. The horrible day in the playground when, goaded beyond endurance by the taunts of the children, he picked up a stick and hit Sterling. He didn't mean to hit Sterling, not Sterling who would sometimes let Alfonso play with him. Alfonso was standing next to Sterling when the other boys laughed, jumping up and down, making up jokes about Alfonso. All that Alfonso could see was grinning mouths and the big stick with a nail on the end lying at his feet. He grabbed the stick and swung blindly. In the sudden silence he looked around and saw the dark blood dripping down Sterling's face. Many nights Alfonso awakens seeing blood.

The teacher sent Alfonso to the principal. She also said she would demand a transfer to another school if that dangerous maniac wasn't removed from her classroom. "It's not safe for the other children," she said, sniffling.

The school was bulging with children. But teachers were scarce. Besides, the teacher did have firsthand experience with Alfonso. So the principal acceded to this teacher's demand. Alfonso was removed from his class and sent home. The principal would recommend a psychiatric examination and a transfer to a special school or institution.

In due course, a letter was sent to Aunt Maggie. A week or so passed before she encountered the postman, who read it to her. Maggie's glasses didn't do her much good. Reading was difficult anyway. The letter informed her: "Alfonso is an emotionally disturbed child who cannot be contained in a regular school setting." The letter suggested that Maggie make an appointment to see Dr. S., the school psychiatrist. Dr. S.'s address and telephone number were given.

The day after Maggie's social security check came, she took Alfonso to see the doctor. The psychiatrist's secretary told Maggie she would have to make an appointment. The doctor just can't see anyone who comes in off the street.

Eventually, Maggie and Alfonso did see the doctor. She had a thick file on Alfonso. She had his medical examination, IQ test, reading scores, and the reports of the teacher, the principal, the guidance counselor, and a social worker assigned to

Aunt Maggie by the outpatient hospital clinic where she went
for treatment of her cataracts. After reviewing all of these papers, she concluded that Alfonso had a "personality disturbance which threatened the safety of other children" and
recommended that he be dropped from the public school rolls.
The psychiatrist's report also states that Aunt Maggie "con-
curred in the recommendation of a D-10 (emotionally disturbed) drop."

No one suggested to Aunt Maggie that she didn't have
to consent or that there were other schools for Alfonso, that he
might have a homebound teacher or supportive therapy in a
mental health clinic. Maggie and Alfonso went home.

From time to time Alfonso would return to school and go
to his old classroom. After a few minutes the teacher would
notice him, summon the assistant principal, and have him
removed.

When all the neighborhood children were in school and
Aunt Maggie was lying down resting, Alfonso wandered the
streets. It was lonely and there was not much to do. Several
times he stole candy bars from the corner drugstore. Sometimes the proprietor would see him and yell; Alfonso would
drop the candy and run. It was a kind of game. Occasionally the
storekeeper would pretend not to see and Alfonso would make
off with some bubble gum.

One day there was a new man behind the counter. When
he yelled, Alfonso was terrified. As he scooted around the
magazine stand trying to get away, he toppled over a whole rack
full of greeting cards, hair lotion, and toothpaste. Alfonso skid-
ded, fell, crawled to the door and into the waiting arms of a
policeman, still clutching the stolen Tootsie Roll. Alfonso was
taken to the police station and transferred to the Youth Study
Center, where he was processed. Aunt Maggie had no phone
and so Alfonso stayed in the center until Maggie received a
notice.

The case of larceny of a Tootsie Roll wouldn't come up for hearing for a long time. The court was months and months behind. We were not concerned about this heinous crime; we wanted to get Alfonso in school as soon as possible.

Alfonso was really at a first-grade level academically. He had been out of school more than three years. Obviously a twelve-year-boy could not be in a class with six-year-olds. Nor could he be with other twelve-year-olds who could not only read and write but also protect themselves in the rough and tumble of the corridors and playground. The school board lawyer and I agreed that he needed a special class for emotionally disturbed children. The school system had a few such classes, but they were all filled. There was no prospect of a vacancy, and besides there was a long waiting list. Meanwhile, Alfonso was wandering the streets. It soon became evident that the school system was not going to find a place for him. I filed a petition in the juvenile court to compel his reinstatement. The school administration then put Alfonso back in his old school in a regular class.

This time he had a different teacher. Of course, his problems were the same, only aggravated. He had been nine years old when he was "excluded" from school. Now he was twelve, still unable to read and unable to cope with groups of children. The school social worker reported:

> *Alfonso will be returning to school—he will have to be in a regular class of fourth graders despite the fact that he does work at a primer or pre-primer level. His I.Q. is a bit too high for him to be placed in an RE (retarded educable) Class, and there is no class for emotionally disturbed children which seems to be available for him.*

This placement was decided at a conference that included the guidance counselor of the Hawthorne School, a supervisor from the Federal Bureau of Assistance, a supervising school counselor, a guidance counselor of the Jackson School, a social worker from Jefferson Hospital, and a social worker from the Child Guidance Clinic.

A month later, Alfonso's fourth-grade teacher submitted the following report:

> *Alfonso's school work indicates that he is an extremely slow-learning child. Academically, he is functioning on a first grade level. He verbalizes surprisingly well.*
>
> *Alfonso has what might be termed a competitive, defensive attitude in order to hold his own with his classmates and peers. His biggest problem is to overcome the temptation to use abusive language when striking back at children who don't readily accept him. Alfonso has few friends though he earnestly tries to take children into his confidence. He has a tendency to dramatize events and find a tragic element in them. Several times he declared to me, in his own inimitable way, that life was really too hard. Alfonso has been involved in numerous fights inside and outside the classroom. From what I have been able to ascertain most of these fights have been started by the other person involved. I don't think he fights with others because he wants to dominate them or because he feels insecure with the group and is trying to establish himself. I think he fights strictly out of self defense. Basically this child's nature is one that is warm hearted and kind. I wonder how I would feel if members of my peer group constantly confronted me with such expressions as "dumb bunny," "retarded," and "crazy."*
>
> *Some physical signs that have attracted my attention and seem to single him out from the rest of my class are: constant making of faces, occasional stammering or stuttering, twitching, and fidgeting, drumming with feet and fingers, and other nervous mannerisms.*
>
> *Alfonso appears to be an angry child, and I am not sure he shouldn't feel this way. To be plagued with injustices, frustration, and feelings of constant failure or inferiority is much more than this child can cope with. I don't think we can expect this immature child to control extreme outbursts of anger; likewise, I don't think he is*

strong enough to inhibit it. I see Alfonso as being a child in an
unbearable situation which he can do nothing to alleviate.

Alfonso was again excluded from the public school system. The school board case review committee wrote to me
suggesting that a petition be filed with the juvenile court seeking to place Alfonso in a residential institution. Such a placement would separate Alfonso from Aunt Maggie, the only
person who loves him. This lonely, friendless child would then
be completely isolated in a world of strangers.

The Child Guidance Clinic reported:

> *We are impressed with the warmth and quality of care given
> Alfonso by his Aunt. However, although she has worked very cooper-
> atively with us, despite her ill health and advanced age, we have been
> unable to find a way in which she could relate differently with Alfonso
> enough [sic] so that he could successfully cope with public school.*

Because the guidance clinic could not remake this loving
old lady so that Alfonso could fit into the Procrustean bed of the
school system, it was concluded that the child be removed from
her. The clinic reported: "She [the Aunt] was never able to
accept this and our impression was that this would represent an
action of abandonment in her eyes akin to Alfonso's earlier
abandonment by mother and father." The suggestion then follows that the placement of Alfonso in an institution be "forced"
on her. The school and the clinic suggested that I, as Alfonso's
lawyer, petition the court to have him removed from Aunt Maggie's home, which was Alfonso's only home, and have him
placed in an institution. But that was not what my client, Alfonso, or Aunt Maggie wanted. I persisted in my suit to compel
the school system to put him in a class for emotionally disturbed children.

If the court commits Alfonso to a mental institution for
children, it will cost the taxpayers more than four thousand

dollars a year. (The average cost of maintaining a child in public school is less than eight hundred dollars a year.) There is no assurance and not much hope that Alfonso will respond to the environment of a strange institution. If Alfonso remains at home—a pariah, excluded from school, illiterate, frustrated, and hostile—he will inevitably encounter the police again. The next time it may not be a theft of a Tootsie Roll or bubble gum and a peaceful surrender to an arresting officer. Alfonso is twelve now. It may cost the taxpayers four thousand dollars a year for the rest of Alfonso's unhappy life to maintain him in jail.

There are countless tax-exempt organizations devoted to the prevention of crime and delinquency. They send out elaborate brochures asking for contributions and describing ambitious programs of community relations, education, discussions of intergroup tensions, and research. These organizations study and survey. They recommend and deplore. They analyze and explore such questions as the psychic effects of the lack of a father figure. But they do not provide care for individual human beings. Nor will they use any part of their swollen budgets to pay for the care of children whose future crime may indeed be preventable through present care and education. Many children are expelled and suspended for misbehavior that is caused by emotional disturbance. Much truancy is the result of the child's inability to endure a classroom situation that does not meet his needs. Children can miss more than one hundred days of schooling before any action is taken to get them back in school. In all of these irregular ways school systems slough off the unwanted problem children.

Where these children are, no one knows. At least five or six came to the Office for Juveniles. Kieth K. sat in the office for two hours smiling vaguely. When I dropped a paper clip, he picked it up for me. He told me that he was "a good boy." He was. He was neat and clean. His distracted mother vacillated between compassion and annoyance. She could not get a babysitter to stay with him while she was at work. Her husband had divorced her because of conflict over the boy. Kieth's mother was young and pretty. Her whole life was slipping away. She knew that unless Kieth received help soon, he would have no chance at all. But there was no help anywhere.

Kieth is one of the many brain-damaged children of the ghetto. Kieth is not stupid or uneducable. He has been in four different schools. He was eight at the time this report was made. He was reading at a third-grade level, arithmetic at a second-grade level. Kieth was seen by a psychiatrist, a psychologist, and a counselor. Neurological studies were made. These showed brain damage. The other reports were as follows:

> *Home status: Mrs. K. loved Kieth, over indulged, later became an emotional problem. Mr. K. left home.*
>
> *Counseling records show that Kieth was too disturbed to help effectively.*
>
> *Adj. to school—He has not adjusted to school—dismissed pending a D-10 drop (for emotional disturbance).*

Kieth did not fit the system and so he was simply put out —put out of school, put out of society. There is no place for him. In a school budget of $234,000,000 there is no money even for a tutor for Kieth.

There is no money for Robert C. either. Robert's mother has six children. The other five are fine. She does not understand why Robert can't go to school. He's not stupid. She sends him to the grocery store, and he brings home the right change. But Robert cannot obey the rules of the school. The school psychiatrist reports that Robert cannot "be contained" in the school. It is an apt expression. The school is a fixed and rigid environment into which the child must fit. Those who cannot contort themselves to conform to the container are rejected.

What happens to these human discards? Many of them fill our prisons. The case of *Commonwealth v. Harris,* decided by the

Pennsylvania Supreme Court in 1968, describes the fate of one such child. He "entered school at the age of six years. He was shuttled from one school to another and finally 'dropped' permanently when he was sixteen years old and enrolled in the sixth grade."

The legislature has appropriated money for emotionally disturbed children. But the school, the city, and the state play a kind of shell game in which the pea of responsibility keeps disappearing. Lift the shell marked "school." No pea. It is the problem of the state. We file suit against the state. That shell is empty too. The city that authorized the school taxes has no authority to compel the school system to educate Alfonso or any other child.

The spokesmen of these public bodies profess the greatest interest in the welfare of children. Just give us money, they say with some justification, and we shall be delighted to educate, care for, and train every child. But in November, 1967, when the school district said that it had no money to educate Alfonso, it was doing many interesting, innovative things. For example:

> *A series of "on the spot" sessions for 120 teachers are being planned with these goals in view:*
>
> *To prepare teachers for leadership roles in the teaching of Constructive Citizenship by:*
>
> *—Providing necessary community and citizenship background based upon actual contact with the community and its leaders.*
>
> *—Studying ways in which the principles of constructive citizenship may be presented more realistically for the pupils in the classroom.*
>
> *—Developing techniques and materials that can be used successfully in the classrooms.*

—Making the community and its leaders aware of the schools' concerns and the direction we are taking.

*The seven two hour after-school (*teachers will be reimbursed*) sessions will begin Tuesday, Nov. 28. They will deal with topics and/or problems unique to* Urban Life *such as: The Child and the Law, Morality in the City, Crime in the City, Juvenile Delinquency, Legal Rights and Citizens' Responsibilities and Cultural and Educational Opportunities available in the Community.* [*emphasis supplied*] [District Communicator, *Bulletin of the Philadelphia School District, November, 1967, p. 3.*]

The federal government allocates large sums of money for education at all levels. It also supports many innovative programs like the Suburban Training Program at the Human Resources Center of the University of Pennsylvania. This one provides free education for white suburban housewives to study the problems of the black urban ghetto. But there is little money to educate the black problem children whom the white housewives study.

The needs of the poor "difficult" children can be avoided by the simple device of putting them out of school. That is one way to balance the budget. Every department is short of funds —welfare, recreation, and the schools. Each of these agencies avoids trouble and stays solvent by excluding Alfonso and many other children. Corrections will be paying for them later.

Significantly, the children for whom there are no classes are predominantly nonwhite and desperately poor. Of the 276 children (noted by the Philadelphia School District as active cases) who were dropped from the school rolls between 1961 and 1968, 147 are Negro and 8 are Puerto Rican. The number of children actually put out of the schools is undoubtedly much higher. The school district admitted that there are more than seventy-five thousand children needing special education who are not receiving it. Similar conditions exist in almost every

school district. Many small communities do not have any
classes for emotionally disturbed or retarded children. Large
metropolitan school districts have insufficient and inadequate
programs.

Middle-class problem children are less frequently put
out of school. Their parents insist that these children be educated. They call, they write, they see their committeemen and
their ward leaders. They get ministers, businessmen, and
prominent citizens to write on behalf of their children. They
confront the school psychiatrist with an opinion from their own
psychiatrist. The less difficult white middle-class children are
accommodated. The more difficult are sent to private schools
with the aid of public subsidies. The white, middle-class parents
of such children besiege the legislature to raise these subsidies
for their children who are in private schools and hospitals. The
legislators, being kindly men and women who love children and
who also want to be reelected, try to respond.

The state contributes fifteen hundred dollars a year toward the education of a child in an approved private school for
the emotionally disturbed. There are several local private day
schools especially programmed for such children. The tuition
charges at these private schools average about four thousand
dollars a year. The parents must make up the difference—about
twenty-five hundred dollars. To some parents this is a crushing
burden. For others, the fifteen hundred dollars is a windfall to
be spent on a new mink coat or sailboat. To those like Aunt
Maggie, who cannot pay the twenty-five hundred dollars, the
state contributes nothing.

These schools, being purely private, do not have to accept every child. They too refuse the more difficult ones. On
some they impose conditions such as regular psychiatric treatment at fifty dollars or one hundred dollars a week and "parental cooperation." Some of these parents live in dread that they
will not be able to meet the fees and that their child will be

expelled or rejected. No private school will even consider en-
rolling Alfonso.

I argued that the fifteen-hundred-dollar subsidy is an
entitlement, a matter of right not a gift of grace. If it is available
to some children, it must be equally available to all. Aunt Maggie and Alfonso are taxpayers. They pay sales taxes on their
meager purchases. They pay all the hidden taxes exacted by the
city, the state, and the federal government. Can a public subsidy
be denied because a person is too poor? Does the equal protection clause prevent this discrimination? Perhaps the courts
might rule that Alfonso is protected by the Constitution. But
neither Alfonso nor Aunt Maggie can afford to sue the state.
The subsidy comes from the state. Aunt Maggie and Alfonso
live in Philadelphia. The sovereign Commonwealth of Pennsylvania may be sued only in Harrisburg, one hundred miles away.
Aunt Maggie and Alfonso do not have the carfare to get to the
local school. How could they get to Harrisburg? If a private
lawyer were to finance such a lawsuit, he might be violating the
canons of ethics that prohibit stirring up litigation. Doubtless
he would be embarking on a long, expensive and quixotic gesture, which at best would result in a Pyrrhic victory. Even if suit
were brought and, after four or five years of protracted appeals,
the school system was ordered to admit Alfonso to a special
class for emotionally disturbed children, it would be too late to
help him. By then he will be beyond compulsory school age and
doubtless beyond educability and treatment.

On a practical level, I urged, give the subsidy to Alfonso
for private tutoring. No. The subsidy can only be paid to a
school for the emotionally disturbed. Very well, the subsidy will
cover only three-eighths of the tuition. Let him go to school for
three-eighths of a year. That is more schooling than he has had
in over four years. But the computers of bureaucracy cannot be
reprogrammed for the Alfonsos of our society.

Aunt Maggie and Alfonso were ordered back to juvenile

court. The judge was handed the ever-growing file on Alfonso. The experts had recommended that Aunt Maggie be forced by court order to surrender Alfonso to an institution. They recommended a school in the same city where Aunt Maggie could visit Alfonso once or twice a month.

"Will the school accept him?" I asked the school district's lawyer.

No one knows. But if it is not that school, it will be another, a hundred or three hundred miles away. And if those schools are overcrowded? (The judge and the lawyers know that there are long waiting lists for every institution.) Then will the court place Alfonso in a correctional institution (jail) for his own protection?

The judge was exasperated by this line of cross-examination.

"Counselor, I can't build a school for this child," he expostulated. He took another tranquilizer. His blood pressure was up again from all this wrangling. There is nothing he can do. Is Alfonso better off on the street or in a jail? Should the judge decide a purely legal question: Must the school system keep Alfonso? It is foolish. The school system will appeal. Alfonso will not be in school this year or next year as the appellate courts duck and dodge the issue. Is it better to seek the lesser evil for the boy? And what is that lesser evil? The school administration and the Department of Welfare were pushing for commitment. How does the judge know what is best for this child or any child? The judge had never even been in juvenile court before his appointment. He knows nothing about these institutions except that they are always full. Meanwhile, he let me argue and cite a New York case. There was really no point in my arguing or the judge's listening. He could not get through the trials on his list by six o'clock. And tomorrow it would be the same thing all over again. Of what use is a legal precedent in such a situation?

"I'll take it under advisement," the judge said, sighing.

"Perhaps you could find a place for him in the public schools," he suggested to the school board attorney. The other cases of emotionally disturbed children were disposed of this way. Did the school system put out one child in order to admit the one for whom the suit was brought? No one knows. No one asks. But it avoids an issue. "It's not *my* responsibility to educate this boy," the judge said pointedly.

The school board attorney reminded the judge that the matter had been carefully studied by the experts.

"There is no room in the school system for Alfonso," the school board attorney replied.

Alfonso, Aunt Maggie, and I left the courtroom together.

"You won't let them take him away," Aunt Maggie whispered.

Alfonso turned to me and asked, "Can I go to school now?"

Chapter Thirteen

A PASSAGE TO FRANKFORD

Innocence or guilt, why mix yourself up? What's the good?

E. M. FORSTER, *A Passage to India*

The trial of Leroy W. caused a stir in the juvenile court-room. It was unusual for two reasons. First, Leroy had private counsel; for a black boy to be represented by paid counsel is relatively rare. Second, there were scores of witnesses, all of whom were white. A Catholic priest was present, a half-dozen pretty, blushing teen-age girls, their blowsy-looking mothers, some with their hair in curlers, others in cotton housedresses and bobby socks. There were several school teachers.

There are seldom any witnesses in a juvenile delinquency case. The assistant district attorney reads the testimony of the witness from the police arrest form. When the juvenile defendant appears in court, the judge will ask him if it is true. He may say No. But because the witness is not there to undergo cross-examination, it is the word of a child—usually an indigent black boy—against a piece of paper reporting the statement of a respectable white citizen. There is little doubt about which is more credible. This procedure violates the due process clause of the Constitution—but it saves time.

"It's the Frankford High School case," the court crier told me with a meaningful nod. I got the message that something special was afoot and went into the courtroom to observe the proceedings. Only in recent years are lawyers permitted to observe in juvenile court. The constitutional guarantee of a speedy public trial does not prevail in many juvenile courts. The visitor must have permission to enter the courtroom. I slipped quietly in the back, where I could take notes unobserved. No one except the court stenographer and the trial lawyer is permitted to take notes in juvenile court. (I do not have the transcript of this trial. The testimony is reconstructed from these surreptitious notes.)

Few Frankford children find their way into juvenile court. Frankford is an old neighborhood, all white, middle-class, solid citizens who own their homes. They seldom find any need to visit other parts of the city. Their friends and relatives live in the area. Frankford is almost the last bastion of small-town nineteenth-century America in the turmoil-ridden metropolis of the 1960's.

The Human Relations Commission, the school board, and the innumerable voluntary organizations who want to "do" something about integration decided that Negro boys and girls should be bussed to Frankford High School. Despite a few protest meetings, bussing of these children began peacefully.

Leroy's case was the first real disturbance. I looked around the courtroom. There was no one from the large and highly paid intergroup unit of experts of the school system. None of the civil rights lawyers was present nor any representatives of the liberal citizens groups that had fought for bussing.

Two scrubbed and neatly dressed black youths were standing at the bar of the court. They could have been brothers. One was Leroy W., the defendant, sixteen years old. The other was his attorney, Mr. B., twenty-five years old, just graduated from night law school and admitted to the bar. The judge was also black; he had been appointed because both parties felt that a Negro ought to be on the juvenile court bench where 90 to 95 percent of the defendants are Negro or Puerto Rican.

The judge looked up and saw me.

"Counselor, do you have a case before me today?"

"Yes, your honor. Numbers twenty-seven and twenty-nine."

"They won't be called until after lunch. You don't have to wait."

"Thank you, your honor. But I'm in no hurry today," I replied and sat down again. Clearly the crier had been right. Something was going on.

The young attorney, Mr. B., asked to see the delinquency petition filed against his client. He read it carefully. This was the first time either he or Leroy had seen the petition or known exactly what crime Leroy was charged with. The petition listed assault and battery, indecent assault, assault with intent to ravish, and attempted rape. There was no time, place, or name of the alleged victim of the attack. No names of witnesses were included. The petition was sworn by the court employee who signed and swore to all the petitions. Of course, this employee had never seen any of the parties and simply stamped the petitions that were prepared by the police. The assistant district attorney took advantage of the pause to read his copy of the petition for the first time.

Leroy's attorney knew the petition was defective on its face and that he should have had a copy of it before the day of trial. To protest now would only antagonize the judge. At best, he would get a postponement. Leroy was in detention. He had been held in the adult jail for ten days, ever since his arrest in the schoolroom. The Juvenile Court Act specifically prohibits holding children in the same jail as adults. But it is an immemorial custom in the city that boys and girls over sixteen are held in the adult jail. The juvenile detention center is more crowded and the treatment there is worse. In adult prison everyone (except those in the "hole") has daily yard period and at least gets outside. The courts knowingly commit youngsters to the adult prison. There would be no point in objecting to such sanctified illegality.

Leroy was arrested without a warrant. That was also illegal. But whenever an attorney protested that a juvenile was arrested without a warrant, there were two standard answers,

"A warrant is not required because the juvenile is not charged with crime but a civil act of delinquency," or "All right, counselor, do you want me to issue a bench warrant now? That will bring him before me promptly." Leroy's attorney evidently decided it would be wiser to waive all of these preliminaries and try to get his client acquitted on the facts.

The complaining witness testified first. Mary Lou B. has reddish hair, fair skin, and freckles. She was wearing a tight green sweater and an uplift bra. She blushed and spoke in a whisper. The courtroom was hushed. Mary Lou said that she was walking from English class to gym. It was between periods and she was late. She went through the little bridge in the fire tower to get to the gym on time. While she was walking through this dark place all by herself he—and she pointed to Leroy and then looked down modestly and paused.

The assistant district attorney sympathetically helped her along. "Now, Miss B., this is difficult for you. We appreciate what you're going through. Just tell his honor what happened."

The judge leaned over with a kindly avuncular smile.

Mary Lou managed to say that he touched her on her behind. A gasp of outrage arose from the witnesses.

According to Mary Lou, that night she told her mother about what had happened and then her mother told—

Leroy's attorney objected to the hearsay.

The assistant district attorney withdrew the question and said he would call the mother.

Defense counsel approached cross-examination gingerly and deferentially. Did Miss B. know the defendant?

Of course, she didn't really know him. Leroy was in her math class and she saw him every day. Naturally, she never spoke to him. Yes, it was dark in the fire tower. She didn't actually see him touch her. It couldn't have been anyone else. She was fully clothed, wasn't she?, defense counsel wanted to know. Mary Lou was horrified and indignant at the suggestion of immodesty. The judge reprimanded counsel and told him to confine his examination to relevant matters and not insult the witness.

If she didn't actually see Leroy, how could she be sure that it was a hand that touched her and not the wall or some object in the passageway that she brushed against?, counsel asked. Mary Lou said she wouldn't have felt the way she did if it hadn't been a hand. Defense counsel wanted to know how she felt. The judge sustained the district attorney's objections.

Mary Lou's mother was the next witness. She was noticeably pregnant. Her skimpy hair was tightly coiled over pink plastic curlers. Her words came out in a torrent. Her innocent child had been subjected to liberties by that, that . . . she had no words to describe Leroy. It all comes from bussing those kids into our neighborhood. Why can't they stay where they belong? The young prosecutor tried to get Mary Lou's mother back to his question. When did she first learn of this incident? Well, she had overheard Mary Lou talking to her friend Cindy on the phone. And like a good mother she listened in. When Mama found out what had happened and who the boy was, she immediately went to the priest, Father X, who was sitting right in the courtroom. There was a big meeting in the church. The group went to the school principal. Mary Lou didn't want to tell. But Father said it was her duty. The school guidance counselor told them to complain to the courts. A week later, Mary Lou came home from school and told her family that Leroy had been arrested. And high time, too, Mama added.

Defense counsel called his one witness, a thin white boy named Walter. Walter said he had been walking from class with Leroy. They were discussing a problem in math. Leroy was telling him how to do it. They had to walk through the auditorium. The girls were sitting there with their legs stretched out in the aisle. He and Leroy had to step over them. They wouldn't pull their legs back. Leroy tripped over Mary Lou and said, "Excuse me," and she giggled. Then all the girls laughed. All what girls?, the district attorney wanted to know. Walter pointed to the five girls in the courtroom and named them. Yes, he knew all of them, all his life. They live in the neighborhood. Walter went on. He and Leroy went to the tower. They stopped a few minutes while Leroy wrote out the answer to the problem. The girls got up and walked past them and into the passageway. Then he and Leroy walked through.

On cross-examination, the district attorney brought out the fact that Leroy walked ahead and Walter behind, that it was dark and Walter couldn't see what Leroy was doing with his hands. Walter said Leroy was carrying his books. The district attorney wanted to know if he had books in both hands. The judge chimed in with the questioning. Walter unhappily admitted that Leroy could have had all his books in one hand. It was possible.

The court called Leroy to the stand. There was no point in claiming the privilege against self-incrimination or the right to remain silent. Leroy denied touching Mary Lou. He said when he and Walter emerged from the passageway the girls were already some distance ahead of them and Mary Lou was giggling.

The court adjudicated Leroy delinquent on all charges and then asked for his school report. The school representative, who had never seen or heard of Leroy until that morning, read from the records. He had been absent only twice this year. He didn't have any grades from Frankford High because he was in jail when the exams were given. His marks from the year before were good. In fact, he was an honor student and that was why he was given the privilege of going to Frankford. She clucked regretfully over his wasted opportunity.

The judge then declared, "We can't have sex maniacs around here." Leroy was ordered back to jail to await neuropsychiatric tests and commitment either to a correctional institution or to a mental institution for an indefinite term. This term was a sentence of five years.

Leroy's counsel, not having had the petition in time to

know the offenses with which he was charged, could not make a technical argument. His plea for mercy and understanding was brushed aside with the suggestion that counsel reprimand his client for such shocking misbehavior and not condone it. The court would help this mentally ill boy by sending him to a psychiatrist. Counsel was rebuked for failing to appreciate the seriousness of the charge.

There is a high school in prison and Leroy could get his diploma there. But he may be required to work during the daytime. Not every boy is permitted to go to high school in Camp Hill, the prison for youths from sixteen to twenty-five. After a day of hard labor he may not have the energy or desire to go to night school. His dreams of college are vanished. If he is sent to a mental hospital, he will not even have the opportunity to get his high school diploma.

The entire trial was over in not more than fifteen minutes. And so ended Leroy's passage to Frankford.

The witnesses thanked the judge. The priest promised to remember him in his prayers. The girls walked out with solemn and dignified mien, surrounding and protecting Mary Lou. They refused to speak to Walter who slunk unhappily after them. Leroy, silent, impassive, was led back to his cell. The young lawyer picked up his briefcase and left. The next defendant was already standing at the bar.

Leroy is one of many black boys and girls who are in jail because they must attend public schools that create situations impossible for them to cope with. Leroy was a victim of integration. Many more boys and girls are victims of segregation. In Philadelphia there are five high schools that are more than 90 percent white and four high schools more than 90 percent black. The educational level in these black schools ranges from 8 to 15 on a scale of 100, and that in the white schools from 27 to 58.

A bright child in a low-achieving school soon becomes

bored, and this boredom usually leads to trouble. "Country" is one of these bright children pushed aside by a school system geared to dullness. (The case is reported from the file. Because no appeal was taken, there was no transcript.) He is a coal-black, big husky boy from Mississippi, one of the very few new arrivals in Philadelphia. Country had lived in a rural community in the South, and had all the naïveté of a country bumpkin among city slickers—hence the nickname. When he ran with the city boys, inevitably Country got caught. The first time, he was released by the court with a stern warning. The school system transferred him from a low-level all-black school to an even lower-level ungraded disciplinary school. There was nothing for him to learn in classes where most of the boys could barely read. He began to play hooky and to try to learn some of the dangerous pastimes of the street.

We met him on his second offense. Country had given money to an old wino to buy liquor for him and his fellow truants. The man bought the liquor but refused to give it to the boys. Country tried to grab the bottle, and the man yelled. The other boys ran and melted away. Country was the only one there when the police arrived.

The school representative in the courtroom reported Country's IQ, his absences, and his transfer. The judge committed him to a correctional institution but agreed to release him in time for the next school term. An appeal would have been futile, since it could not have been heard before the boy was released. And he was guilty of an offense. Country desperately wanted to learn. The correctional institution, however, would not let him attend school classes for the first month of his imprisonment. During this time he was tested, classified, and processed. When Country was released, we arranged for him to be transferred to a school with an accelerated college preparatory program. Once he was in this school, Country had no further encounters with the law.

Truancy is one of the major causes of commitment to jail

for poor black teen-agers—bright, stupid, and average. These children are usually not formally charged with truancy on the delinquency petition. But if there is some evidence that a child may be guilty of an offense, a poor school record is often the deciding factor in the decision to institutionalize him. This was the avowed policy of Philadelphia Judge Juanita Kidd Stout. *The Wall Street Journal* quotes her as saying, "I don't care who disagrees with me. If a gang member with a bad school report comes before me, he's going to jail." Many other judges follow this principle. The school system that fails to teach a child or places him in the wrong class does not have to answer to anyone for wasting the taxpayers' money and destroying the child's life chances. The law—which is supposedly there to help the child —is put to work against him.

Chapter Fourteen

HALVING THE CRIME RATE

An ounce of prevention is worth a pound of cure.

We lawyers in the Office for Juveniles were appalled at the number of children arrested and brought to trial on charges of delinquency. Although the national arrest figures show that one-third of all those arrested are under the age of eighteen, in Philadelphia and other big cities children account for almost half of the arrests. After a few months we realized that a large percentage of these children had not committed any offense for which an adult could have been arrested.

Perhaps a third of the cases involved runaway, incorrigibility, truancy, and curfew violation. These are not penal offenses, but the children were being arrested, tried, and sentenced just as if they had robbed or raped or murdered. These children were in court because they had problems, but problems that "the law" could not solve.

In attempting to analyze the conditions that resulted in an accusation of delinquency, we did not reach the orthodox conclusions. Among current researchers, Sheldon and Eleanor Glueck have cited such factors as "careless supervision by mother" and "aestheticism" as causes and characteristics of delinquents (*Problems of Delinquency* [Boston: Houghton Mifflin, 1959] pp. 152–170). It takes considerable temerity to suggest that the problem of juvenile delinquency may have other roots. Significantly, the Gluecks did not mention reading problems, although they carefully analyzed the IQ's of "delinquents" and "nondelinquents" (*Problems of Delinquency*, p. 83).

Without being unduly simplistic, our office found two overriding problems—aside from race and poverty—present in children accused of delinquency. The first was not the home but the school. Almost every one of our children had difficulty adjusting to the Procrustean bed of the school system. Some slum children, contrary to widely held belief, were too bright. They were bored in third grade, and the boredom increased every year. So did their misbehavior. By high school a child with an IQ of 130 was often put in an ungraded disciplinary school. Some children could not or would not learn to read. Others simply could not sit still. Still others were too lethargic. They just sat, and learning passed them by.

We in the Office for Juveniles began to question our clients about their performance in school. Very few, we discovered, had any liking for school, and many had very poor academic and school attendance records. We made an analysis of one hundred consecutive cases. Problems with school had become part of the record in ninety-four of these files. Eighteen children were school dropouts. Eleven of these eighteen were unemployed. Thirty-two children were not at their normal grade level. Fourteen were in special classes or schools— classes for retarded educable children or special schools for problem children. In these schools, there are no separate grade levels and standards of achievement. Thus 67 percent of this sampling of children were not at normal grade level in school. Of course, even the regular classes in regular schools in slum areas are at least two years below national standards.

We also discovered that many of the children we represented—regardless of their school grade—could not read a simple letter. More than a few sixteen-year-olds could not even read a printed form telling them how to get to the office. The public school system lent us a set of graded readers, from primer to sixth grade. As part of our case preparation interview, we gave every boy and girl a quick reading test. The second-grade reader was beyond the grasp of many boys fifteen, sixteen, and seventeen years old.

Judge Charles Wright of the Philadelphia Juvenile Court finds that at least 78 percent of alleged juvenile delinquents are functional illiterates. Among a sample of one hundred cases, twelve children tested as absolute illiterates. He points out that children reading at less than second-grade level are in high school.

No wonder they play hooky from school. In 1970—four years later—U.S. Commissioner of Education James E. Allen, Jr., is urging that the teaching of reading be a priority in the public schools.

The result of truancy was often incarceration in a correctional institution where the child had no schooling at all. Were these boys better off not going to school in jail than not going to school at home?

We began to look at the school laws. Every state has a compulsory school attendance law. The longer the child is required to stay in school, the more advanced the state is considered to be. But youths of seventeen who have been in school for eleven years under such laws have not received the equivalent of a fourth-grade education. It is a waste for the child and the taxpayer.

The reasons why Johnny can't read are endless. We lawyers concluded that one reason, never mentioned, could be the school attendance law itself.

Compulsory school attendance laws operate like a penal sentence. They prescribe the number of hours, days, and years a child must spend in school. When he has served his time, he is released regardless of his skills or lack of them. Often the most ignorant are permitted to leave school early and are encouraged to drop out at or before legal school-leaving age. Possibly a different type of attendance law should be drafted, one that makes legal school leaving dependent upon skills rather than time served. If a child is functionally literate, reasonably well informed and employable at sixteen, why must he remain in school another year if he prefers to get a job? Conversely, just because he is seventeen, should he be permitted to leave if he cannot read or function in the adult world? Such a law would give the child an incentive to learn and the school an imperative to teach him.

Those who did attend school regularly were bored and idle the greater part of the day. In Philadelphia, high school is over at two thirty. These boys and girls told me they had very little homework. And besides, they had one or two study periods in school when they could do all their assignments. There just wasn't enough for them to do. Most of the crimes they committed occurred in the long hours between school closing and bedtime. We concluded that three changes in the school program could materially reduce juvenile crime:

1. An incentive school-leaving law.
2. A longer school day.
3. Homework assignments to be done after school hours.

Correlatively, the school buildings should be kept open for study, use of the library and the gym until at least 6 P.M. These changes would not make school more interesting, more relevant, or more effective in teaching poor slum children. Many children would still be bored and play hooky, and there would still be school-initiated complaints. Obviously, new teaching methods, smaller schools, and better teachers are needed. But these three proposals could be adopted quickly and alleviate the problem.

School problems are not the exclusive prerogative of the poor. Many middle-class and rich children play hooky, get into trouble at school, get disciplined, and even get expelled. But they do not come to the juvenile court because of these difficulties. The nonindigent parent of a child having problems in school has choices open to him. He can persuade the principal to transfer his child to another, more sympathetic teacher; he can move to a community with a different kind of school system; he has a wide range of private schools from Montessori to military academies, to fit the needs of his particular child. In many families the children go to different schools because of their different requirements. The poor child is a captive in a rigid unresponsive system. The nonindigent parent does not have community control of his suburban school. He does not even have control of the private school to which he pays thousands of dollars of tuition. Few nonindigent people would want to be saddled with the responsibility of control of the schools. Few are competent to make the many decisions involved in operating even one small school. The nonindigent, however, have one right that the indigent do not have. They have the fifth freedom: freedom of choice.

Any large urban community could at little, if any, additional cost, establish several geographically co-extensive school systems based on different educational philosophies and practices. The indigent as well as the nonindigent would then have the right to choose the school system best suited to the needs of each child. How many public schools would cease operations if parents could arrange to send their child to a different school?

Perhaps reduction of school problems would materially reduce delinquency. We do not know for sure.

The experience of the Office for Juveniles was that most crimes occurred accidentally—without plan or premeditation. They were the result of hours and hours of idleness. Private prep schools have a carefully structured day for the scions of the wealthy—rigorous academic classes, compulsory after-school sports, compulsory extracurricular activities, and supervised evening study hall. A school day that is over at 2:30 P.M. as in Philadelphia, or even at 3 or 3:30, is not long enough for a teen-age child. Nor is a nine-month school year with three months of absolute idleness.

The boys we encountered were not interested in playing basketball or being taken on outings. They wanted jobs and self-respect. They longed for maturity. Little in their school day answered these needs. Why not experiment with such programs and find out what happens when idleness and boredom are alleviated?

The other major problem of our clients was physical illness. Sickness is endemic among the poor; the ghetto child is just plain sick a good part of his life. Of course, we lawyers were in no position to diagnose these ailments or to obtain treatment for these children. The only time any of our clients saw a doctor was in the hospital after an accident, a stabbing, or a shooting. I am convinced, however, that stomachaches, headaches, untreated or badly treated injuries contribute materially to their problems. Disfiguring facial scars, severe malocclusion causing speech impediment, impaired vision and hearing, and brain damage were common. I do not know the incidence of such ailments in the general population. Repeated recurrence of these maladies among three thousand poor children must, I feel, be extraordinarily higher than in the population at large. If these children had adequate medical care, perhaps they could respond better to the requirements of school and society.

Our brief experience also indicates many simple areas of crime prevention that could be explored. Self-service stores invite shoplifting. So do unguarded school buildings. Nights and weekends, most public schools are left untended. The children know that these buildings are filled with desirable objects from magic markers to television sets. There is often no night watchman to chase them away. New York reports thefts and vandalism in the public schools estimated at three million, two hundred thousand dollars in 1967. Similar proportionate losses occur in Philadelphia and other big cities. Some children told us they went in and out of the schools three and four times during a single weekend, carrying away loot. Some of it we were able to locate and return. Much more just disappeared. Justice Benjamin N. Cardozo enunciated the doctrine, Danger invites rescue. This means that a rescuer was relieved from liability for any negligence while effecting the rescue. Forer's variant is, Carelessness invites theft. Yielding to such temptation should not necessarily be punished as severely as deliberate crimes.

The single most popular juvenile crime is larceny of automobiles. It accounts for almost half of juvenile arrests. In 1968, 815,000 automobiles were stolen in the United States, and there is a steady increase in auto theft every year. Almost two-thirds of the thieves were under the age of eighteen. Two-thirds of the boys in the Robert F. Kennedy Youth Center at Morgantown, West Virginia (admission requirement: conviction of a federal crime), were there for stealing an automobile and driving it across state lines. My random sampling of teenage children indicates an astonishing number of arrests for stolen cars. An eleventh-grade history class at John Bartram High School consisted of twenty-five students—twelve boys and thirteen girls. Six of the boys and nine of the girls were black. From their clothing and appearance it was obvious that these students were not at the poverty level and could not have been clients of the Office for Juveniles. Nine of the boys had been arrested at least once for larceny of automobile, and one of the girls. They all claimed that they were simply "passengers" in the car that had been "borrowed" by someone else.

The common-law definition of larceny is "the felonious taking and carrying away of personal goods of another with intent to convert them to taker's use and make them his own property without the owner's consent." Few if any of our clients had such an intent. All they wanted was to "borrow" a car for a brief joyride. They could not afford to keep it. They couldn't even afford to buy gas. They usually abandoned the car near where it had been taken, so that the owner could easily reclaim it. Some owners withdrew the charges after getting the car back. (Several automobile owners, after visiting the Office for Juveniles to discuss their cases, not only withdrew the charges but also employed the boys and took a continuing interest in them. This was one of the extralegal benefits that accrued from having live witnesses in the courtroom instead of written reports.)

The boy who takes a car usually goes around the neighborhood and picks up all his friends to share in the fun. When the police see a car full of black teen-agers, they immediately stop the car and arrest everyone. Occasionally, if the car is stopped by the curb, they will arrest the boys and girls standing around the car. This runs up the crime rate, clogs the judicial system, and unnecessarily gives many children an arrest record. The assembly-line trial proceeding rarely impresses the defendants with the majestic impartiality of the law.

Two interesting legal questions are implicit in this practice. Is the temporary taking of a car really larceny? Are the passengers, who had nothing to do with taking the vehicle, guilty of any offense? Although thousands of children are arrested for larceny of automobiles each month, the high courts of the land have not passed upon these legal questions. Nor has society considered any practical remedies. I know and the judge knows that if he releases the boys charged with auto larceny, in all likelihood they will "borrow" another car when the opportunity arises. Little will be accomplished by locking them up. The desire for a car will be just as strong after they are released from the institution as it is before they are committed. It is an unending cycle of "borrowing," arrest, trial, detention, and then repeat.

For the young male in urban America, the desire for an automobile is frequently stronger and more insistent than the desire for food or sex. In a materialistic society an automobile may be both a sexual symbol and a status symbol, as well as an irresistible object. Significantly, there are almost no cases of auto larceny by a female.

The desire for a car transcends age and economic condition. Wealthy, rational middle-aged men who are not professional car racers pay more than fourteen thousand dollars for a bloodred Ferrari that will go over one hundred and fifty miles per hour. The reason? "All men believe any girl would like to sit beside her man in a Ferrari; and if this is *not* true, it is nonetheless part of the Ferrari mystique which each 'client' thinks he is buying—it makes them feel younger and stronger, emperor and daredevil at one and the same time" (R. Daley, "That Blood Red Ferrari Mystique," *The New York Times Magazine,* July 25, 1965, pp. 22–23). Among the Ferrari clients have been Governor Rockefeller and Adlai Stevenson.

A boy's desire for a means of locomotion is apparently universal. In Russia, where cars are scarce and well guarded, theft of bicycles is a common juvenile offense. Among the common offenses in Israel are auto theft and, on communal farms, driving a tractor without permission. The desire of the young men of Mali to acquire a motor scooter is causing not only larceny but social problems. Those who can afford motor scooters find them more desirable than wives. The girls of Mali are complaining.

Laws cannot curb desires. Despite the prohibition against the sale of alcohol, American adults simply could not resist the urge to drink. The massive educational program publicizing the dangers of cigarette smoking does not seem to have appreciably reduced smoking by mature, intelligent adults. Nor have the severe penalties for possession of marijuana curbed "pot" smoking among well-educated middle-class teen-agers and young adults.

Because boys apparently cannot resist the desire for an automobile, a way should be found to gratify it legally. When one considers that nearly 45 percent of the urban male Negroes aged fifteen to twenty-one are unemployed, it is apparent that the black teen-ager has no reasonable hope of legally acquiring an automobile or legally obtaining the use of a car. Most of these boys could be satisfied by the use of a car for an hour or two at a time. Of course, no commercial rental agency would lease a car to such a boy. In fact, most agencies will not lease cars to minors no matter how affluent they may be or what security they give.

A noncommercial organization for crime prevention could, however, establish a Hertz for Hoods and rent cars on an hourly basis to boys of legal driving age.

The boy in the dashiki has Technicolor dreams of himself in a shiny car, a pretty girl by his side. Black is beautiful; so is a red Ford. He wants racial pride and self-respect, and he also wants a part of this affluent world around him. He should be able to make this modest dream come true, for one hour a week, by lawful means.

In the Office for Juveniles we found no easy answers to crime and delinquency. We did, however, see these obvious and feasible steps that could be taken. But the crime rate continues to rise, and so does the number of young people in jail. There are more commissions, more surveys, more studies and recommendations. But no one listens.

Chapter Fifteen

WHEN THE BATTLE'S LOST AND WON

Who lose today may win tomorrow.

CERVANTES

On Friday, November 17, 1967, two hundred armed, helmeted, and booted policemen under the personal direction of Philadelphia Police Commissioner Frank Rizzo attacked and beat scores of unarmed black high school students. Commissioner Rizzo himself ordered the attack. "Get their asses,"* he told his men. The policemen charged down the street, indiscriminately clubbing everyone in their path. Boys and girls were knocked to the ground. Girls were dragged along the street by their hair. A club was broken over a boy's back. Father Bevins, a white minister, was clubbed when he tried to protect a black girl who was being beaten to the ground. Forty-two children were arrested. Many of them were badly injured. Commissioner Rizzo's comment was, "What can you do when you turn them [the police] loose?"

Immediately I met with my staff. Two of the lawyers and one investigator had been at the scene. Harvey Schmidt, the new executive director of Community Legal Services, had gone to police headquarters with our staff to see about the release of scores of children. Judge Adrian Bonnelly, upon application of our attorneys, directed that all the children be released to their parents pending the filing of charges. The children were home. They and their parents were outraged and demanding redress.

*Quotations are from the transcript of the federal trial: *Heard v. Rizzo*, U.S. District Court for the Eastern District of Pennsylvania (Civil Action No. 4451).

I begged the children and the adults to "cool it." The children were out of jail; we would defend them when their cases came up for trial. This did not satisfy either the children or their parents. In juvenile court, they would be faced with the usual hopeless proceeding in which the child would be lucky to escape imprisonment and the policemen would not even have to answer for their behavior. They would be told to sue the individual policemen for damages. Such suits were a farce, they told me.

This time they were determined to be the accusers, not the accused. This time they wanted to sue the police. They wanted action in the courts, and they wanted it now. The alternative was to return to the streets.

They wanted to know if they could trust any court of law. I talked to them about the United States Supreme Court. Nine white justices have outlawed segregation in the public schools, I told them. "But we go to all-black high schools," they replied.

It was the situation in the schools that had been the cause of the dreadful events of November 17. These children and many adults were beaten and injured when the black high school students of Philadelphia had gone to the school administration building to protest the inferior education they were receiving in the public schools. In the City of Brotherly Love there are ten high schools with a majority of black students. These schools had the greatest number of substitute teachers and the greatest overcrowding. The higher the percentage of black students, the lower the test scores. The national average on the standardized tests is 50. Philadelphia's average was 29. In the schools with more than 80 percent black students, the scores were below 15. Gratz High School, with 99 percent black students, scored 10. Gratz, with a capacity of 2,750, had 3,551 students. These children had a real grievance and they knew it. (These figures, from the Philadelphia School District, were included as Appendix C in the Jurisdictional Statement on appeal to the United States Supreme Court.)

"If you go back to the streets, you may be beaten again,"

I warned. Some of the children had been badly injured, and I feared what might happen the next time. Commissioner Rizzo was planning to buy two armored vehicles that closely resembled army tanks. The police had all manner of sophisticated weapons. The children had only their bodies. "Try to let the law work for you, not against you," I suggested. "We are civilized people. The law exists to resolve differences without force, to protect the rights of the defenseless, to ensure the safety of all of us." They listened politely. I looked at their dark, intelligent, troubled faces. Many were bruised and scarred. They asked if they could go into another room and discuss it by themselves.

The children agreed to refrain from violence and try the law. They persuaded the adults to do the same. About one thing they were very clear: They wanted to sue Commissioner Rizzo and the policemen who had beaten them. We realized, of course, that this lawsuit would not be popular with a large segment of the community. But we also knew that if we whose function it was to represent poor children did not seek the protections of the law for them, we would be derelict in our duty and failing in our professional obligation. Canon fifteen of the Canons of Professional Ethics is clear:

> . . . *No fear of judicial disfavor or public unpopularity should restrain him [the lawyer] from the full discharge of his duty. In the judicial forum, the client is entitled to the benefit of any and every remedy that is authorized by the law of the land, and he may expect his lawyer to assert every such remedy or defense. . . .*

There were other practical countervailing considerations. We were overwhelmed with routine work. How could we undertake such a difficult case? If any action was to be brought, we knew that we would have to do it ourselves. There would be no help from any agency. Our function was to give poor children every legal avenue of redress available to a paying client. If we refused, their only recourse was more violence. We could not turn them away or limit their remedies.

This was not our first acquaintance with these particular students. A number of them had come to the Office for Juveniles some time before the riot on November 17. Teen-agers frequently came to the office for advice and information. These young clients had wanted to know if it was legal to distribute leaflets on the streets of Philadelphia. They were informed that it was, but that the leaflets should not be obscene, defamatory, or incite to crime. Their leaflets were simply going to announce a peaceful demonstration. They planned to go to the school administration building and to meet with the superintendent and present their grievances. They asked to have an attorney accompany them. They knew that the school administration would have its lawyer present at the conference. They had quickly grasped the concept of legal counsel and were using the office in precisely the same way that a business tycoon uses his lawyer. They wanted advice beforehand, and they wanted their counsel with them at negotiations.

Mrs. Almanina Barbour agreed to go. She was inside the school administration building meeting with Superintendent Mark Shedd and these students when the riot occurred on the street. They saw it all from the windows of the room in which they were conferring.

The school administration had known all about the plans for the meeting. In fact, some time before the seventeenth, school officials had consulted with Lieutenant George Fencl, head of the civil disobedience squad of the Philadelphia Police Department, to make arrangements for police to patrol the gathering. And, of course, the police were well aware of the plans.

No one from the school administration suggested an earlier meeting or a different time or place. There was no reason why Superintendent Shedd could not have met with the students on Tuesday, Wednesday, or Thursday and thus obviated the reason for the demonstration. He could also have arranged for the students to meet with him after school in one of the school auditoriums where he could have addressed a large gathering. The high schools are equipped with public address systems. An announcement like this could have been made and every black student in Philadelphia would have got the word, if Mark Shedd had wanted a conference with student leaders. Instead, he proceeded to make arrangements with the police department for a demonstration.

The day before the demonstration, several of the student leaders had encounters with the police. Scarlet, a very pretty high school senior, a girl who not only was a good student but also had a part-time job, was harassed by policemen when she was passing out leaflets announcing the demonstration. They threatened to arrest her, but when she stood firm and demanded to know what the charge was, they let her alone.

Two boys passing out leaflets were stopped by other police officers in the early morning of November 16. They were taken to the police station. The boys were never told that they were under arrest. They were never questioned. The officers admitted that they were not investigating any crime. The officers were armed; the boys were not. Kennieth H. testified that he was struck by a policeman and that his glasses were broken.

Officer Mims' testimony at the trial with respect to the incident was patently ridiculous. I cross-examined him at length as he insisted that the boy had injured himself. My last question and his answer were:

Q. And is your testimony that Kennieth—in the presence of four police officers grabbed Officer Feldman and then hit himself on the nose, knocking his own eyeglasses off; is that your testimony?
A. That is my testimony.

Kennieth was not released from the police station until his mother agreed not to prefer charges against the policeman. On Friday morning, November 17, Mr. Charles R. Colgan, coordinator to the Office of Integration and Intergroup Cooperation of the school system, toured the black high schools. He testified that everything was peaceful. It was a bright sunny morning. The TV news cameras had no difficulty in photographing the events that soon occurred. The school administration had been ready and waiting for the students to gather at the school administration building. So had the police and the newsmen.

I decided to bring a class action on behalf of all the indigent schoolchildren of Philadelphia in the federal court under the Civil Rights Act. The case on which I placed my greatest reliance was *Dombrowski v. Pfister*. In 1965 the United States Supreme Court had decided that a plaintiff threatened with prosecution under a state statue that was unconstitutional on its face, or unconstitutional in the manner in which it was applied, could get an order from the federal courts enjoining his prosecution if that prosecution would have a "chilling effect" on the exercise of his First Amendment rights.

The black schoolchildren had gone to the school administration building to ask for a better education. This was clearly an exercise of free speech, one of the preferred First Amendment rights. The children were now charged with delinquency, a violation of the Juvenile Court Act. That statute, both on its face and in the way it was daily applied by the judges, violated every principle of constitutional law. Certainly the brutal beating of these children "chilled" thoughts of future petitions to the school administration. William M. Kunstler, the distinguished civil liberties lawyer from New York City, had represented Dombrowski. At our request, he came to Philadelphia and gave us his pleadings and briefs and he returned again to argue some of the questions of law. Kunstler came at his own expense and gave most generously of his time.

I didn't sleep for two nights. Mrs. Barbour, my first assistant, and I finished the Complaint in Equity seeking declaratory and injunctive relief on Tuesday morning. We were asking the federal court to convene a special three-judge court to consider the constitutionality of the Juvenile Court Act and several other statutes, to enjoin the prosecution of the children, to restrain the police from beating or otherwise intimidating the plaintiffs and from refusing to give them proper protection, and to appoint a special master to direct the affairs of the police department "until such time as that department can be so reorganized as to protect the lives and property of all citizens of Philadelphia equally and impartially" without regard to race, economic status, or moral values. Oscar N. Gaskins and Stephen Sheller, members of the Philadelphia bar, represented the adults who had been beaten and arrested and the one nonindigent juvenile. They copied our complaint with appropriate substitutions of names. Both actions were filed at 3:59 P.M. on Tuesday just as the clerk's office was closing. Because our clients were indigent, we had to petition for leave to file and appear *in forma pauperis.* The Office for Juveniles had no money to pay for anything, not even overtime. Our two dedicated secretaries typed all night, after working all day, to finish these numerous papers.

At four o'clock that Tuesday, I attended the regular monthly meeting of the board of Community Legal Services. There were the usual routine statistical reports. Finally, about three minutes before five, I was asked if I had anything to say. As I recall, I again pleaded for more lawyers. The board members were putting their papers in their briefcases. They had heard that before. I then stated loudly and clearly, "I want you to know that I have just now filed suit in the federal court on behalf of the black students who were beaten by the police last Friday."

William R. Klaus, the president of Community Legal Services, said, "Good."

In a large room full of lawyers, not one person asked me what kind of an action I had filed, against whom, or for what remedy. They picked up their briefcases and left.

It was not my custom to discuss the cases in the Office for Juveniles with the director, Mr. Harvey Schmidt, and he had never expressed the slightest interest in knowing anything more than appeared in the regular monthly reports. The case against Commissioner Rizzo, however, was of exceptional importance legally and in the community. I told Mr. Schmidt briefly what I was doing and asked him if he wanted his name on the complaint. Neither he nor his assistant, Jerome Bogutz, had had much experience in the federal court and they were eager to have an opportunity to do so. Neither of them did any work whatsoever in the preparation or trial of the case or in the tremendous amount of paper work involved.

Mr. Schmidt signed the complaint. I do not know whether he read it. It is certain that the details of its contents reported in the newspaper the following morning upset him. Mr. Klaus also read the paper. Although neither Mr. Klaus nor Mr. Schmidt had been able to spare the time before to come to the Office for Juveniles and see the extent of our problems, they both now found time to call an emergency meeting. Robert D. Abrahams, Mr. Schmidt's predecessor as executive director of the Community Legal Services, also appeared. Messrs. Klaus, Schmidt, and Abrahams were unanimously of the opinion that our federal court action was unwise. "You are jeopardizing our chances for getting funds from the city council," Mr. Klaus told me. (It was not until two years later that the city council appropriated meager funds for the Defender Association to take over the defense of poor children.) They wanted the complaint amended or withdrawn. I pointed out that a lawyer cannot amend a complaint or withdraw it unless he obtains the consent of his client. This was brushed aside as a mere technicality. Call those kids in and tell them what to do, I was instructed.

This was the grossest interference with the lawyer-client relationship. In granting the Charter of Community Legal Services, Judge Raymond Pace Alexander had carefully ruled that this corporate structure could not interfere with the relations between lawyer and client, that even though the lawyer's salary was paid by the corporation, he owed his duty to his client and he was subject to the canons of ethics just like any other lawyer. But this "technicality" did not bother Messrs. Klaus, Schmidt, or Abrahams.

The children were called into the office by Mr. Schmidt. I spoke to them and explained what they were being requested to do. Again, they asked for time to confer and decide. They went to another room. I do not know what happened in the other room. Very shortly thereafter Mr. Schmidt came and handed me their signatures on the amended complaint. The request for a special master to reorganize the police department was deleted in the amended complaint. This amendment of the complaint was immediately announced to the press by Mr. Klaus, although it had not been filed with the court. I did not see my clients again until the morning of the hearing.

Judge John Lord was designated to hear our application for a three-judge court, a requirement when a complaint charges that a state law is unconstitutional. At this time I intended to make an oral application to file the amended complaint.

Mr. Schmidt, Mr. Klaus, and Mr. Joseph N. Dubarry, III, a well-known member of the bar and a member of the board of Community Legal Services, were on hand to observe the proceedings. So were several hundred black citizens and our plaintiffs, the schoolchildren. As I came down the crowded corridor to the courtroom, the children were waiting for me. They asked if I would talk to them for a few minutes. In substance, they wanted to know if I were their lawyer in exactly the same way as if they were paying me a fee. I assured them that this was our relationship: They were the clients, I was the attorney.

"You mean that if you do something we don't like we can fire you?" they asked.

"Absolutely."

"Well," said Albert, the spokesman, in some embarrassment, "we don't want to change the complaint. We appreciate all your help but we want the case the way it was. We want Mr. Rizzo out. So"—Albert took a deep breath—"we fire you."

"Come into the court and sit right behind me," I told them. "I'll be at the counsel table. You can speak to me. I shall tell the court just what you have said and then call upon you to speak for yourselves." They smiled nervously. We filed into the crowded courtroom. As soon as court was convened I requested leave to make an application. Judge Lord and everyone else expected it would be the amendment of the complaint that had been announced in the press. He said he would defer that until other matters were taken care of. All kinds of preliminary motions and arrangements were ruled upon. He decided that a three-judge court should be convened. He then turned to me for my application. I stood up and asked for leave to withdraw as counsel. Judge Lord was aghast. Why? My clients did not wish to amend their complaint. They wanted a lawyer who would be free to represent them according to their wishes.

Judge Lord, who was doubtless having visions of a black-power militant taking over the case and disrupting the court, asked me if I couldn't persuade the children to change their minds. I assured him that these young people were very intelligent. They knew what they wanted. They had been beaten by the police many times; they were continually harassed; and they wanted the remedies prayed for in the complaint. Judge Lord requested me to remain in the case until the children obtained other counsel.

Messrs. Klaus and Dubarry were shocked. They feared Community Legal Services would lose the confidence of the black community if it didn't represent the children. I was ordered to go and get them back. It is a clear breach of the canons of ethics to solicit clients. I never did so in private practice. I did not intend to solicit poverty clients either. Now that we had shown what kind of an action to bring and that it was clear that the black people of Philadelphia strongly supported it, there would be many lawyers who would be willing to try the case for the publicity value. I was perfectly satisfied that the children would be able to find a lawyer who would carry on the case without a fee. It seemed to me desirable that they should do so. But this was not what the Community Legal Services board wanted. They were concerned with their image and with getting more money from the federal government and the city. They thought they needed the support of the black citizens. Schmidt was deputed to round up the children and bring them back to the fold. He did so.

Before agreeing to continue to represent the children, I obtained a letter from Mr. Klaus as president of Community Legal Services authorizing me to represent the children in accordance with their wishes and my own judgment on how to handle the case. On December 5, he wrote me a "Dear Lois" letter stating, ". . . In view of the attention of the community now fixed on this matter and the threat of adverse reaction in the poverty community which would *virtually destroy the program's* identification with that community, [emphasis supplied] you are authorized to proceed with the case under the original complaint." He agreed that there would be no further interference by the board with the lawyer-client relationship pending the establishment of a special advisory committee of the board to go over future actions before they are instituted. Of course such a committee would make it impossible for any poverty lawyer to function like a lawyer. Few attorneys of stature would agree to practice under such conditions. But there was no time to discuss this new proposal. The case was listed for trial. I agreed to try the case, along with Mrs. Barbour.

The trial began on December 11 to a packed courthouse. Armed, uniformed guards patrolled the corridors. The plaintiffs had difficulty getting into the courtroom. (I later learned that some of the spectators were being paid with federal funds to attend the trial as a "learning experience." These people were paid more per hour than we two poverty lawyers who were trying the case.)

The court dismissed our complaint as to the judges of the juvenile court, employees of the probation office, and the attorney general. We had named these people as defendants in their official capacity simply to ensure that the children would not be prosecuted for delinquency, or confined under the all-embracing powers of the Juvenile Court Act, while this trial was proceeding. No charge of impropriety was made against any of these officials. Counsel for all defendants agreed that no action would be taken against any of the children until the federal case was concluded. The remaining defendants were the police commissioner personally, unnamed policemen, the mayor, the managing director, and the district attorney in their official capacities. This distinction is important. Rizzo and the policemen were being sued not only for what they did officially but also for the personal excesses of brutality and incompetence. The others were simply nominal parties not charged with any personal misbehavior.

The three judges assigned to hear the case were Francis L. Van Dusen, newly elevated to the Court of Appeals, E. Mac Troutman, and John Lord. Judge Troutman did not utter a single word during the thirteen days of trial. Judge Lord spoke very little. Judge Van Dusen was in control.

Certain facts that were not disputed were reduced to this stipulation, which was made a part of the record:

> On November 17, 1967, at approximately 11:00 A.M. certain white and black adults and school children made a presentation for improvement in the school system to certain members of the school administration in the Board of Education building at 21st and Winter Streets. There was a discussion among members of the Philadelphia School Administration Staff and Lt. Fencl of the Civil Disobedience Squad as to arrangements of policing the demonstration of November 17 on the evening of November 16. From approximately

10:00 A.M. on, including during the time the above-mentioned meeting was going on in the Board of Education Building on November 17, school children assembled in the vicinity of the Board of Education Building at 21st and Winter Streets. Subsequently police officers of the City of Philadelphia, and during the progress of the meeting inside the School Administration Building, arrested certain of the juveniles and adults who were outside the building. At least one person who was inside the building and came outside the building was arrested after he came outside the building.

Also included as part of the pleadings was an affidavit by Spencer Coxe, executive director of the American Civil Liberties Union of Greater Philadelphia, detailing case after case in which individuals who were passing out peace leaflets, driving cars with antiwar stickers, or attending peaceful street rallies had been arrested and interrogated. These people were asked questions about their political beliefs. Some were beaten. The affidavit, which was carefully drawn by Burton Caine, an able volunteer lawyer, showed an unmistakable pattern of police harassment, violation of First Amendment rights, and brutality. It was interesting that the Civil Liberties Union, with a tiny staff and very little money, had files and files of complaints against the police. The Philadelphia Fellowship Commission, an organization that has been in existence more than thirty years and has an annual budget in excess of three hundred thousand dollars, whose purpose is to protect and promote equal treatment of Negroes, had not a single complaint.

The first witness called by the plaintiffs was Frederick D. Holliday, an administrative assistant to the superintendent of schools. Mr. Holliday is a soft-spoken, well-educated, light-skinned Negro. He had been with the school system more than seventeen years and had been promoted on merit. He held a very responsible position. He was highly respected. No one could question his veracity.

Mr. Holliday testified that he was in the conference with

the students, school staff, and board members, about thirty people in all, on the morning of November 17. The conference was proceeding well. Many students were standing outside on the sidewalks. Some were walking in the streets. They were singing and chanting cheerfully. Traffic was not impeded. Many of the children were carrying their school books. At about 12:15 P.M., the people in the conference room looked out of the window. The room is on the street floor. It is on the corner and from its large windows they had a good view of everything that was happening on both streets.

He saw "policemen lined up approximately five deep on the east side of Twenty-first Street—approximately fifty in ranks." The policemen were armed with riot sticks and guns. Some wore helmets, boots, and leather jackets. At that time the children were standing still watching the policemen. At Superintendent Shedd's request, Mr. Holliday and one of the students went out to speak to the policemen and ask them to move one block east of the building. As he stepped out of the building, Mr. Holliday was grabbed by a policeman who swung his stick and then threw Mr. Holliday to the ground. Mr. Holliday said that he did not see a single child fight the police.

The police, on signal from Commissioner Rizzo, charged into the children and ran down the streets beating everyone in their path. While this was happening, some of the children climbed in the windows of the school administration building seeking sanctuary. There was no damage to any school property inside or outside the building. Not even the shrubbery was damaged. The children inside the building were weeping.

Some time later in the afternoon, after Mr. Holliday returned to the building, he showed Commissioner Rizzo his clothing that had been torn by the police. Mr. Rizzo responded, "I have a tailor in South Philadelphia. I will give you his name." Mr. Holliday was asked for the record to state his race. He hesitated for a very long moment. I could almost see his thoughts, a middle-class Negro who had by effort and ability climbed very high on the ladder of his profession, who had never identified with any movements. He sat very straight in the witness chair as he crossed his private Rubicon. "I am black," he said.

The Reverend H. H. Nichols, a respected Negro minister and vice-president of the school board, testified that he was out on the street with Commissioner Rizzo when the police attacked the children. He too had been in the conference room. But when he saw the policemen lining up in formation and saw Commissioner Rizzo get out of a car carrying a long nightstick, he put on his coat and hat and went out to speak to Mr. Rizzo. He persuaded Mr. Rizzo to give the nightstick to someone else. They stood on the street corner together for about five minutes. During this time there was no disorder. The Reverend Mr. Nichols turned to go back to the building and then, he testified:

> *I saw this charge of police into the crowd and young people ran down Twenty-first Street with some of the officers pursuing them and hitting them over the head as they ran south on Twenty-first Street going towards Market. . . The one order that the Commissioner [Rizzo] gave was to move the crowd and his terminology was to "get their asses". . . I challenged him along with a fellow board member, who was present . . . to show us one stone, one bottle, one brick [that had been thrown]. . . . He was not able to show us anything. . . . The police were beating a girl whom I do not know, and I saw a white Episcopalian minister step between and saw him manhandled, and I walked out and said to the two officers and a lieutenant who was with them, "Officer, is it really necessary to treat this man this way?"—and this lieutenant said to me, "Shut the hell up or we will beat the hell out of you.". . . I went back to Commissioner Rizzo and at that time they were taking a young man out of the bus. . . . He had been beaten and was out and they put him on a stretcher. . . .*

Mrs. Mary Struve, a white supervisor in the school system who had taught for twenty-five years, saw the entire riot from the window. She came forth as a volunteer witness. She first saw the policemen massing on 21st Street.

"The next thing I observed," said Mrs. Struve, "after looking at the children and their freezing, their consternation at the massing of the police, was that the police were going through the people on Twenty-First Street indiscriminately swinging their clubs . . . I was there long enough that as the crowd dispersed because the children were pursued as they ran, the crowd had pretty well dispersed, and we saw cops, policemen, returning, swinging their sticks and smiling as if their job was finished. . . . It's pretty hard to see children knocked to the ground. I was able to observe a clergyman. That was noticeable because of his collar, being dragged by the policemen. I was conscious of kids falling and sticks swinging. It was so repulsive it was hard to look at."

The children who had been beaten testified. Their testimony was corroborated by the photographs taken by the newspapers and by the TV motion pictures. There was no difficulty in identifying these very witnesses in the pictures showing police beating them, blood dripping down their heads as they were dragged along the street and thrown into police vans. Every witness testified that he or she would be reluctant to engage in any street meeting for any purpose after this experience.

On the second day of trial, I called Police Commissioner Rizzo to testify as on cross-examination. This was one reason for making him a defendant. The plaintiff can call the defendant as a hostile witness, examine him, and not be bound by his testimony. It took little perspicacity to know that the city would not put the hot-tempered, arrogant police commissioner on the stand. If we wanted his testimony, we would have to call him as our witness. It was important to call him early in the case. My clients were under arrest and would have to stand trial. Their alleged misconduct would constitute the pretext for the police action. If we knew what they were charged with having done, our witnesses could refute this in their testimony.

Esquire magazine described Rizzo:

> *Intelligent and tough, he is a living argument for the view that a discreet but hard line is the only way. He sent bus loads of riot-ready cops cruising quietly around Philadelphia last summer, and he's kept them going ever since. Aided by a large budget, a well-stocked arsenal and power at City Hall, he has so far been able to keep the lid on the City of Brotherly Love. But he's training anti-sniper squads to shoot from helicopters, just in case. "We may have a riot here," he says, "but it will be the shortest riot in history."* [Esquire, *Vol. 69, March, 1968, p. 74.*]

Commissioner Rizzo's answers were in character. He refused to give his address. My second question was: "Would you state your educational background, sir?"

The answer: "Yes. I am a high school dropout."

The court refused to permit me to question him about the qualifications for the various ranks of police supervisors. In fact, these officers require a high degree of formal education. There are police academies to train and educate policemen in sociology, psychology, and intergroup tensions. The President's Commission on Law Enforcement and Administration of Justice recommended that police departments should take immediate steps to establish a minimum requirement of a baccalaureate degree for all supervisory and executive positions (*The Challenge of Crime in a Free Society,* 1967, p. 110). Because Rizzo's conduct and judgment were at issue in the trial, his qualifications for this very important position, we thought, were relevant. The court ruled otherwise.

The commissioner testified that he ordered six hundred men into the area, that there were one hundred and fifty policemen lined up along the curb of 21st Street, one of the two streets abutting the school administration building. The police were lined up across the streets. Cars were parked on both sides of the street. Thus, the children standing outside the building were trapped. They had no means of egress. If the police really wanted to disperse the crowds, they had not given the children a way to leave. Instead, they were chased, caught, and beaten. Such a deployment of police personnel violates the guidelines set forth in the FBI manual *Prevention and Control of Mobs and Riots.* The rules for quelling a riot are clearly set forth on page 86 and require that an order be issued "directing the people to disperse and leave within a prescribed time and insuring an avenue of escape for them." At no time was an order given to the crowd to disperse. Commissioner Rizzo admitted that he did not order the children to move. He testified, "I took complete command. I gave the orders and I only gave one order." The commissioner arrived at the scene at noon. He testified that at 12:34 P.M. he gave the order to his men "to move in and disperse." In response to my questions as to what the police did by way of dispersing the crowd, Commissioner Rizzo stated, "I am sure that they swung their nightsticks occasionally—there comes a time that a policeman must defend himself even against a woman—I saw some force used on girls." He stated that most of the people around the school administration building were juveniles and that 95 percent were nonwhite. He described this gathering of students as an undisciplined mob.

The commissioner was asked: "Well, would you consider it an undisciplined mob of black power demonstrators or of children?"

Answer: "It don't make no difference to me what color they were."

Commissioner Rizzo had been quoted in the press as saying that black power must be crushed—"The only thing they understand is force . . ." He explained this quotation by saying that when black power resorts to violence, to killing or burning our city, it must be crushed. I then asked this question:

Q. Did you see any person in this group of predominantly children around the administration building attempt to burn down the city? A. No.

Commissioner Rizzo testified that when he arrived he saw "a mob, an undisciplined mob." He testified that bricks, bottles, and barricades were thrown. Although he testified that the streets were choked with people and traffic was blocked, he had no difficulty in looking down the street and observing what was happening a block away. Commissioner Rizzo stated unequivocally, "I to this day have no knowledge of any students [who were injured] with the exception of one who was treated in the school infirmary. Our police records reveal no injury to students. In fact, your honor, we have about twenty detectives out visiting the various hospitals to come up with hospital slips and information to tell us who these injured students were or are. We have no knowledge as to any injured student."

The arrest sheet put in evidence *by the defense* showed that three children were taken to the hospital. Several children testified that they were beaten by the police and then taken to the hospital in police wagons.

Ronald Miller, a white reporter and newscaster for WCAU-TV, was on the scene from nine in the morning until after one. He testified that he did not see any objects thrown. He saw white policemen beating black boys and girls and also beating a white minister.

After the crowd was "dispersed" around the school administration building and many people had been beaten and arrested, those who remained decided to walk to police headquarters about fourteen blocks away. When they arrived at police headquarters, another attack occurred. Robert H. Finkel, one of our staff attorneys and a former assistant district attorney, testified about this episode. Many more people were beaten by the police at this time.

Commissioner Rizzo also testified as to the activities of the civil disobedience squad and the intelligence unit, which maintain files with respect to all kinds of people who have not committed crimes and who are not criminal suspects. He told the court, "We [the police department] have all kinds of files. We have files on the Ku Klux Klan, the Minute Men, the Sons of Italy—you name it, we have it." An interesting disclosure for citizens of a free country.

Every statement made by the commissioner was flatly refuted by the testimony of twenty-seven eyewitnesses. Although the various policemen who testified as well as the commissioner referred to their photographs, none was offered in evidence.

A crucial part of our case involved the unconstitutionality of the Juvenile Court Act as it was administered in the Philadelphia Juvenile Court. There was testimony that many of the children appearing in juvenile court were not represented by counsel. This was eight months after the United States Supreme Court decision holding that a child has a constitutional right to counsel. The assistant district attorney who was defending the city and the police commissioner agreed that the following statement describing the juvenile court practices was correct and could be presented in evidence.

1. At the Youth Study Center intake interview neither the child nor his parents is given a written statement of the charges against him.

2. The arresting officers are not required to be present and the child is not permitted to confront his accuser if the accuser is a police officer at that time.

3. The hearing official is not a judicial officer or learned in the law.

4. The rules of evidence are not applied in the determination of whether or not to hold the child for a court hearing.

5. A summary, which does contain some direct quo-

tations, but is not a verbatim transcript, is made of the hearing and forwarded to the juvenile court judge who has this information at the hearing [trial] and may use it to test the credibility of the child.

      6. The child is not advised of his right to counsel until the end of the interview.

      7. The Youth Study Center [the detention center] is a security institution akin to a prison in which the children are incarcerated.

      8. The current records of the Youth Study Center indicate that children are detained there for periods of many months pursuant to orders of the juvenile court entered under the aegis of the Juvenile Court Act on charges including incorrigibility, truancy, runaway, protection, which are not offenses in the penal code.

Every one of these points was a clear violation of the principles established in the *Gault* cased.

      The Supreme Court had held that a child was entitled to be represented by counsel and to avail himself of the privilege against self-incrimination. The court had also specifically ruled that a child is entitled to adequate notice of the charges against him and that he is entitled to appeal.

      The Supreme Court had excluded from its decision questions of detention because these were not involved in the problems that Gerald Gault encountered in Arizona. It was reasonable to infer that the principles of due process and fair treatment, which the Supreme Court held applied to juvenile court trials, would also prevail in deciding the legality of the detention practices of juvenile courts. We therefore attempted to get this question in issue before the federal court. In offering in evidence the records of the Youth Study Center, I made this argument: "I am attempting to put in evidence here material that specifically relates to the unconstitutionality of the Juvenile Court Law, because I believe that it could not be doubted that a law which permits the holding of a child in prison for three hundred and fourteen days on the grounds that the child is a runaway would be unconstitutional, if not on its face, as applied." The records of the Youth Study Center, showing many detentions for over three hundred days, were admitted into evidence. Although these records, which the defense agreed were an accurate factual report, were admitted in evidence, the court evidently did not consider such incarceration of children illegal.

Other evidence that we thought was pertinent and significant was not admitted. We had many experts who had agreed to testify for our clients without fee or expenses. Alton Lemon, a Negro sociologist employed by the North City Congress, would have testified that police brutality toward black boys and girls was causing a rising residuum of hostility that if continued could not be contained. Dr. Igor Kopytoff, a cultural anthropologist, would have testified as to the importance of ethnic identification and racial pride in the development of stable societies and stable individuals. Dr. Nicholas Poussaint, the noted Negro psychiatrist, and Dr. Alvin Reiss, the distinguished sociologist from the University of Michigan, agreed to testify. We urged the court to hear these witnesses for the following reasons:

—school children are taught that America guarantees equality of treatment, but black adolescents are not treated as equals; they are harassed by the police and denied due process of law.

—repressive police measures contribute to civil disorder and violence.

—the operation of the Philadelphia Police Department is discriminatory and promotes disorder.

The court refused to hear the testimony of these witnesses unless it could all be presented in one day, including cross-examination. This was a patent impossibility.

This, in substance, was our case: twenty-seven eyewitnesses, scores of photographs, court records, forms, evidence as to the operation of the juvenile court and the police department. The defendants produced only a few police officers whose testimony was thoroughly discredited by our rebuttal witnesses.

After hearing the testimony of all these witnesses and seeing the news photographs and TV movies, no one doubted the fact of police brutality. As Assistant District Attorney Michael Rotko put it, "The court will have to decide . . . is it better to have less brutality and more disorder."

Judge Van Dusen said in chambers but on the record, "We know that when children are treated brutally . . ." disorder will be promoted.

A mere recital of the evidence is only a fraction of the totality of the trial. Many extraneous things occurred during the course of the trial that were unprecedented. I received several evening telephone calls from Washington wanting to know why this suit was being brought. Was it true, as Commissioner Rizzo had reportedly said, that I wanted to abolish the police department? Of course this was not true, as anyone could see from reading the complaint.

In the courtroom equally strange things happened. Three black adult plaintiffs who wore their felas (small skullcaps of African origin) as a matter of conscience and racial pride were not permitted in the courtroom. Their testimony was taken in chambers. This occurred in William Penn's Philadelphia. Just three hundred years before this trial, William Penn had been held in contempt of court for not removing his hat in a court in London. Shortly thereafter he moved to America, where he founded the colony of Pennsylvania and the city of Philadelphia on principles of liberty.

Graffiti were found in the men's room. The court was very indignant. One night after the court sessions were over, defecation was found in one of the judge's chambers. The most extraordinary security measures were invoked. Armed guards with walkie-talkies paraded up and down. The black children who were both plaintiffs and witnesses were kept in a locked room under surveillance and not permitted in the courtroom. Policemen who were defendants and witnesses were in the courtroom in large numbers. Three black teen-agers were held in contempt of court for allegedly failing to rise as the judges were leaving the room or failing to rise fast enough. They were held in jail. After a hearing before Judge Thomas J. Clary, all three children were discharged.

The graffiti [Black is best, fuck the rest.] on the walls of the men's room were copied and placed in evidence as a court's exhibit. I objected that there was no evidence that the plaintiffs had written on the walls. Judge Van Dusen overruled this objection with the following remarks:

JUDGE VAN DUSEN: Do you doubt that they [graffiti] were caused by this suit and the breadth of the allegations which you made in the complaint and the people who brought the suit?

MRS. FORER: There has been no evidence that any person who brought this suit—there is no evidence who committed these acts of vandalism. There is no evidence as to who—

JUDGE VAN DUSEN: Well, there certainly is some evidence. It requires an inference, but there is evidence that "Black is best" was written all over the lavatory, in two places in the hall, and do you mean to say that you think this suit had nothing to do with that?

MRS. FORER: I am saying that I think there is no evidence that any of the plaintiffs in this action had anything to do with this. No evidence has been produced, nor has there been evidence produced as to the persons who have threatened the life of counsel by repeated phone calls and by very unpleasant anonymous missives in the mail. *

*This is an exact reproduction of one of dozens of postals and letters that were sent to me every day:

Well you slovenly jew-bitch i hope the day is not far away when one of these nice-niggers cuts your throat from ear-to-ear it would improve your look's you ugly kike. you make me vomit, the jew-bastards like you—promote another "hitler"—to bad he was not properly prepared. (democrat)

JUDGE VAN DUSEN: Well, are you suggesting that the defendants or the court had anything to do with threatening the life of the counsel?

MRS. FORER: Of course the court had nothing to do with it.

JUDGE VAN DUSEN: It just seems to me it is so obviously the sort of reaction which will result from somebody who alleges in broad language that the entire police system is to be scrapped* and enjoined from being carried out by the persons managing the police department; that the entire juvenile court system is to be declared null and void, in the emotional considerations, the emotional times in which we live—do you think it surprising that threats do not come to counsel who bring a suit like this. . . ."

On January 9, 1968, after eight days of testimony, the court entered an order separating the complaint into two parts: those allegations dealing with violations of civil rights and those dealing with the unconstitutionality of the state statutes. We were given the right to file an amended complaint dealing with the civil rights aspects of the case within ten days. This part of the case would then be heard by one of the three judges sitting alone. At this time the court had already filed an opinion in the middle of the case, *before* hearing all the testimony, in which it held that Commissioner Rizzo's actions were justified. If we did not care to amend the complaint, the court said it would allow only one more day of testimony.

We chose not to forego our rights by attempting to present all the evidence in one more day. This was clearly an impossibility that the court well recognized. Nor did we wish to forego our rights on appeal. Therefore, we asked for an extension of the time in which to file an amended complaint so that we could appeal the propriety of that order. This was denied. We did not file an amended complaint. The court ruled against

*This is a gross misconstruction of the plaintiffs' prayer for the appointment of a receiver for the police department to restore law and order.

us in a final opinion handed down on January 30, 1968. I promptly filed a notice of appeal in the United States Supreme Court.

The United States Supreme Court affirmed the trial court without affording us an opportunity to file briefs or present oral argument.

My clients and their parents were not surprised. They had not expected any other result. The parents were pleased that their children were not in jail and that they had not been harassed any further.

Was the lawsuit ill-advised, as Messrs. Klaus, Schmidt and Abrahams said? Many months later, I still do not think so. The prompt filing of the lawsuit staved off more violence. There was no further street confrontation. No other children were injured. The day by day newspaper accounts of the trial, almost a running transcript, enlightened the public about the operations of the police. The mayor canceled the authorization for the purchase of the two armored vehicles ordered by the police department. The police department instituted a bureau of citizens' complaints. The mayor belatedly instructed the city solicitor to appeal the decision of the state court declaring the police advisory board unconstitutional. All of the charges against the children were quietly dropped. Some reforms were instituted in the juvenile court. We obtained much of the relief we sought although the courts ruled against us on every issue.

The most important point I wanted to make was this: the poor ghetto child can make the law work for his benefit. In this I failed totally.

Chapter Sixteen

THE FALL

Some rise by sin and some by virtue fall.

WILLIAM SHAKESPEARE, *Measure for Measure*

The lawsuit against Police Commissioner Rizzo gave Harvey Schmidt, the director of Community Legal Services, and William R. Klaus, president of the board, an opportunity to get rid of the Office for Juveniles.

Both Mr. Klaus and Mr. Schmidt were uneasy in their exposed positions with Community Legal Services, the organization responsible for the Office for Juveniles. They were not accustomed to the criticism and pressures to which people in government are subjected. They panicked at any adverse comments and were always conscious of the "image." Mr. Klaus was wont to call press conferences and to discuss cases and methods of operation. I was present at one such press conference and considered it inappropriate. I was not in the habit of discussing litigation with the press. The personal relations between Mr. Klaus and Mr. Schmidt, a Negro attorney, were correct and formal. Mr. Abrahams (the director before Mr. Schmidt) had known most of the lawyers on the board for many years. They respected him as one of themselves—a wealthy, middle-class establishment lawyer. I, too, had known most of the board members for years and years. We were on first name terms. They looked upon my involvement with the poverty program as a quixotic gesture. From time to time, Mr. Klaus would assure me that he really sympathized with poor Negroes. It was the other members of the board who hadn't seen the light and become liberals like him.

The Office for Juveniles was caught in a pincers play by the juvenile court and Community Legal Services. The court wanted to give token compliance with the Supreme Court decision in the *Gault* case. They also wanted to do business in the same old way. Community Legal Services wanted to oblige the court and the city politicians, retain their funding, get a little money from the city council, and not rock the boat. None of the other divisions of Community Legal Services caused much trouble. The area offices were limping along, not disturbing anyone, helping a few people. The area attorneys were never invited to board meetings, so no one knew of their many complaints and dissatisfactions. The unhappy clients had no one to whom to complain. The criminal division was simply the old Defender Association with a few new frills like a social worker and prison counseling. The defender had never offended anyone except perhaps some disgruntled clients. The consumer advocate was busy organizing community groups. Community action programs were the favorite innovation of the Office of Economic Opportunity. It was thought in Washington that by setting up organizations of black ghetto dwellers under the tutelage of a bright young lawyer, society would be peacefully restructured to eliminate poverty. Daniel P. Moynihan (in "The Professors and the Poor," *Commentary*, Vol. 46, August, 1968, p. 19) characterizes the community action idea as "the purest product of academia and the Ford Foundation." None of these activities disturbed anyone. The young lawyers found it exciting to go to meetings with what they naïvely assumed was "the black community." It was much easier and pleasanter than trying cases all day every day. The area attorneys who were sufficiently dissatisfied and who could afford to leave did so. Similar weariness prevailed at the criminal division. In every division and at every level of Community Legal Services it was clear that Mr.

Schmidt was determined not to offend the board, the court, or city hall.

The Office for Juveniles did not fit into the pattern of acquiescence. We insisted upon objecting to illegal actions that affected our clients. And we kept asking for more lawyers as the number of clients soared. Everyone promised more help. Just keep going until fall, we were told in the spring. The city council will appropriate money for lawyers for the children. September came and went. So did October. The juvenile court judges did not ask city council for money. Neither did Community Legal Services or the bar association.

Shortly after the *Gault* decision, there had been a big meeting of juvenile court judges, leaders of the bar, officers of Community Legal Services, the district attorney, the defender, the director of Community Legal Services, and myself. Herman Pollock, head of the Defender Association, presented a paper showing how to avoid the *Gault* decision and have lawyers only for those children the court had already decided to commit to institutions. Judge McGlynn took a dim view of this suggestion. What everyone wanted soon became clear.

"Just put one lawyer in each of the four juvenile court rooms and let him take all the cases. That's what the defender does and there are no problems," I was told. The Supreme Court had held, decades before, that the right to counsel means that the accused has "the guiding hand of his lawyer every step of the way" (*Powell v. Alabama,* 1932). Counsel also means adequate representation, a presentation of all the evidence on behalf of one's client, motions, argument, and appeal. Failure to inform a client, no matter how guilty, of his right to appeal is a valid ground for reconsideration under the Post Conviction Hearing Act. Under the system proposed by the judges, a child would not see his lawyer until he came into the courtroom. If the case were continued for any reason—and more than half of all juvenile cases are continued at least once—he might have a different lawyer the second time. How could the second lawyer represent the child when he would not know what happened at the first hearing? I refused to agree to such a scheme, which would give the appearance but not the substance of legal representation. It would also deprive the child of his right to appeal on the ground that he had not had counsel.

In early November, 1967, I wrote to the juvenile court saying that regretfully our office could not accept any more clients. If the judges wished to appoint counsel for indigent children, they would have to appoint members of the private bar. Except for a small panel of volunteers, it was obvious that few lawyers would accept such appointments without compensation. If the members of the bar had been urgently requested to take appointments without fee, many of them might have done so. But the last thing the juvenile court judges wanted was for each child to have his own court-appointed lawyer. With thirty or forty different lawyers, no judge could get through forty cases in a day.

My decision was countermanded by Harvey Schmidt. He and his former law partner, Judge Clifford Scott Green, then head of the juvenile court, decided that the Office for Juveniles, with only five lawyers and two secretaries would represent some 90 percent of the sixteen thousand children tried in juvenile court each year. There was no doubt in anyone's mind that at least 90 percent of the children were indigent. There was no one to object to this arrangement on their behalf. Everyone was satisfied to let the Office for Juveniles carry the whole burden. But we persisted in our refusal to accept more clients than we could represent. Any private lawyer who accepted cases that he could not possibly try would be subject to censure and disbarment. We believed that even though we were salaried lawyers hired to represent the poor, the canons of ethics applied to us. We were not willing to be relegated to second-class status at the bar and we were determined not to give our clients inferior representation. The issue was joined but there had been no confrontation.

It was clear that as long as the Office for Juveniles had a measure of autonomy it would not quiescently subside into a traditional agency for the poor. None of us had ever been a part of that new managerial class in America that makes its living from the miseries of other people. We saw what happens to both the managers and the managed. Every day in the courthouse we saw the bored, disdainful middle-class public employees—black and white—interviewing the poor. The large, badly lighted, badly ventilated waiting rooms were crowded every morning. Hundreds of poor people sat waiting for their numbers to be called. It is easy to forget that these are individuals with pride, love, sensitivity, and capacities for pain and hope. If a person interviews fifty or sixty people in a day, all with similar complaints and problems, their identities merge. They lose the quality of uniqueness that every person has. We were determined to resist this dehumanization.

If we were there to provide a legal defense, it had to be a thorough defense. Mr. Schmidt realized that the only way to placate Judge Green, Mr. Klaus, and the politicians was to abolish the Office for Juveniles. While I was in federal court trying the case against the police commissioner, Mr. Schmidt canceled our lease. (The excuse given was that the building that housed our office was for sale. It had been for sale when we entered into the lease. More than two years after the lease was canceled, the premises are vacant. The building is still for sale.)

The Office for Juveniles had occupied two floors over an auto body repair shop, at a rental of one hundred dollars a month. This included heat, which was intermittent. We had six rooms, a powder room, and a bathroom. We were one block from the juvenile court and one and one-half blocks from the detention center. The space was inadequate, but the office was conveniently located for the lawyers and, more importantly, for the clients. Without consulting any of us, Schmidt ordered the Office for Juveniles moved to the central office of Community Legal Services, where we would be physically under his surveillance and he could direct the assignment of cases and the office procedures. It was more than a mile from the juvenile court, and there was no direct public transportation from the central office to the court. We were given three windowless cubicles in a very expensively renovated garage. The waiting room was unheated. Four people could barely squeeze into this little area —actually just a vestibule. The clients stood outside in rain and snow waiting to get into the office. There were not enough people to type essential letters, but a clerical staff was set to dismantling our filing system and merging it into the general files, thus destroying unique data on juvenile delinquency, recidivism, treatment, trials, and pretrials.

Mr. Schmidt announced that things would be done differently now. Clients would have to make appointments in advance. If a poor woman spent carfare and came to the office, she could not see a lawyer. A receptionist would give her an appointment several weeks later. Of course, if her child was in jail, he would stay there until she came for her appointed visit. Poor people do not run their lives by clocks and calendars. They do not have diaries and datebooks. We knew that many people would lose the slip of paper or forget the date. Very few of our clients had telephones. They could not call to cancel or change an appointment in case of illness or some other emergency.

To Mr. Schmidt, however, such hardships on the parents and children were unimportant. This was to be an efficient streamlined operation. Every cog in the macine had its limited function. The receptionist made the appointment. The interviewers interviewed. The lawyers appeared in court. I protested that the lawyer should talk to the client once financial eligibility was established. Schmidt assured me that he had hired two lawyers to do the interviewing. This was interesting, because he had previously told me that there was no money for more lawyers for the Office for Juveniles.

I met the two "lawyers." One was a sad young woman who had flunked the bar examination. She had been in the bottom quarter of her class in law school. No one on the faculty would recommend her for litigation—which was 95 percent of our work. She was not recommended for research or drafting of documents. The other lawyer was a Cuban who had been a member of the bar in Cuba. His English was sketchy and uncertain. Not more than 5 percent of our clients were Spanish speaking. Most of the Puerto Rican children spoke better English than he did. He planned to go to law school in America. I checked over their first few interview sheets. Most of the important questions—Was the juvenile arrested with a warrant? Previous record? Names of eyewitnesses—were left blank. In the space for "offense charged," the Cuban gentleman invariably wrote "felony."

The clients were given numbers. The interviewers emerged from their cubicles every few minutes to call out the next number. Of course, the clients responded to this attitude. In eighteen months of operation in our office over the repair shop, there had not been one act of vandalism, theft, or misconduct. Hundreds of children—many charged with the most serious crimes—had been in the office. They used the same toilets as the staff. They were in and out of the private offices. Often when I would get a phone call to hurry to court in an emergency, I would rush off without my pocketbook. One of our clients would run down the stairs after me to bring it to me. Not one penny, not one ashtray, not one piece of equipment or supplies was ever taken. Not one word was ever scribbled on the walls. But within two weeks of the move, a child was accused of stealing from a secretary's purse. The police were called and the client was arrested in the law office.

While there was great and understandable consternation over this larceny, there were certain other monetary matters about which I was deeply concerned. How much was the poverty program paying for these dreadful new offices? How much was paid for the renovation? Were these two "lawyers" receiving the salaries designated for attorneys? No one would give me this information. I discovered that at least one lawyer assigned to the criminal division was carried on the payroll of the Office for Juveniles. I also discovered that half of the salary for the social worker was assigned to the Office for Juveniles. We had never seen him. When we complained about the problem of getting to the court from the office, we discovered that there were cars and drivers on the payroll to take Schmidt and other dignitaries to meetings. They would ferry us back and forth to court, Schmidt said. This seemed to be horribly extravagant and inefficient.

It was clear that the Office for Juveniles would no longer be a law office. Naturally I resigned. The entire staff wanted to resign with me. They all wrote strong letters of protest over the destruction of the Office for Juveniles. These were addressed to Klaus and the board of Community Legal Services. None of us ever received a reply. I urged the staff to stay on until they got other employment. I also hoped that they would be able to see that some of the children were properly represented. The staff left, one by one. The backlog increased. Months later the defense of juveniles was transferred to the Defender Association and city council appropriated funds for this purpose.

The new arrangement for processing clients was contrary to everything that the legal services program was designed to accomplish. But the Office of Economic Opportunity was totally disinterested in the destruction of the program and in the fate of the children of Philadelphia. All of us wrote to Earl Johnson, then the head of the legal services branch of O.E.O. He was addressing a high-level group in Philadelphia that week and agreed to see us for fifteen minutes. He gave us ten minutes. All of the lawyers from the Office for Juveniles came to his hotel to meet him. He had a cup of coffee with us and promised to look into the matter. None of us ever heard from him again. Legal representation of children was soon "phased out."

The Committee on Professional Guidance of the Philadelphia Bar Association advised me that it was my ethical obligation to carry forward the cases in which I was counsel even though I was no longer receiving a salary. At my own expense, I continued to represent many of the children. I also carried forward the appeal in the *Rizzo* case. Community Legal Services refused even to type the jurisdictional statement of forty-three pages and an appendix of greater length.

I believe the Committee on Professional Guidance was right. A lawyer cannot withdraw from a case just because he is not paid. He cannot abandon a client in the middle of a case. These are obligations that a person assumes when he becomes a lawyer. He is not a bricklayer who is paid by the hour. On the other hand, he does not have the protections of a bricklayer— no union, no contract, no fringe benefits. This also is the worst of both worlds. It will become increasingly difficult to obtain able attorneys to accept employment in the agencies for the poor under such degrading and burdensome conditions.

The significance of these events transcends what happened in Philadelphia. It indicates what can happen in any community under these anomalous programs. The Office for Juveniles was attempting to do exactly what it was created for, namely, to give the poor the same kind and quality of legal representation that the rich can purchase from private counsel. I feel reasonably sure that, if my sons had been beaten and injured by the police and then charged with resisting arrest, I would have sued the city and the police commissioner. And I believe that most middle-class parents would not have sat meekly by if their boys had been beaten, injured, insulted, and falsely accused of engaging in illegal activity.

The courts would not have been so hostile to a private lawyer who was representing such clients for a fee. The fact is that the federal judges were particularly antagonistic to us because we were acting as quasi-public employees. The same wrath was not vented on private counsel even though they, too, were serving without fee. Judge Van Dusen made very clear the distinction between a lawyer representing a client and a lawyer who is paid a salary by an agency. At the end of the seventh day of trial, at a conference in chambers, he suggested that the complaint be amended to delete the request for a receiver for the police department. Judge Van Dusen addressed Mr. Gaskins (private counsel for the adults) as follows: "Now, I don't want you to withdraw anything that you feel you have to press. Sometimes lawyers have to press things that they may advise their clients against, but that they feel aren't so unreasonable that they can say we will withdraw rather than press them, do you see? But if your view is, as it apparently is here, I would think you would want to go on record as changing this number eleven [the prayer for a receiver], and I would think it is something *that Mrs. Forer particularly would want to think about several times because she, to a certain extent, is representing a nonprofit corporation* and this is a pretty drastic paragraph to have in there" (emphasis supplied).

This was precisely the difficulty. I thought I was representing my clients—the poor black children. The court and Mr. Klaus thought that I was representing Community Legal Services. Despite the fact that there have been legal aid programs for more than half a century, the relation of lawyer to indigent client has not been clarified.

It cannot be forgotten that although Mr. Schmidt is a Negro, Community Legal Services was a predominantly white middle-class organization. The one successful Negro lawyer on the board either dissented or abstained on the votes taken with respect to the lawsuit against the police commissioner. The destruction of the Office for Juveniles was not voted upon by the board.

I am convinced that the lawsuit against Commissioner Rizzo would not have angered so many people if the plaintiffs had not been black. A sizable section of the white community expressed its hostility to black people in communications to me and to the public press. The attitude was made explicit by one policeman who refused to let an injured boy, the brother of a Negro policeman, make a phone call. "Niggers like you don't have no rights," he told the boy. Among better educated citizens it was phrased more politely. Judge Van Dusen continually berated me for "wasting" the time of the court. The clear implication was that the rights of poor black children were not worthy of the time of three exalted federal judges who could have been hearing antitrust suits or accident cases.

The lawyers who represent the poor, the black, or the unpopular will, of course, not be very popular themselves. They cannot be effective if they are employees of agencies that reflect popular sentiments and hostilities. A lawyer cannot serve the establishment and the poor. A lawyer cannot give his undivided loyalty to the board that pays his salary and to the client who is the recipient of charity. This is the lesson it took me so long to learn.

Chapter Seventeen

THE POWER STRUCTURE AND THE POOR

If all the world were just, there would be no need of valour.

PLUTARCH, *Lives*, Agesilaus

My first lesson in how to represent the poor should have prepared me for the decision to abolish the Office for Juveniles. When we opened the office, Herman Pollock warned the lawyers not to file any papers (motions to dismiss, etc.) because we would have to live with the judges. Mr. Pollock had been head of the Defender Association for years. He knew what was expected of lawyers for the poor. In 1966, Mr. Pollock was not only head of the Defender Association but also in charge of the criminal division of the antipoverty legal services program for Philadelphia. This was the result of a sixteen-month power struggle.

It began in the spring of 1965, shortly after the cases of Wendell and his friends, the boys who were jailed for the alleged obscene phone call to Judge Stout. The release of the boys had been widely reported in the local press. My phone rang constantly with requests from frantic indigent parents for attorneys for their children. Neither the Legal Aid Society nor the Defender Association would represent children. There was no place for these people to turn except a name in the newspaper.

I learned of the possibility of help for them from a report in the April 15, 1965, bulletin of the American Bar Association announcing a conference on Law and Poverty. This was the beginning of the Office of Economic Opportunity's program funding legal services projects. Immediately I wrote to Theodore Voorhees, a member of the Philadelphia bar who was president of the National Legal Aid and Defender Societies and a member of the steering committee on law and poverty. A copy was sent to Sargent Shriver, director of the OEO.

The letter stated in part:

> *May I call your attention to an aspect of the problem of legal services for the poor—counsel for indigent children charged with delinquency. Nowhere is the inequality of treatment of rich and poor more evident than in the juvenile court. Children are less able than adults to know their rights and to protect themselves. The child represented by counsel is seldom declared delinquent, except for the most serious offenses. Even then, if his parents are financially able to pay for his treatment or education, he will not be committed. But the vast majority of children who appear before the juvenile courts are poor, non-white, semi-literate and without parents or friends who are sufficiently knowledgable or financially able to secure counsel for him . . . I urgently request you to bring this pressing problem to the attention of the Steering Committee.*

On May 5, the OEO sent me a form to apply for a grant. Believing that this was an appropriate undertaking for the bar association, not an individual practicing lawyer, I called Marvin Comisky, chancellor of the Philadelphia Bar Association. He invited me to a meeting to discuss the project with members of the Public Service Committee of the bar association, Mr. Pollock, Robert Abrahams (director of the Legal Aid Society), and Charles Bowser (director of the Philadelphia antipoverty program). It was agreed that an application for a pilot project grant for legal services for children be made under the sponsorship of the Philadelphia Bar Association and the local antipoverty program. I was requested to draft the application. Following the familiar pattern for the furnishing of legal counsel to the indigent, I proposed the establishment of a special law office for poor children.

The first agencies in the United States to provide free or

low-cost attorneys for the poor were established at the turn of the century. Legal counsel in criminal cases was not a matter of right then; lawyers were provided for the deserving poor as a matter of grace and philanthropy. From the inception of the program, the leaders of the bar gave money (but not very much) to hire special lawyers to represent the poor. The wealthy members of the bar could have given their own services without cost. But wealthy law firms are geared to wealthy clients and big fees. Occasionally the press reports the size of fees paid to law firms by government agencies. Mayor Joseph Alioto of San Francisco is reported to have received a fee of $2.3 million. Southeastern Pennsylvania Transportation Authority, a public body, paid $1,227,000 in legal fees to four Philadelphia law firms. Drinker, Biddle and Reath, one of the law firms, received $637,000, almost twice the amount requested to provide legal representation for all the indigent juveniles in Philadelphia.

Obviously, wealthy law firms found it easier and cheaper to establish special law offices for the poor and turn the whole problem over to a few hired hands. Such separate law offices became the norm for legal representation of the poor.

Because both the Philadelphia Legal Aid Society and the Defender Association had disclaimed any interest in representing children in juvenile court, we proposed that a new agency be formed under the direction and sponsorship of the bar association. This proposal was submitted to the chancellor on May 14, 1965. Suddenly, on May 17, the Defender Association sprang to life and, according to a letter from Herman Pollock, declared that "if funds were made available, the [Defender] Association should assume the task of supplying legal representation independent of other professional or civic organizations." The scent of money had pricked the nostrils of the establishment agencies.

By the middle of June, 1965, the Philadelphia Bar Association had approved the proposal I drafted and agreed to have it funded through the association's charitable foundation, which was already sponsoring a bail project. On the urging of the Legal Aid Society and Defender Association, this application was withdrawn so that a comprehensive proposal covering civil, criminal, and juvenile representation could be substituted. It was not until the spring of 1966 that the second proposal was submitted. Operations did not begin until September, 1966.

The Office of Economic Opportunity recognized that because legal representation was a right, it should not be dispensed like a charity. The clients should have some measure of control over the program. The antipoverty program never really grasped the nettle of this issue. If the client was to have the same legal rights as a paying client, then the superstructure of a charitable board to administer the program, hire and fire the lawyers, and set policy would be irrelevant. On the other hand, there was little disposition to give the client the money and let him retain his own lawyer. Only the state of Wisconsin was funded to provide a program called Judicare (after Medicare) in which private attorneys were paid by the Office of Economic Opportunity.

The language of the antipoverty law provided a median position. The act required "maximum feasible participation" by the poor. This provision was inserted by a couple of idealistic youngsters, and to this day no one knows what it means or what it accomplishes. (See Moynihan, *Maximum Feasible Misunderstanding,* Glencoe, Ill.: Free Press, 1969.) In providing lawyers for the poor people of Philadelphia, this "participation" requirement was met by creating a new nonprofit corporation called Community Legal Services, Inc. It was governed by a board of directors, one-third of whom were representatives of the bar association, one-third representatives of the Legal Aid Society and Defender Association, and one-third representatives of "the poor." The old agencies against which the poor had been protesting for so long were clearly in control. The representatives of the poor were merely window dressing giving token compliance with the act. Similarly, in most other cities, the old-line agencies quickly assumed control of the anti-poverty legal services programs.

The result was clearly foreshadowed at the National Conference on Law and Poverty, which was held from June 23 to June 25, 1965, in Washington , D. C. The conference was composed of lawyers and politicians. There were few Negroes, except for Washington employees of the Office of Economic Opportunity. No poor people were visible. This was obvious to everyone. In his opening remarks, Lewis F. Powell, of Virginia, president of the American Bar Association, alluded to the elite nature of the conferees. Powell said, "I took a look at the registration list for this conference. I must say it is notable both in terms of the numbers of delegates and particularly so in terms of your positions in your respective communities—in legal aid, in social service, and in the organized bar. I am reminded of a definition of the term 'upper crust.' Obviously, it is not appropriate really for a meeting dedicated to the poor. But it was told last February at a meeting of the fellows of the American Bar Foundation and it may amuse you. 'Upper Crust' was defined to be a bunch of crumbs held together by a lot of dough."

The lines were quickly drawn between the reformers who wanted to create a "great society" and the establishment. Hubert Humphrey, then Vice-President, welcomed the delegates. He told them, "We're not trying to do the job the way it used to be done because the way it used to be done just didn't get the job done. We have to experiment. We have to seek new talent. We must call on people to use their initiative . . ."

Voorhees took up the cudgels for the status quo:

> *A number of our friends, some from the law schools, others in active practice, have suddenly come forward with advice, criticism, even strictures on Legal Aid.* . . . Our established position in the community *and existing goodwill, our expertise, the availability of our staffs as a cadre for a much broader enterprise, seem to us, in toto,* to provide assurance that any rival service will have to be

extremely good to enter into successful competition. [*emphasis supplied*]

In Philadelphia as in many other cities, no rival service was ever given the opportunity to prove itself. Robert Abrahams, director of the Legal Aid Society, was appointed director of Community Legal Services. He agreed to serve for one year. The offices of Community Legal Services were opened in the same building with the Legal Aid Society and the two programs were meshed. Herman Pollock, director of the Defender Association, was put in charge of the criminal division. Legal services for children was tucked away as a minor sideline of the criminal division, although later it was treated as a separate entity. I was requested to take charge of this phase of the program.

It was not an easy decision to make. I enjoyed my private practice. It was interesting and lucrative. I had misgivings about being the employee of an agency for the poor. However, I could not resist the opportunity to try to bring due process into the juvenile court.

Fortunately, there were three excellent experienced lawyers who were also willing to embark on this quixotic experiment: Mrs. Almanina Barbour, a seasoned trial lawyer practicing in the law office of United States Congressman Robert N. C. Nix and his son (since elevated to the bench); Mrs. Ellen Q. Suria, one of my former students at the University of Pennsylvania Law School, an honor graduate, who had served as a clerk to a federal judge and had had several years of practice; Ronald M. McCaskill, an able young lawyer from Howard University Law School, who had worked with the Civil Rights Division of the United States Department of Justice. Our two devoted secretaries, Phyllis Brown and Brenda Lum, were lured away from Congressman Nix and the American Civil Liberties Union. All of us took substantial reductions in income (more than 50 percent for some) in order to work for this program.

We were later joined at different times by three able, dedicated lawyers—Richard Ash, Arthur Cortese, and Robert Finkel. There were never more than five lawyers on the staff at any one time. Mrs. Barbour, Mr. McCaskill, Miss Brown and Miss Lum are Negroes. Although the board and the executive directors worried a great deal about integration of the staff and "relating" to the black community, the Office for Juveniles was united by a concern for "our children." We were a cohesive, happy little family.

With the influx of federal antipoverty money, the Legal Aid Society and the Defender Association promptly enlarged their offices. The Defender Association purchased an expensive and extensive library, even though its offices are located one block from city hall, which has a magnificent law library. The directors and staffs of these agencies received salary raises. They had pensions and other fringe benefits. The new antipoverty staff attorneys were limited to a maximum salary of fifteen thousand dollars per annum. They, of course, had no pension or retirement benefits. Harvey Schmidt, a Negro attorney and former political appointee, was made assistant director. A year later, when Mr. Abrahams resigned, he was made director. Mr. Klaus, president of the board, reported at a board meeting that both Schmidt and I attended that no one else was willing to take the job at that salary. On this understanding, the board ratified the appointment of Mr. Schmidt. All employees except Mr. Abrahams were required to give up their private practice. This was no hardship for Mr. Pollock; he didn't have any. Nor did most of the employees of the Legal Aid Society and Defender Association. It did not discourage the recent law school graduates. But it was a severe impediment to getting a competent experienced staff. The salary limit of fifteen thousand dollars created a serious problem. This sum is the same as the beginning salary paid by Wall Street firms to youngsters just graduating from law school. Leading law firms in other cities were meeting that pay scale and also giving new employees the entire summer as a paid vacation to study for the bar examination. These firms offered not only a secure future, good salaries and bonuses, but also excellent training under experienced lawyers.

Community Legal Services set up a so-called law office in each of the city's twelve poverty area offices. That is, a lawyer was given a chair, a desk, and a telephone. He had no secretary, no lawbooks, and no other lawyer with whom to consult. He was expected to give on-the-spot advice to any poor person who came in off the street, meet the eligibility standards, and live in the poverty area. The clients' problems were many and varied. They involved the commercial code, real estate transactions, installment sales, bailments, leases, opening judgments, divorce, custody, support, extradition, claims in other states, answers to libel and trespass actions, accident claims, evictions, distraint on household goods, pension rights, veterans' benefits, social security problems, landlord and tenant problems. A lawyer with decades of active practice could not resolve all these questions without some study and much investigation. But law school graduates, some of whom had not even passed the bar examination, were put in those offices and expected to function.

The criminal division of the poverty law program simply expanded the operations of the Defender Association. A lawyer was posted in the magistrates' court (police court) to cover preliminary hearings. His duty was to go back in the cellblock and call out, "Anybody need a lawyer?" He would stand by the client as the magistrate set bail. It is important for the statistical report to show a large volume of clients even if one doesn't do much for them. The defendants quickly learned the eligibility standards and came within them. No one knows how many of these people could have retained private counsel.

Many indigent defendants, advised by other inmates, steadfastly refused to be represented by the Defender Association, believing that they could do better without that kind of lawyer. The Defender Association's practice is to have the client questioned by an interviewer. His case is tried by an attorney who picks up the file the night before and tries all the cases listed for that courtroom on that day. It is a rarity if the trial attorney has seen the client before the morning of the trial. (The operations of the Philadelphia Defender Association are described in a comment, "Client Service in a Defender Organization: The Philadelphia Experience," 117 *University of Pennsylvania Law Review* 448 [January 1969].) Most law offices for the poor operate in this manner.

During more than a quarter century of practice, I had heard lots of grumblings and complaints about the Defender Association and the Legal Aid Society. I knew that legal aid refused to represent plaintiffs in divorce actions. Divorce was presumed to be a luxury for the rich, and a charitable agency does not provide luxuries for the needy. The fact that under the law anyone who has grounds for a divorce, regardless of economic status, is entitled to bring such an action was irrelevant in the considerations of the philanthropic citizens serving on the board of legal aid. There were numerous complaints about the Defender Association by prisoners. But one is always inclined to discount the complaints of disgruntled clients. Besides, they were getting something for nothing and should show a proper sense of gratitude. Like most members of the bar, I had never seen either agency in operation.

Like most practicing attorneys, I had appeared in juvenile court only infrequently. When middle-class parents retained me to defend their child, he was invariably discharged (acquitted) after a brief, gentle hearing. This was the result regardless of whether the girl was caught red-handed shoplifting, whether the boy had been driving a stolen car or carrying a gun or had severely injured another person in a fight. If windows were broken or a restaurant vandalized, the parents paid the bill and the boys went home with kindly admonitions from the judge.

Before opening the Office for Juveniles in 1966, I spent

a week or two in the Defender Association's office to learn the filing system and the mechanics of the operation. I saw the lawyers hurry in at nine o'clock, grab their files, and rush to court. They returned late in the afternoon. But the secretaries left on the stroke of five thirty. If a pleading or brief was due the next day, it could not even be typed. There was signing in and out. This was like a factory with a time clock and an assembly-line division of functions. This was not the kind of law office I wanted.

The Defender Association's office was located more than a mile from the juvenile court and the detention center. I insisted that the Office for Juveniles have its own headquarters near the court. We managed to obtain such a location. Our office did not meet the standards set forth in the National Legal Aid and Defender Association *Handbook of Standards for Legal Aid and Defender Offices:* "A small library . . . a few suitable pictures for the wall, or a flower vase or two . . . draperies or venetian blinds." The Office for Juveniles didn't have enough filing cabinets, paper, manila folders for the files, or even paper clips or chairs. The clients often had to set on the stairs or the floor.

Despite its obvious limitations, the office was loved by the staff and the clients. The children and their mothers didn't have to pay extra carfare to reach the office. The lawyers could get back and forth from court easily. There was never a sign posted outside, although one was promised. Even without curtains and flowers, over three thousand children found their way to the office in a year and a half.

Clients began to come the day we opened the office, although there was never a public announcement. No attorney ever solicited a client—a practice that would have been contrary to professional standards. Word spread swiftly not only among the poor but among the staffs of agencies that deal with children. Public and parochial schoolteachers and counselors, welfare workers, prison wardens, and workers in children's shelters and playgrounds sent children and their parents to the office. Two white policemen brought little Gary into the office and urged that we attorneys "do something" to protect him. Gary L. was nine. His black face was tearstained and his body raw with welts. His mother's paramour had beaten the boy with the cord to an electric iron. Several young assistant prosecuting attorneys sent distraught mothers to the office with secret scribbled notes explaining why their boys were held in jail and why the orders were illegal. Social workers from many public and private institutions called from telephone booths to seek help for children in their institutions. Some called anonymously. Others gave their names and asked that we not disclose the source of the call. All of them feared they would lose their jobs if it became known that they had revealed these abuses. Yet they took the chance and called. Some employees in children's instituions asked to meet me in remote places where there was little likelihood of their being seen. These dedicated souls would come on their day off and bring documentary proof of mistreatment of poor children.

Several doctors called to get protective orders on behalf of battered babies so that these infants would not have to be returned to the parents who had abused them. Other doctors came to us for court orders permitting life-saving operations on children whose parents could not be located or refused to give consent. Other doctors phoned (asking for anonymity) to get permission to perform abortions on twelve- and thirteen-year-old victims of incestuous rape. After we obtained the necessary court orders, the doctors operated without fee and all of the girls recovered quickly.

We received several calls from a jail warden who requested us to get new trials for boys who protested that they were innocent. And after much effort, we were able to get these boys released.

At first we encountered resentment and hostility from the court employees—the clerks and criers and guards. We took up a lot of time. Many days we were still trying cases at seven in the evening. Of course, the court employees had to stay until we were through. Their attitude was that all these kids were probably guilty; their mothers were lazy and immoral. The juveniles would be better off in institutions. What was all the fuss about notice of charges, evidence, proof of guilt? Day by day, as we tried the cases carefully and properly, all of us came to realize that easily two-thirds of the children brought to court were not guilty of the charges. Many of the court employees quietly referred children to the office. A number of judges called asking us to protect a child in cases involving children's property rights or custody fights over children. All of these people were struggling, as we were, against the juggernaut of a system that seemed blindly and impersonally to crush any child in its path.

The school system, the welfare department, the institutions for children, and the juvenile judges were keenly aware of the activities of the Office for Juveniles. Some were friendly; others hostile. Only the directors and the board of Community Legal Services were disinterested in our activities and problems.

Every month we presented a report to the board listing the number of cases and describing special problems and successes. Arrest without warrant, police brutality, and jailing of children by probation officers were three important problems that we repeatedly called to the attention of the board. We implored them to meet with the police commissioner, the bar association, the judges, and concerned civic groups to initiate reforms. We went directly to officials of the bar association. We spoke to many people. But no one listened.

The meetings of the board of Community Legal Services were largely devoted to a numbers game. How many new clients did each office have that month? One of the twelve area offices consistently showed an incredible case load. This was obviously the result of the exceptionally able and dedicated attorney, Manuel Gomez, who was also bilingual. Mr. Gomez saw over

675 clients a month. He was never given any help. Other areas
had a consistently low clientele. Some as few as fifty or seventy
client interviews. It was never suggested that the lawyers might
not be doing a satisfactory job, that they were too inexperienced, or that they were unwilling to work the long hours
and make the efforts to help their clients that Mr. Gomez made.
Instead, there was much discussion about hiring a public relations firm. Serious consideration was also given to buying expensive vehicles to provide mobile law offices to cruise through
the slums, like mobile public libraries seeking out clients.

After the first few months, only one or two representatives of the poor bothered to attend these perfunctory meetings. Nothing of importance was acted upon. The busy lawyer
members gave one hour a month. On the stroke of five they
picked up their briefcases and left. The advice and opinion of
the poor was seldom sought. It was apparent to them, as it was
to us, that despite the elaborate and expensive elections for the
representatives of the poor, they had no influence or control in
the antipoverty program. Control was firmly held by a troika
composed of the political machine, the establishment, and a
small group of middle-class Negroes. These three groups were
primarily concerned to maintain the status quo.

Only two lawyer members of the board visited the Office
for Juveniles—the president, William R. Klaus, and the late
Francis Hopkinson, Jr. They came together, for one brief inspection. One representative of the poor took the time and
spent the carfare to visit the office. Abrahams came to the office
once, and only at my frantic urging. The day after the *Gault*
decision holding that every child accused of delinquency had a
right to a lawyer, Judge Joseph McGlynn of the juvenile court
sent us all the children without lawyers who came before him.
The other judges continued to try children who had no counsel,
as Judge McGlynn did in the succeeding days. On November
12, 1967, six months after the *Gault* decision, Juvenile Court
Judge Samuel H. Rosenberg (according to an article in the
Evening Bulletin) stated that he would continue to try juveniles

without counsel. "Let them take an appeal to a higher court," he said. And this unconstitutional practice continued.

On May 16, 1967, the day after the *Gault* decision, however, some forty children plus their parents and friends came pouring out of the courthouse and over to the Office for Juveniles. They were sitting on the floor, on the stairs, and lining the street. The local press photographed the bedlam. Four lawyers and two secretaries to handle all these cases! When Abrahams arrived, picking his way through the mob, he remarked, "You should put up a sign, 'Leave your guns and knives outside.' " He did not provide any additional personnel or funds. He did not transfer people from the consumer's office, which was trying to develop a theory of "advocate planner," or from the civil division to help meet the desperate needs of the children, the courts, and the administration of justice. He did not seek additional funds. Neither did the board of Community Legal Services or the bar association. The mayor, the governor, city council, and the state legislature paid not the slightest attention to complying with the ruling of the Supreme Court.

Because we were in court all day every day, we began to understand the problems of the judges. They are faced with an impossible situation, vast numbers of people with problems for which a court of law has no answers. Judge Joel L. Tyler of New York City, in an interview with Sidney Zion of *The New York Times* (August 25, 1968), characterized the work of the judge as "generally degrading and dehumanizing."

> *"You sit on that bench," Judge Tyler said, "and you get this terrible sense that you can't help anyone who could be helped. Sometimes you look at a young man or woman and you feel that if someone could really get hold of them maybe something good could come of their lives.*
>
> *"But the system is just too big, the individual is nothing, the lawyers are ciphers and the judge turns out to be a virtual mechanic more often than not."*
>
> *. . . [Judge Tyler criticized] the lawyers for the Legal Aid*

Society, who handle most arraignments ("They don't fight hard enough"), and the facilities of some of the parts of the Criminal Court ("The traffic courts are a disgrace; the Brooklyn Criminal Court is a rat hole").

"The day I was sworn in," the judge said, "my mother was walking on air. . . .

"Her son was a judge. Well, friend, one week later I was ready to quit."

Doubtless many of the judges feel that way. At first they protest. Then they simply succumb to the system. Although many would like to quit, few are willing to renounce the salary and the power. Many are lesser political figures who were rewarded for faithful party services with these appointments.

The esteem in which the judiciary is generally held may be illustrated by two comments. The late United States Congressman William J. Green, Jr., political boss of Philadelphia County, once said to me, "What's a judgeship? Just a job and a headache for me." Former Governor George M. Leader of Pennsylvania was asked to press for enactment of a statute giving retired judges full pay. He asked in good faith, "Why should a judge be treated differently than a charwoman?"

All the problems of criminal courts are compounded in juvenile court. Many leading attorneys will not accept an appointment to this court. The more senior judges adamantly refused to sit in juvenile court. Some of those who did sit had ambitions. They made the headlines by "getting tough" with hoodlums. They were busy on the lecture circuit, television, and radio berating the children. And they wrote articles about the beneficence of the juvenile court.

Every lawyer who dons the black robes of judicial office and ascends the bench assumes inordinate powers. Few people can resist the opportunity to tyrannize over those who cannot strike back. The lawyer in private practice in a big city does not appear in court before the same judges day after day. But the lawyers for the poor do. The judges can with impunity let out their frustrations on these attorneys. If they strike back, the hapless client may be injured. If they fight the judges within the rules, they may find themselves without a job. It only takes a word from an irate judge to a practicing lawyer who is a member of the board of an agency providing counsel for the poor.

A highly successful trial lawyer who practices in a community where there are only three judges shamefacedly told me that when a judge mentioned one day on the golf course that his lawn needed mowing, two lawyers promptly went over to cut the judge's grass. Just a friendly, neighborly gesture to a fellow who can exercise unbridled power.

Even when a lawyer in private practice regularly appears before the same judge, there is not a great similarity in his clients. The lawyer who every day appears on behalf of indigent black kids finds that the judge holds one child answerable for the sins of another. If the lawyer asks for acquittal for lack of evidence, the judge may say, "You *always* claim they are innocent. What about that boy yesterday who stabbed a man?" Or if the judge lets the defendants in the first three cases go, despite violations of the law, the fourth case is sure to be doomed. The judge often says, after a plea for mercy, "But I just let those other kids go home!"

It is difficult to be firm with a judge who can make one's day miserable. It requires delicacy and fortitude to prevent a judge from taking over the examination of your client. It is tactless and gauche but necessary to object to the "helpful" comments of the court. Knowing all these things, the staff of the Office for Juveniles unanimously decided to disregard Pollock's sage advice to "live with those judges."

We were determined to give our young clients the same quality of representation that we would give to a fee-paying adult client. We discovered that it took even more time and effort to represent a poor child than a wealthy adult. Few ghetto children speak easily to strangers. They look out warily from

behind iron prison bars or across the barriers of race, generation, and poverty.

Even when the child and his parents want to cooperate,
it takes a long time to get the relevant facts. These clients are
not sure what papers they signed; they do not keep records.
They are vague as to time and place. We learned that the only
way to fix the time of an event, often crucial in establishing
defense to a serious criminal charge, was by the TV program
that the child or the witness was watching. Even dates are uncertain. On occasion we had to ask the TV station to find out what
day a certain episode in a program had been played.

One trial may take only fifteen minutes. But another may
require a whole day or several days. To be adequately prepared
for trial—or even filing a pleading—there must be an investigation of the facts. In a delinquency matter this includes the previous court record and social, medical, mental, and emotional
problems of the child. Hospital and school records have to be
obtained. There may be pretrial motions and trial briefs required. In many cases an appeal should be taken.

A brief glance at certain figures gives one pause. The
handbook of the National Legal Aid and Defender Association
sets a standard case load maximum of nine hundred "matters"
per attorney per year.

Like most limitations, this one is often exceeded because
there is not enough money to hire more lawyers. Simple arithmetic reveals the kind of service that can be given under such
a case load. Allowing for holidays, vacations, and lunch periods,
a salaried lawyer for the poor on a forty-hour week works about
1,680 hours per year. This allows an average of less than two
hours per "matter." It is impossible to provide the indigent
with constitutionally adequate representation, including the
right to appeal, under such a case load.

Cost is not an infallible test of value. It is, however, some
indication. There is a minimum expenditure below which one
cannot provide meaningful service. The annual report of the

National Legal Aid Society bears this legend: "Quality of Service: A Lawyer Competent—Independent for Every Need." The 1967 report states: "In 1967, organizations furnishing legal assistance on civil matters reported a total of 791,304 cases with a gross cost of operations of $29,106,259. Defender offices reported a total number of criminal cases of 465,023 with a gross cost of $17,899,295." Again, simple arithmetic yields an average of thirty-seven dollars per civil matter and thirty-eight dollars per criminal case. A good deal must be taken off for overhead, publicity, and the national organization, which is not engaged in the business of representing poor people. More accurate cost figures can be obtained from a local office. The Defender Association of Philadelphia handled 28,307 "matters" in the year 1967-68. (The figure is from the Philadelphia Defender Association *Annual Report, June 1967–June 1968*.) Of these, 12,962 matters were magistrate hearings that probably did not consume more than five or ten minutes each. There were 15,345 other matters, including trials, appeals, and post-conviction hearings. The annual budget was $180,000. Rough arithmetic indicates that the Defender Association spent an average of less than twelve dollars per matter, including overhead—rent, paper, salaries, telephone, administration, transportation expenses, conferences, meetings, and reports. It is cheap. But is it justice?

The average salary of a lawyer for the poor is eighty-five hundred dollars a year. (Compare this with the Criminal Justice Act hourly rate of ten to fifteen dollars paid for retained counsel, according to Dallin Oaks, "Practices and Policies under the Criminal Justice Act," *Legal Aid Brief Case*, October, 1968, p. 13). This is far less than the salary of a government lawyer or a lawyer employed by a large law firm. The work is much harder and more exhausting. No matter how dedicated he is, a lawyer cannot maintain a workload of nine hundred matters for very long and still give each client the time, attention, research, and investigation his problem requires.

The cost of such niggardly provision for lawyers for the poor is immeasurable. The cost to the unfortunate client and his family is obvious. The cost to the public in appeals and retrials is not inconsiderable. On a dollar-and-cents basis, it might be cheaper to provide adequate representation at the first trial.

In many law offices for the poor, law students are being used as staff lawyers. They prepare cases; they go to court and represent clients even though they have not been admitted to practice. Law students are now permitted to represent *indigent* clients in court in thirteen states. But they are not permitted to represent paying clients. Students are considered a cheap source of legal labor (they are sometimes paid for this work—usually from a grant). I have reason to doubt that the public is getting a bargain. Certainly the client is not. The Office for Juveniles had its quota of law students. Programs were set up with the faculties of the law schools so that a certain number of students would appear at certain times. No member of the faculty supervised their work. No one from the law schools inquired whether the work was satisfactory or whether the student learned anything.

We attempted to utilize law students in three ways: as observers in court, to do the paper work at the office, and to research difficult problems. There was an enormous amount of paper work—motions to suppress, petitions for habeas corpus, petitions for rehearing, appeals. The students had never seen such documents. Even when given a form and a file, they could not be trusted to draw up the papers. Crucial averments would be omitted. Our attempt to use the law students for research was a failure. Our problems were on the frontiers of the law. There were no exact precedents. The students simply did not know how to develop a doctrine by analogy and build a persuasive argument from other areas of the law. If there was no precedent, they stopped the legal argument and turned to a windy mixture of sociology and psychology heavily sauced with "policy." The Brandeis brief, which contains hard facts and statistics, was practically unknown to our students.

Many of the young lawyers for the poor are fired with enthusiasm and idealism. Many are very bright, but few have had any trial experience. Often they graduate from law school without ever having been in a courtroom, without ever seeing a pleading. They are plunged into practice at once. Large law offices can afford to train their young people. They expect to have them for years. It is a good investment. A shorthanded, overworked poverty law office cannot afford the luxury (at public expense) of training a lawyer for six months or a year.

In the Office for Juveniles we had many young volunteers who frankly admitted they had never been in any courtroom before. We had to give them briefing sessions. They were instructed to ask for a recess in case of difficulty and call the office. Many a time, I would get such a hurry call for help. The plight of the inexperienced young lawyer and his clients is aptly described in Howard James' *Crisis in the Courts:*

> *In Philadelphia, for example, I watched several public defenders* [*in Philadelphia at that time the office was not a public defender but a voluntary defender*] *in night court . . . They were obviously doing their clients more harm than good. One was shy, inarticulate, and badly bullied by the magistrate. Every three or four minutes he had a new client assigned to him. . . . I found a similar pattern across the country, with many a defender's office simply a do-it-yourself training ground for would-be trial lawyers.*

The National Legal Aid and Defender Association proudly proclaims that it provides "competence" and "independence" on the part of lawyers. Both qualities are essential. Neither is really possible under the existing structure of legal services for the poor, despite the good intentions and integrity and ability of individual lawyers. Dissatisfaction is spreading from the clients to the lawyers and the courts.

Richard H. Kuh, former chief of the Criminal Court Bureau of the Manhattan District Attorney's Office, described the operations of the New York Legal Aid Society in an interview with David Burnham of *The New York Times* (February 11, 1968). Kuh said:

> . . . [*T*]*he case* [*of Thomas Grapshi*] *presented for review a "serious defect of even the best institutionalized legal services for the indigent—an aspect of such services that sharply differentiates them from the legal service that is available to the wealthy."*
>
> *Grapshi—poor—was obliged to proceed to disposition of the charges pending against him while represented by an attorney in whom, as he repeatedly informed the trial judge, he had absolutely no confidence, he said. . .*
>
> *Grapshi, the lawyer said, "was caught in the crusher of two massive and overworked institutions: the Criminal Part of the Supreme Court, necessarily concerned with disposing of a large volume of criminal cases, and the criminal branch of a large agency assigned by the court to represent him . . . through a series of attorneys. . . ."*
>
> *On January 9, 1967, after a number of preliminary hearings, Grapshi explained to Justice Gustave G. Rosenberg that he did not want the help of the Legal Aid lawyer who was representing him.*
>
> *"The attorney now representing me in this case has never yet had a full discussion with me regarding this case," the brief quoted the defendant as having said.*
>
> *"I only saw him a couple of times in the bullpen, never for more than a few minutes," he continued. "All he had to say to me is that I should plead guilty in view of my past record. I have a past record, Your Honor, but I am not guilty of this charge. I am convinced that the present attorney is not concerned with protecting my interests and my defense."*
>
> *Grapshi then requested that the Legal Aid lawyer who represented him in the preliminary hearings be reassigned to him.*

The defendant's statement that he had been told to plead guilty
—advice that is not uncommon—was immediately denied by the
unwanted lawyer who was representing Grapshi.

Exactly one month later, after a prolonged series of additional
hearings, the defendant—still represented by the lawyer he objected
to—withdrew his not guilty plea and pleaded guilty to the original
indictment. He was sentenced to two and a half to three and a half
years in prison.

The Grapshi case is not uncommon.

The forced guilty plea understandably causes much resentment on the part of the indigent client and his family. LeRoi Jones, in *Four Black Revolutionary Plays,* (Indianapolis: Bobbs Merrill, 1969), has a scene which brought much bitter laughter from the black portion of the audience when I saw it performed. In the play *Great Goodness of Life,* Mr. Court Royal, a Negro postal employee, is arrested. This dialogue follows:

COURT ROYAL: No. I have an attorney. If you'll just call or
adjourn the case until my attorney gets here.
VOICE: We have an attorney for you. Where is the legal aid
man? . . .
ATTORNEY BRECK: Pul-plead guilty, it's your only chance. Just
plead guilty, brother.

Neither the courts nor the legal profession have acknowledged the problem of the right of choice of counsel. A poor defendant in a criminal case has a constitutional right to counsel. It must be adequate counsel. Can such representation be adequate if the client has no choice? The lawyer-client relationship is one of trust and confidence, often likened to that of priest and penitent. A client can have little trust or confidence in a lawyer he has never seen until the morning of trial. But at present he must accept whatever lawyer is provided for him, regardless of his personal likes or dislikes, the incompetence, laziness, or indifference of the lawyer. This is true whether the lawyer is furnished by an agency for the poor or appointed by the judge.

Should the indigent client in a civil or criminal case have the right to choose his own attorney? One's view of the problem may depend on his attitude toward the poor. The sociologists who argue among themselves about the poor refer to a little colloquy between F. Scott Fitzgerald and Ernest Hemingway. Fitzgerald is supposed to have said, "The rich are different from us." Hemingway replied, "Yes. They have more money." We do not know whether the poor are really different from us or whether if they had more money, they would be just the same. We never really believe in either theory. And so, like the atheist who prays on Sunday, we try a little of both. We provide a lawyer for the poor client but then impose a guardian agency over him so that the client will not really be in control of the case.

The independence of lawyers for the poor is often severely restricted. Such lawyers must think about the policy of the organization that employs them, the effect of this case on other cases. They cannot give single-minded attention to the needs of the client. Sometimes they are limited by the policy of the organization. At other times they are limited by fatigue, despair, and lack of preparation. It is difficult to represent a client whom one has never seen before, whose life history and problems one is unaware of. Often such a lawyer has only a sketchy idea of the facts in the case from an incomplete file. Both the lawyer and the client are severely disadvantaged in this situation.

Many of these problems in representation of the poor would be eliminated by a strict adherence to the canons of professional ethics, which apply to representation of nonindigent clients. These rules of conduct for lawyers, while not laws, are binding. The penalty for breach of the canons may be disbarment and concomitant disgrace. Canon thirty-five reads as follows:

> *The professional services of a lawyer should not be controlled or exploited by any lay agency, personal or corporate, which intervenes between client and lawyer. A lawyer's responsibilities and qualifications are individual. He should avoid all relations which direct the performance of his duties by or in the interest of such* intermediary. *A lawyer's relation to his client should be personal and the responsibility should be direct to the client.* Charitable societies rendering aid to the indigent are not deemed such intermediaries. [*emphasis supplied*]

Whether or not a charitable society is "deemed" to be an intermediary, it is in fact not merely an intermediary between the poor client and his lawyer but a barrier to understanding and representation. This ethical problem of lawyer-client relationship is seldom mentioned. Nor are the problems of adequacy of representation and qualifications. A lawyer in private practice would be severely censured if he accepted more clients than he could adequately represent. A lawyer in private practice would be censured if he represented a client in a field in which he had no competence. And, of course, a person not admitted to practice would be guilty of a crime if he went to court to represent a nonindigent client. "Poverty lawyers" openly admit that there is a new set of ethics for them. Mort Cohen of the Brooklyn poverty law office was quoted in *The New York Times* (June 2, 1968, p. 59) thus: "You need a different set of ethics for a poor man's lawyer."

The only ethical problems that appear to concern O.E.O. and the lawyers for the poor are advertising and solicitation of clients. Although the Office for Juveniles managed to become known among the poor without advertising, much time and money supplied by O.E.O. (the taxpayers) has been spent to advertise the existence of free legal services. Advertising by lawyers is forbidden by the canons of ethics. So is stirring up litigation. It was unreasonably feared that solicitation of clients by poverty law offices would arouse the condemnation of the bar association. Obviously, there is no objection on the part of practicing lawyers to having an agency provide services for people who cannot pay fees or urging them to litigate. The Standing Committee on Ethics of the American Bar Association accordingly ruled in opinion 992: "Offering publicly to tender legal services without charge to citizens who are unable to pay for them is not unethical."

What troubled us in the Office for Juveniles was a very different question: Is it unethical to hold out to the public that free legal services are provided and then furnish something materially different and inferior to what the client would receive from a lawyer in private practice? This is a kind of consumer fraud on the poor. Its consequences are far more devastating than the sale of mislabeled and overpriced meat or a TV set that falls apart after a few weeks—the problems that so exercise the lawyers for the poor.

There is no quick, cheap panacea. But there are several simple and obvious changes that could be made at once:

1. The lawyers for the poor should be qualified members of the bar.

2. The lawyers for the poor should have adequate time and resources to represent their clients properly.

3. The client should have the choice of counsel so that the lawyer is directly answerable to the client and not to the board of the poverty agency. This can be accomplished in many ways. There can be several law offices primarily engaged in representing the poor, and the client can choose from among the offices. Once he becomes a client, he must be a client of a particular lawyer who assumes responsibility for his case. The poor should also have a free choice of any counsel in private practice who will then be paid on an hourly or on a case basis, much like Medicare.

4. Neither advertising nor solicitation is necessary or appropriate. Poor clients, like rich clients, will soon find the lawyers who provide competent representation.

Financing of legal services is a difficult problem no matter who represents the poor. However, I believe that less administration and advertising and more direct representation will prove less costly.

Antipoverty legal services programs have been widely hailed as a challenge to the profession and an answer to the needs of society in eliminating poverty. John W. Gardner, former Secretary of Health, Education and Welfare, addressing the American Bar Association on August 6, 1968, expressed the rhetoric of optimism so prevalent among government and foundation officials:

> *The possibilities for the lawyer interested in community service are enormous in scope and variety precisely because he brings to the assignment such extraordinary potentialities as negotiator, advocate, planner, organizer, appraiser of the legality of administrative actions, student of constitutional questions, drafter of legislation and so on.*

Appraising administrative action and drafting legislation are important. But it must also be remembered that "the poor" are individual people with individual problems. The solutions are also individual. Mr. Jones's front door was battered down by a policeman. Jones needs fifty dollars to repair or replace the door and for the damages to his house. Tyrone is put out of school. An order compelling the school to educate Tyrone is required. The sheriff is about to take Mrs. Coleman's furniture away to satisfy a summary judgment. Each of these problems requires a lawyer for a client. A bureaucracy to prevent fraud, to check on abuses of government, and to receive complaints —whether it be called a consumer advocate, a mayor's office for complaints, or an Ombudsman—cannot substitute for lawyers who have the time and skill to represent Jones, Tyrone, and Mrs. Coleman.

In its brief life, the Office for Juveniles struggled against the courts, the poverty agency, and the pressures of time and numbers to give some three thousand ghetto children the same single-minded devotion that the lawyer in private practice is enjoined to give his client. But such legal representation slows the courts and disrupts the system.

Community Legal Services decided to turn its attention from representation of poor people to projects of law reform. It is easier and pleasanter to sit in an office and devise statutes (which may never be enacted) than to do the hard grubby work of battling in court on behalf of poor people. O.E.O. is busy subsidizing such law-reform programs. Duke University received a grant of $113,275 on July 5, 1968, to provide "technical assistance in legislative research and drafting"; the University of Pennsylvania Law School on July 18, 1968, received $1,303,313 of O.E.O. money for a hundred fellowships in legal services; and Harvard Law School received $133,358 for "giving law students an insight into the legal problems of the poor." This public money allocated for antipoverty programs is really financing middle-class students and wealthy law schools instead of providing services for the poor. But the courts and the police are much happier now that the lawyers for the poor are making studies and gaining insights instead of fighting on behalf of poor clients. And so are the directors of the antipoverty agencies.

Chapter Eighteen

SEEKERS AFTER TRUTH

Research, *n.* diligent protracted investigation, especially for
the purpose of adding to human knowledge; studious inquiry.

Funk and Wagnalls New Standard Dictionary of the English
Language

From the experience of OEO, we have learned the value
of having in the Federal Government an agency whose special
concern is the poor. We have learned the need for flexibility,
responsiveness, and continuing innovation. We have learned the
need for management effectiveness.

PRESIDENT NIXON, *January 19, 1969*

The true function of legal research should be to show the
way to achieve a just society. But today research is big business.
The favorite subject of study at the moment is "the poor."

Almost every day some middle-class white recipient of a
grant calls me for information. One man is studying prisons.
He had never visited one before he received his grant. He wants
a few stories of brutality to spice his report. Another team of
legal researchers is working on "the right to treatment." Do I
know of any child who is not receiving therapy in an institution?
It is easier to ask someone than to go and find out. A team—
a young man and a young woman—from Johns Hopkins University are studying race and violence. They came to visit me in
Philadelphia. I offered to introduce them to some black community leaders. Oh, no, they told me in shocked dismay. Didn't I
know that white field workers don't interview Negroes? The
black team would be in Philadelphia in a few weeks but they will
not speak to me. These sweet young people were formerly a

kindergarten teacher and a government civil servant. Dickinson
School of Law is having a forum on how white lawyers can relate
to the problems of the poor client. A social worker, who is a
panelist, calls for suggestions on what he is to tell the audience
about "the poor." He admits that the agency for which he works
(supported by the local United Fund) has no indigent clients.
But he is the expert. Lincoln University is running three weekend seminars for public officials on treating the poor with dignity. Will I please come and tell them of some of the
unconscious or subconscious slights unknowingly inflicted on
the poor? The seminar is intended to change the attitudes of the
governors toward the governed. The law schools have special
funds to teach courses in "poverty law." Of course, no one
really knows what this new concept—poverty law—is. Villanova
University Law School fills the gap in professional ignorance by
inviting practicing lawyers to come and lecture (without fee) to
the students. Similar makeshifts are in contemplation in a number of law schools, including Harvard Law School, which have
grants to develop clinical courses in law. There are even grants
to teach people how to get grants. The Ford Foundation, according to *The New York Times* (December 16, 1968), granted
three and one-half million dollars to help local groups get
money from government and private agencies.

The commercial press is getting in on the act. The editor
of a national magazine is doing a piece on poor children. He
writes that he has done all the research and he has the conclusions. Now can I please give him a few illustrative incidents? A
Pulitzer Prize winner taking a quick turn around the country
comes for a few choice quotations and some leads to a juicy case
or two for his next book.

All of these people are making studies. They think they
are doing research. But, as many of them readily admit, they
already have the answers. They are just looking for supporting
data. This medieval scholasticism of deductive reasoning led to
firm scientific conclusions that the earth is flat.

Examining the facts first and then drawing conclusions

is more difficult. Sometimes facts are stubborn. People refuse to behave in the ways that they are supposed to. It is much better to avoid actually seeing the poor and to work through middle-class intermediaries who will give the expected responses. It is easier to relate to a white middle-class lawyer who has had poor clients than to go into court and see what actually happens to the poor when they do not have a lawyer or when they are rushed through the turnstile poverty law offices. If enough of these intermediaries are questioned and the answers tabulated, the researcher can build up impressive statistics that appear to support his conclusions.

The establishment—judges, professors, and bar associations—suddenly have awakened to the fact that the poor are not fairly treated in court. Of course, this has been true for decades. But now there is financial support for those who will do research and write reports.

Typical of such proliferating studies is *Juvenile Gangs,* a monograph by Gilbert Geis (President's Commission on Law Enforcement and Administration of Justice, 1965). In his introduction Dr. Geis reveals frankly the inspirations for much of this research:

> *For another thing, research is still in a very tentative stage, with numerous contradictory findings and unexplored questions. . . .*
>
> *Such integrative work is, in fact, proceeding apace.* The sudden availability of federal and foundation funds for field research with delinquent gangs precipitously thrust social scientists into investigations which are beginning to rival the ethnographic work undertaken by anthropologists. *The contributed papers, which form the major basis for the present statement, indicate the extensive nature of research work being done in various places with different gangs. "My gang does it this way," uttered at gatherings of social workers, sociologists, and psychologists, seems to be heard as often these days as the traditional anthropological statement that "In my tribe, this is the way it is done."*

*Attempts to assess and to summarize even a fractional part
of the literature and to elicit training guidelines must, almost of
necessity, be a tentative effort. . . . [emphasis supplied]*

The subjects of research on law and poverty are endless.
There are obvious fragments of the problem such as bail,
prison reform, consumer frauds (currently the "in" subject),
welfare rights, characteristics of delinquency, and community
action organizations. These peripheral subjects are important.
But the amelioration, without a real cure, of one inequity leads
to worse diseases. The release of indigent prisoners without
bail and consequent multiple arrests of persons awaiting trial
leads to "preventive" detention. Requiring a due process hearing with counsel in juvenile court leads to proposals to avoid the
juvenile court and use "social agencies." The growing backlog
in the courts leads Judge Bernard Botein and others to propose
siphoning certain cases out of the courts. The requirement of
counsel and jury trials in criminal cases is so time-consuming
that it compels the courts, prosecutors, and lawyers for the poor
to insist on guilty pleas.

The New York Times of February 2, 1969, reports that
judges are requiring "prosecutors with defense lawyers to *dispose* of as many cases as possible by accelerating the negotiations of guilty pleas and lengths of sentences." Similar
programs of forced guilty pleas are being instituted in many
large cities. The accused who are represented by the agencies
for the poor will doubtless be those most likely to plead guilty
regardless of actual guilt or innocence. The right to a fair and
impartial trial under these circumstances has reached the van-
ishing point.

These same stultifying processes inhibiting reform are
already in operation in juvenile court. Scarcely six months after
the United States Supreme Court held that children were entitled to some constitutional rights, the experts began to recommend that the juvenile court be sidestepped and children again
be siphoned off into agencies that are not subject to the judicial

requirements of fundamental fairness. It is an easy device for token compliance with the Supreme Court decision without making necessary fundamental reforms, particularly when the court itself suggested nonjudicial handling of juveniles. The task force report *Juvenile Delinquency and Youth Crime* made the following recommendations:

> *Recommendations to improve our system of* planned nonjudicial handling *for* reputed *delinquents fall into three categories: First is the further limitation of referrals into the juvenile court system and the ability of that system to accept such referrals. Second is the creation and the strengthening of alternative agencies and organizations to deal with putative delinquents. Third is the development of an improved capacity on the part of the police and juvenile court system to make appropriate dispositions and refer* putative delinquents to alternative agencies and organizations. [*emphasis supplied*]

The concept of putative or assumed felons is utterly contrary to American law and seemingly repugnant to the Constitution. Who is a putative delinquent, and how is such assumed delinquency to be determined if not by a court that hears evidence of misconduct? Many careful and painstaking studies have been made of children in correctional institutions, comparing them with "nondelinquent" children. It is of course assumed that every child in a correctional institution has committed a crime and that those who are free have not. Innumerable characteristics of these children have been measured, including "strength of handgrip, sensuousness, cyanosis, gainful employment of mother, lack of cultural refinement in home,"* but neither race nor school performance was consid-

---

*Sheldon and Eleanor Glueck, *Problem of Delinquency* (Cambridge, Mass.: Riverside Press, 1959) pp. 59, 65. Despite evidence to the contrary, scholars assume that it is possible to identify "predelinquents" and to prevent future criminality. See Winifred E. Cavenagh, *The Child and the Court* (London: Gollancz, 1959) p. 221: "Early prognosis of future criminality could lead to early action to prevent the development of the delinquent tendencies."

ered. These data are collated and analyzed. But how meaningful
are they? Computer men have a saying, "Garbage in—garbage
out"; the results of the computations depend on the input—on
the assumptions. All studies in this area assume that the prison
inmates—adult and juvenile—have actually committed crimes.
Our experience, limited as it is, does not support this comfort-
able assumption. The figures are further skewed because the
poor are more likely to be arrested and prosecuted and convicted than the nonpoor. What all this research on delinquency
shows is simply the characteristics of children likely to be arrested. This soon becomes a self-fulfilling prophecy. (Note that
the Juvenile Aid Division of the Philadelphia police uses such a
study of characteristics of delinquents to assist them in making
arrests.) Without more meaningful information, there is no
basis for identifying "putative" delinquents.

There is some evidence that more careful judicial hearings, as contrasted with informal proceedings or the standard
five-minute juvenile trial, may drastically reduce the number of
adjudications of delinquency and the number of commitments.
The brief experience of the Office for Juveniles is indicative of
a fruitful line of research. In May, 1966, before the Office for
Juveniles was opened, thirty-eight boys were committed to the
Philadelphia Youth Development Center North. In May, 1967,
only fourteen were committed. At that time the Office for Juveniles was in full operation. In February, 1968, just before the
office closed, the Youth Development Center North was at only
half capacity. The Youth Development Center South, with a
capacity of 120, had only 40 inmates. This amazing reduction
in population was explained by Stanley Brody, then deputy
secretary of the Department of Public Welfare of Pennsylvania.
"There has been a subtle influence on all correctional people
and law enforcement officers to be sure that a kid really ought
to be booked," he said. "I've always felt more kids were committed than should have been."

An able young sociologist studying the files of the Office

for Juveniles while we were in operation, to help us analyze our clients' problems, discovered that fewer than 3 percent of our clients got into trouble after their contact with the office. Many of these boys and girls expressed a determination to go back to school; some said they wanted to become lawyers. Whether they succeed, what happens to them next, no one will ever know, because when the office was abandoned its files were dispersed. Since the closing of the Office for Juveniles, the correctional institutions are filled beyond capacity. We do not know whether more careful judicial proceedings (such as the Office for Juveniles had tried to enforce) or nonjudicial, informal referrals are better for the children and for society. Surely it is worth finding out.

Meanwhile superficial or irrelevant studies and hasty junkets by researchers continue. They result in rash proposals for change. For example, Judge Orman W. Ketcham, after a ten-day foundation-financed visit to England, lauds the British juvenile court system in which lay volunteers sit as magistrates with the powers of judges to commit children to institutions (*The Philadelphia Inquirer,* March 9, 1969). A study by Martin Gold and Jay R. Williams financed by the National Institute of Mental Health concludes, on the basis of 847 children studied, that the fact of apprehension of guilty juveniles encourages rather than deters future delinquency. It is proposed that juvenile court judges, instead of deciding cases on the basis of the child's conduct, determine the "risk" on the basis of demographic characteristics of the group ("The Effect of Getting Caught," *Prospectus,* December, 1969, pp. 1-38).

Breast-beating acknowledgments of injustice to the poor are also plentiful. Judge J. Skelly Wright deplores the injustice to the poor in an article called "The Courts and the Inner City" (*The Detroit Tribune Magazine Section,* May 26, 1968, p. 3). A typical reaction of kindhearted and uninvolved lawyers is expressed by Seymour Rembar in *The End of Obscenity* (New York: Random House, 1968, p. 213):

*Meanwhile, the procedures of the criminal law went forward. . . .
I went to court on these matters, to a court I had never appeared in
before and had visited only once or twice. . . . Each time I saw it in
action, I was struck by the contrast with courts as we generally think
of them. The difference is enormous, and disheartening. This is poor
man's law; we have not yet achieved democracy in the dispensation
of justice.*

Responsible proposals for basic reform of the system creating
these injustices are scarce. It takes considerable temerity for a
practicing lawyer to make suggestions on the basis of his own
experiences. Today any serious recommendation, even for the
amendment of a single statute, must be presented as conclusions based on scholarly research. The shrine of scholarship is
academia; only there can its true acolytes be found. The practicing lawyer, who knows at firsthand the techniques and problems
of litigation, the difficulties and costs of legal representation,
and the delays of the courts, is rarely consulted. He is busy and
does not have time to attend endless conferences. He receives
no grants to enable him to participate in think tanks. Seldom
does he know the high priests of the foundations or the immutable rites of the research vocation.

There is an accepted format for any scholarly work: Review the existing literature, record interviews with people in
authority, calculate percentages, extrapolate figures, check
against control groups, present conclusions. Simply to assimi-
late the bulky accumulation of literature and data on any subject
requires an entire team plus supporting personnel. Such a staff
requires a grant, a foundation to make the grant, and a tax-
exempt entity to receive the grant. Research has become divorced from action and experience as a result of this process.
The O.E.O. legal services program, by establishing separate
units for law reform and legal research as opposed to the practice of law and the representation of the poor, has perpetuated
and widened the schism.

The researchers are selected by the donors in a circular process that results in a closed community in which those who should be the critical original thinkers and reformers are a part of the establishment and reflect the currently accepted views. For example, the community action programs, a concept devised by the Ford Foundation, were recently evaluated by an "independent" study of war-on-poverty-programs financed by the Ford Foundation (*OEO News Summary,* February 17, 1969). The heavy financial support of research, conferences, symposia, dialogues, and papers acts as a deterrent to the presentation of unorthodox ideas. There is an astonishing similarity in the "innovative" programs recommended by institutionalized research.

In an age when even students and poets are paid to write or tape-record their thoughts, a person must be moved by extraordinarily strong convictions to undertake a study or the presentation of a proposal without institutional support. The solitary thinker with his little portable typewriter is as obsolete as the solitary scientist experimenting in his cellar. The volume and methods of research are formidable obstacles to reflection, to observations of reality, and to original thought. We are locked into the status quo by the institutionalization of the very research that is deemed to be a condition precedent to change.

Despite the large sums spent on research, our ignorance of the nature of the litigational process is abysmal. We do not have even the foggiest notion of the dimensions of the problem. Although crime reporting is incomplete and open to some question as to accuracy, the Uniform Crime reports give at least minimum figures. In 1965, 4,955,047 arrests were reported by agencies covering a population of 134,095,000. Because the population of the United States was approximately 180 million, there must actually have been more than six and a half million arrests. Every one of the arrested persons had the constitutional right to the guiding hand of counsel beside him from arrest through trial, appeals, and post-conviction applications.

At least 50 percent of the adults arrested and more than 90 percent of the juveniles were indigent and entitled to counsel at public expense. How many courtrooms, how many judges, and how many lawyers are needed simply to handle criminal and delinquency cases? How much will it cost? No one knows. There are only three hundred thousand practicing attorneys in America. Not many of them are able or willing to engage in the hard, unremunerative work of representing these people.

What training and qualifications should these litigation lawyers and judges have? We do not know. Many cases have to be tried a second and a third time because of the ignorance or ineptitude of the judge or lawyer. What is the role of the law schools in preparing lawyers and judges to perform these essential tasks? Are the law school professors, many of whom have never tried a case, equipped to teach the lawyers? Should there be special training for judges before they are appointed or elected? Who should be their instructors?* We do not know. Little study of these basic questions is being undertaken.

We know even less about civil litigation. We do not know how many civil claims are filed or how many valid causes of action the poor must forego because they cannot afford to litigate. Poor people have many legal rights—not simply entitlements to welfare and public housing. They have rights to social security, veterans' benefits, pensions, claims for accidents and injuries, damages to their property and persons by the police, by citizens, by the government in urban renewal displacement, and condemnations for all purposes. In the Office for Juveniles we found that children had many civil causes of action that were lost, with tragic consequences, because of ignorance and poverty—the right to attend school, the right to all kinds of government benefits for dependent children, and claims for innumerable injuries, medical malpractice, and inheritance rights.

*See, for example, Ralph Nader's attack on the law schools, *Harvard Law Record*, November 7, 1968, p. 1. See also Lois G. Forer, "Training the Lawyer," 47 *American Bar Association Journal* 354 (1961).

There are valuable legal remedies available to those who can afford them. A man owing millions of dollars can be legally relieved of his debts by court action. But bankruptcy is too expensive for the poor. There has been little research into the matter of making existing substantive and procedural rights accessible to everyone. If, in fact, such laws are only for the rich, they violate the equal protection clause of the Constitution as certainly as laws for "whites only."

Access to the courts is not free. In order to sue one must pay costs and filing fees. The poor can be relieved of this expense only at the discretion of the court and upon submitting to the indignity of filing a pauper's oath. Although all manner of sophisticated cost-benefit analyses are made in this country, we do not know the costs of the operation of the courts or the costs to the taxpayers and the litigants. There has been no conscious policy decision by the voters as to whether these costs should be borne by the taxpayers like the cost of police protection or by the litigants like user taxes on toll roads. Should the defendant bear the cost of his prosecution? Often he does. Should industry bear the cost of its regulation? Often it does not. The civil courts are used to a great extent by individuals and corporations to prosecute claims for money damages. But the cost of the entire system is borne by all the people, including the poor, through direct and indirect taxation. Often the poor are debarred from the assertion of valid claims by the filing fees, witness fees, the cost of printed briefs, and the formidable expenses of litigation.

The only fact of which we are certain is the delay in bringing cases to trial. In Detroit a litigant waits thirty-two months from the filing of suit for trial. In Los Angeles and Philadelphia he must wait fifty-five months. Obviously, those in dire need surrender their rights for whatever settlement they can get. Those who can afford to wait years and years, to delay, and to appeal may avoid paying just obligations. They may by endurance and expenditure of vast sums prevail in the assertion of their rights.

The system of litigation continues to function in civil cases only because a large segment of the population is excluded from access to the courts. It continues to function in the prosecution of crimes only because the majority of defendants cannot afford to assert their constitutional rights.

Proposals to reduce delay and expense by sloughing off certain types of cases on nonjudicial agencies are popular. Generally it is suggested that negligence cases and juvenile delinquency (both of which especially affect the poor) be handled this way. The new agencies may be as costly as the expansion of judicial facilities. We do not know. And will they be more or less fair than the courts? These questions are seldom asked. Nor are other fundamental questions often posed.

Is our time-honored adversary system of trying cases the best, fairest, and most efficient way of deciding questions of fact and law? Dean John Henry Wigmore called it the "sporting theory" of justice. In criminal cases the power of the state with its enormous resources of investigation, subpoena power, and lawyers is arrayed against the accused. Often he is in jail and unable to go about and make his own investigation of the facts. He usually lacks the power to obtain witnesses; he often knows little of the ways of the police or the criminal world.

It is no more sporting for the state to try a poor defendant who has no counsel or inadequate counsel than for a hunter to shoot wild animals with a high-powered telescopic automatic rifle from a protected jeep. It is not very sporting either for a large finance company to sue the poor purchaser of overpriced, inferior merchandise who has either no counsel or inadequate counsel. Even assuming that good counsel with sufficient time and resources could be provided, is the process valid? In civil litigation it is difficult to assess whether the result of a trial is fair or just, whether the award was too large or too small. But in criminal cases there is a readily ascertainable standard.

Does our system of trial convict the guilty and acquit the

innocent, or vice versa? Scarcely a week passes that the press does not report the chilling discovery of an innocent person serving a sentence for a crime he did not commit. In 1942 Professor Edwin M. Borchard's book, *Convicting the Innocent* (Hamden, Connecticut: Archon Books) shocked the legal profession with documented accounts of many innocent people who had been tried, convicted, and jailed or executed. No substantial changes were made in the method of criminal trials. Often these unfortunate people were represented by the special counsel for the poor and had a "fair trial." Are these cases aberrations, or do they occur so frequently that we should reexamine the system? The fact is, we do not know.

The limited experience of the Office for Juveniles would indicate an alarmingly high incidence of error in trials of delinquency. The legal researchers have not considered testing the results of trials against a standard of fact. There is nothing sacred or immutable about the testimonial method of proof. How reliable is testimony under oath by witnesses whose memories have dimmed over months and years while waiting for trial? Are there better ways of finding the truth? We do not know enough about the litigational process to make sound recommendations for change.

Are the courts being misused and overburdened with the trial of issues that should be resolved by the legislature or the executive? There is little research into this question. It would be interesting to know the number of judicial days and the cost of trying essentially political cases such as the prosecution of Dr. Benjamin Spock. How much time of trial and appellate courts and the United States Supreme Court has been expended in the fruitless effort to define pornography? Is litigation the best means to reapportion voting districts, to compel manufacturers to meet government standards of safety, and to pursue a host of other public questions?

Mr. Justice Frankfurter observed, "Our society, now more than ever, is a legal state in the sense that almost every-

thing that takes place will sooner or later raise legal questions."
Must all of these questions be tried in the courts in the traditional manner by means of a specific case litigated in the adversary system of trial? We might inquire into the possibility of
advisory opinions on issues of public policy. Such decisions, if
authorized by statute, could save a great deal of court time,
expense, and infinite hardship on a large class of persons
affected by a Supreme Court decision that is not rendered until
four or five years after litigation has begun. The judge-made
doctrine of judicial parsimony, which restricts the courts from
deciding the broad issues implicit in a case and limits them to
the narrow, often anomalous facts of the particular case, suggests the need for reexamination. Such decisions often promote more litigation instead of resolving issues.

Perhaps we are overusing or misusing the courts as an
instrument of social change. Responsible research might consider whether the legislature can't better provide a coherent
system of statutory revision than the courts can offer through
the incomplete aleatory processes of litigation. The executive
branch of government has the duty to enforce the law responsibly with due regard for the rights of the citizen. Dangerous
drugs, defective machinery and war matériel, overreaching
subordinate public officials, and a host of other problems that
now go to the courts might more quickly and effectively be
remedied by executive action.

If the government responsibly enforced consumer protection laws, it would not be necessary for the individual to
seek redress through the long, complicated process of class
actions.

Reliance on the United States Supreme Court as the
principal protector of individual liberties appears to be unwise
and unjustified. The record of the United States Supreme Court
from the Dred Scott decision and the Korematsu case (which
upheld the legality of the internment of innocent Americans of
Japanese ancestry in World War II) to the present time suggests

the need for other and more effective means of protecting the rights of the individual. The emphasis on the United States Supreme Court in the legal profession would also appear to be undue. That court decides on the merits only about four hundred cases a year. A single juvenile court judge may decide four hundred cases in a month. Each one involves the life, liberty, and future of a child. Each case may determine whether the child grows to normal adulthood or becomes a criminal, a pervert, or a person unable to live in an open society. The public, the bar associations, and the law professors largely ignore the qualifications—scholarly, ethical, and temperamental—of these judges. The significance of the lower judiciary must be better understood, since these are the courts which affect the lives of countless Americans.

In attempting to frame a just and appropriate legal system for children, we are also in a quagmire of conflicting theories and astonishing ignorance. Do early learning projects increase the ability of slum children or not? Do IQ tests measure anything but the ability to take the test? Iconoclasts cite studies in which children perform in accordance with the teacher's expectation regardless of IQ scores. What is the role of the public school—to teach? and if so, what? to develop the whole child? to integrate society? to prepare the child for a job? We try to do a little of everything, but never enough.

Certain important questions, however, are never asked. Who is a child? Should the age of adulthood be twenty-one, eighteen, sixteen? When is the average young person mentally, physically, and emotionally mature? We do not know. What, if any, rights should a child be denied? And what rights should the legal system guarantee to him? At present there is no Bill of Rights for children. They can be deprived of a home, education, essential medical care, and liberty with few corresponding protections. There are appallingly few avenues that the law affords a child for the assertion of basic human needs and rights.

It is necessary to make radical changes in the entire juvenile justice system. But we lack the essential information on which to base intelligent choices.

While scholars study and reports proliferate, the unending ranks of the poor are whisked through the courtrooms on the conveyor-belt legal system for the poor. Every day in the Office for Juveniles we saw injustices perpetrated on our clients and their families by all phases of the legal system—arrest, treatment by police, intake, juvenile court trial, testing, detention, probation, and institutionalization. We also became aware of a rising level of hostility toward the dominant society. I cannot forget Taylor McB., a black boy who refused to speak to me. His mother had come to the office the morning of his trial. I went down to the dark cellblock where he was locked up. Taylor stood behind bars and said, "I don't want to talk to you." His mother and the Negro guard finally persuaded him that even though I was white, I wanted to help him. After he told me his story, I was able to get him released.

I thought of Taylor and of many other boys and girls when I read the Philadelphia *Evening Bulletin* on September 27, 1969, which reported a juvenile case. A black boy who had been held in temporary detention five months was brought to trial and committed to a correctional institution. At the trial his mother wept and protested that he was a good boy. The assistant defender who represented him, when questioned by the reporter, replied that there was nothing newsworthy about the case. "I think," he said, "it [the commitment] will be excellent. She's not the right kind of concerned parent." As she left the courtroom, the mother cried, "Well, you win again. It's your laws, your rules, your regulations—"

The young, the nonconformers, the poor, and the black have found neither redress for wrongs nor protection of rights in the legal system. They have taken to the streets, to the gangs, and to the politics of confrontation. Dr. John Spiegel of the Brandeis University Lemburg Center for the Study of Violence states it very simply:

It seems evident that if a subgroup like the Negroes of America* feels itself excluded from and penalized by the value system of the over-all society, then it will experience a sense of alienation and of resentment sufficient to justify violent retaliation, provided it has the power to retaliate. The dominant society can respond either by an over-powering show of force—calling out the National Guard, for example—or by attempting to reduce the sense of injustice and alienation. [Paper presented at the Fifth Annual Regional Leadership Conference, December 3–4, 1966, Hartford, Connecticut, p. 10.]

To reduce the sense of injustice requires drastic changes in the legal system as it operates on the poor and the young—although this significant cause of alienation is often ignored. *Newsweek,* in its "Twelve-Point Program for Action, The Negro in America" (November 20, 1967), made no mention of the administration of justice as it affects Negroes. This continued disregard of one of the most exacerbating problems of race and poverty is probably the result of general ignorance of the hasty, brutal, and degrading treatment of the poor by the courts. Significantly, *Time* magazine, reporting on Black America 1970 in the April 6, 1970, issue, points out that there is a gross disproportion of blacks arrested, jailed, and convicted and that they receive heavier sentences. *Time* explains that "few black defendants can afford skilled lawyers."

More information about the actual operation of the litigation system for the poor is essential if we are to find ways to equalize the treatment of rich and poor before the law. But the impetus for meaningful studies will come from the matrix of firsthand experience, not from projects dreamed up in foundation offices, or hasty flying field trips of a day in one court, a morning in a prison, or an afternoon in a storefront poverty law office. Accurate information cannot be obtained from second-hand responses to questionnaires, but only from close and continuous personal observation and study.

---

*Youth is also a subgroup of society.

We neglect these problems of the legal system at our peril. Thirty percent of Americans are poor. More than 11 percent of Americans are nonwhite. More than half of all Americans are under twenty-five years of age. Although juveniles do not have money or political power, they will make their demands known to a disinterested adult world, if necessary by the force of their young bodies.

The late W. C. Fields once said, "A man who hates children can't be all bad." American society has masked its hostility to the young with conventional expressions of affection for children. The citizens of Youngstown, Ohio, permitted the public schools to be closed for weeks rather than authorize additional taxes. Similar revolts against paying for services for children are occurring in many cities. Recently the antagonism toward youth is becoming overt. It is only barely concealed in demands for "law and order." Almost everyone—young and old, rich and poor, black and white—would like to live in comfort and security. Those most lacking in any sense of personal security are poor black boys and girls. Their world has neither law nor order. They receive little protection from the police or the courts. Law is used harshly and punitively against them.

All around them, black youths see the rich and the powerful, private citizens and government officials, openly defying the law with impunity. The school board in Clairton, Pennsylvania, announced the return to daily Bible readings and prayers in public schools, despite a ruling by the United States Supreme Court. "The worst they can do is to get an injunction to stop us," Robert Le Frankie, superintendent of schools, is quoted as saying (*Evening Bulletin* [Philadelphia], January 23, 1969, p. 3). Similar announcements of intention to violate the law are made by mayors, governors, and judges. Attacks on the courts are made by policemen, public officeholders, and other judges who happen to disagree with a decision. Prosecutors and lower court judges openly announce their defiance of Supreme Court decisions. This type of lawlessness is endemic. Those who demand law and order do not define the terms. Tyranny is often supported by law. There can be order in jails and in concentration camps. It is more difficult to achieve domestic tranquillity among free people, particularly when a sizable and self-conscious minority is denied equality of treatment by the very agencies of law established to ensure equal justice.

In less than five years since the anti-poverty program was instituted, lawyers, judges, and scholars have acknowledged—and without objection accepted—the fact that there is not one law and one system of justice for everyone in America. It is admitted that there are two legal systems: the standard legal system and the secondary legal system for the poor. There are special lawyers for the poor and special ethics for poverty lawyers. The fact is seldom mentioned, but for the poor there are quick trials and long sentences. Little, if any, effort is being made to close the gap between the substantive law and procedures in the standard legal system for the nonindigent and the law and procedures actually available to the indigent. Nor is there much interest in bridging the gap between the lawyers engaged in the regular practice of law and those who represent the poor. On the contrary, the law schools and the research centers are busy teaching and writing about this other jurisprudence, poverty law. Special courses are given for those who intend to practice poverty law. It is no longer a gap but a chasm that separates the law for the poor and the law for the nonpoor. Government money, foundation grants, and expenditures by social institutions are perpetuating and institutionalizing apartheid justice, two separate and unequal systems of law in the United States.

In 1965 the O.E.O., with the best of motives, engaged in a headlong rush to set up law offices for the poor all over the country and to move in with the techniques of litigation to cure the problems of the ghetto. The establishment agencies for the poor were eager to receive this federal largess. Only one cau-

tionary voice was heard, and it was disregarded. William Pincus
of the Ford Foundation warned lest the expenditure of all this
money institutionalize a separate system of law for the poor.
But no one listened.